# Publisher's Note

For the first time in one book, the author proves conclusively that:
1. A group of financiers, representing international bankers headquartered in London, met secretly at Jekyll Island, Georgia in November, 1910 for two weeks, during which time they drafted the banking act, later known as the Aldrich Plan and/or the Federal Reserve Act, in order to gain control of the money and credit of the people of the United States.
2. When the Federal Reserve System was set up in 1914, the financiers who had written the Federal Reserve Act purchased the stock of the twelve Federal Reserve Banks, and had themselves appointed to key positions on the Federal Reserve Board of Governors and the Federal Advisory Council.
3. The financiers were then able to launch World War I, with the financial banking provided by the Federal Reserve System. When Germany wished to withdraw from the war in 1916, they set up the "Belgian Relief Commission" to feed Germany so that she could continue the war.
4. These financiers simultaneously financed the Communist Revolution in Russia in 1917, supported the bankrupt Soviet Government during the 1920s and 1930s, and financed Hitler's rise to power in Nazi Germany in 1933.
5. These financiers exercise daily control over the volume of money and the value of money in the United States, by buying and selling government securities through the Federal Reserve Open Market Committee.
6. The Reagan Administration is directly influenced by these financiers through Vice President George Bush, son of the longtime senior partner of Brown Brothers Harriman; Secretary of State George Pratt Schultz, of the Schroder-Rockefeller controlled Bechtel Corporation and Secretary of Defense Caspar Weinberger, also of the Schroder-Rockefeller controlled firm, Bechtel Corporation.

## ABOUT THE COVER

The cover reproduces the outline of the eagle from the red shield, the coat of arms of the city of Frankfurt, Germany, adapted by Mayer Amschel Bauer (1744-1812) who changed his name from Bauer to Rothschild ("Red Shield"). Rothschild added five golden arrows held in the eagle's talons, signifying his five sons who operated the five banking houses of the international House of Rothschild: Frankfurt, London, Paris, Vienna, and Naples.

# SECRETS OF THE FEDERAL RESERVE
# The London Connection

By

Eustace Mullins

First Edition

Published by:  Bankers Research Institute
P.O. Box 1105
Staunton, VA 24401

## BOOKS BY EUSTACE MULLINS

MULLINS ON THE FEDERAL RESERVE
THE FEDERAL RESERVE CONSPIRACY
DER BANKIER VERSCHWORUNG DER JEKYLL ISLAND
THIS DIFFICULT INDIVIDUAL, EZRA POUND

*(Mr. Mullins was designated the only authorized biographer of Ezra Pound by letter from him dated July 24, 1958.)*

Library of Congress Catalog Card No. 83-072665

Copyright 1983
by
Eustace Mullins

Dedicated to two of the finest scholars of the twentieth century

GEORGE STIMPSON

and

EZRA POUND

who generously gave of their vast knowledge to a young writer to guide him in a field which he could not have managed alone.

## ACKNOWLEDGEMENTS

I wish to thank my former fellow members of the staff of the Library of Congress whose very kind assistance, cooperation and suggestions made the early version of this book possible. I also wish to thank the staffs of the Newberry Library, Chicago, the New York City Public Library, the Alderman Library of the University of Virginia, and the McCormick Library of Washington and Lee University, Lexington, Virginia, for their invaluable assistance in the completion of thirty years of further research for this definitive work on the Federal Reserve System.

# About the Author

Eustace Mullins is a veteran of the United States Air Force, with thirty-eight months of active service during World War II. A native Virginian, he was educated at Washington and Lee University, New York University, Ohio University, the University of North Dakota, the Escuelas des Bellas Artes, San Miguel de Allende, Mexico, and the Institute of Contemporary Arts, Washington, D.C.

The original book, published under the title *Mullins On The Federal Reserve*, was commissioned by the poet Ezra Pound in 1948. Ezra Pound was a political prisoner for thirteen and a half years at St. Elizabeth's Hospital, Washington, D.C. (a Federal institution for the insane). His release was accomplished largely through the efforts of Mr. Mullins.

The research at the Library of Congress was directed and reviewed daily by George Stimpson, founder of the National Press Club in Washington, whom *The New York Times* on September 28, 1952 called, "A highly regarded reference source in the capitol. Government officials, Congressmen, and reporters went to him for information on any subject."

Published in 1952 by Kasper and Horton, New York, the original book was the first nationally-circulated revelation of the secret meetings of the international bankers at Jekyll Island, Georgia, 1907-1910, at which place the draft of the Federal Reserve Act of 1913 was written.

During the intervening years, the author continued to gather new and more startling information about the backgrounds of the people who direct the Federal Reserve policies. New information gathered over the years from hundreds of newspapers, periodicals, and books give corroborating insight into the connections of the international banking houses.*

While researching this material, Eustace Mullins was on the staff of the Library of Congress. Mullins later was a consultant on highway finance for the American Petroleum Institute, consultant on hotel development for Institutions Magazine, and editorial director for the Chicago Motor Club's four publications.

---

*The London Acceptance Council is limited to seventeen international banking houses authorized by the Bank of England to handle foreign exchange.

# Table of Contents

Page

Chapter One *Jekyll Island* ................................. 1
Chapter Two *The Aldrich Plan* ............................. 10
Chapter Three *The Federal Reserve Act*....................... 16
Chapter Four *The Federal Advisory Council* .................... 40
Chapter Five *The House of Rothschild*........................ 47
Chapter Six *The London Connection* ........................ 63
Chapter Seven *The Hitler Connection*........................ 69
Chapter Eight *World War One* ............................. 82
Chapter Nine *The Agricultural Depression* .................... 114
Chapter Ten *The Money Creators* ........................... 119
Chapter Eleven *Lord Montagu Norman* ...................... 131
Chapter Twelve *The Great Depression*........................ 143
Chapter Thirteen *The 1930's* .............................. 151
Chapter Fourteen *Congressional Expose* ...................... 171
Addendum ............................................. 179
Appendix I ............................................. 181
Biographies ............................................ 186
Bibliography ........................................... 190
Index ................................................. 194

# Congress of the United States
## House of Representatives
### Washington, D. C.

Texarkana
November 23, 1953

Mr. Eustace Mullins
American Petroleum Industries Committee
50 West 50th Street
New York 20, N. Y.

Dear Mr. Mullins:

    I want to thank you very much for your letter in which you refer to Col. Allen's column about an investigation of the Federal Reserve System.

    Your book is among the few books that I have on my desk, Mr. Mullins, that I often refer to. It is a very fine book and has been very useful to me.

    When I return to Washington, if you are down that way, I would like to have the privilege of seeing you and visiting with you.

    Thanking you again for the book and for your letter I am

                        Sincerely yours,

                         Wright Patman

[U. S. Congress, 1929-1976; House Banking & Currency Committee, 1937-1976.]

---

Other testimonials from many business and political leaders praising my book on the Federal Reserve System included the following:

...I am very grateful that your book called to my attention those long-ignored Congressional Hearings on the 1929 stock-market crash...

                        Col. Robert R. McCormick,
                        publisher,
                        The Chicago Tribune

...your book has been and I am sure will continue to be very useful to me. However, I would appreciate your not using my name in connection with it until appropriate legislation can be prepared to remedy some of the abuses of the Federal Reserve System.

                        Sen. Robert Taft,
                        Republican majority
                        leader in Congress

**Sixty-third Congress of the United States of America;**

**At the Second Session,**

Begun and held at the City of Washington on Monday, the first day of December, one thousand nine hundred and thirteen.

## AN ACT

To provide for the establishment of Federal reserve banks, to furnish an elastic currency, to afford means of rediscounting commercial paper, to establish a more effective supervision of banking in the United States, and for other purposes.

*Be it enacted by the Senate and House of Representatives of the United States of America in Congress assembled,* That the short title of this Act shall be the "Federal Reserve Act."

*[Signature: Champ Clark]*
Speaker of the House of Representatives.

*[Signature: Thos. R. Marshall]*
Vice President of the United States and
President of the Senate.

*Approved 23 December, 1913.*

*[Signature: Woodrow Wilson]*

*Facsimile of portions of first and final pages of Federal Reserve Act of 1913*

*The above facsimile is reproduced from page 60 of "HISTORICAL BEGINNINGS.... THE FEDERAL RESERVE", published by the Federal Reserve Bank of Boston in its seventh printing, 1982.*

# Foreword

In 1949, while I was visiting Ezra Pound who was a political prisoner at St. Elizabeth's Hospital, Washington, D. C. (a Federal institution for the insane), Dr. Pound asked me if I had ever heard of the Federal Reserve System. I replied that I had not, as of the age of 25. He then showed me a ten dollar bill marked "Federal Reserve Note" and asked me if I would do some research at the Library of Congress on the Federal Reserve System which had issued this bill. Pound was unable to go to the Library himself, as he was being held without trial as a political prisoner by the United States government. After he was denied broadcasting time in the U.S., Dr. Pound broadcast from Italy in an effort to persuade people of the United States not to enter World War II. Franklin D. Roosevelt had personally ordered Pound's indictment, spurred by the demands of his three personal assistants, Harry Dexter White, Lauchlin Currie, and Alger Hiss*, all of whom were subsequently identified as being connected with Communist espionage.

I had no interest in money or banking as a subject, because I was working on a novel. Pound offered to supplement my income by ten dollars a week for a few weeks. My initial research revealed evidence of an international banking group which had secretly planned the writing of the Federal Reserve Act and Congress' enactment of the plan into law. These findings confirmed what Pound had long suspected. He said. "You must work on it as a detective story." I was fortunate in having my research at the Library of Congress directed by a prominent scholar, George Stimpson, founder of the National Press Club, who was described by *The New York Times* of September 28, 1952: "Beloved by Washington newspapermen as 'our walking Library of Congress', Mr. Stimpson was a highly regarded reference source in the Capitol. Government officials, Congressmen and reporters went to him for information on any subject."

I did research four hours each day at the Library of Congress, and went to St. Elizabeth's Hospital in the afternoon. Pound and I went over the previous day's notes. I then had dinner with George Stimpson at Scholl's Cafeteria while he went over my material, and I then went back to my room to type up the corrected notes. Both Stimpson and Pound

---

*See bibliography for personal identification of background.

made many suggestions in guiding me in a field in which I had no previous experience. When Pound's resources ran low, I applied to the Guggenheim Foundation, Huntington Hartford Foundation, and other foundations to complete my research on the Federal Reserve. Even though my foundation applications were sponsored by the three leading poets of America, Ezra Pound, e.e. cummings, and Elizabeth Bishop, all of the foundations refused to sponsor this research. I then wrote up my findings to date, and in 1950 began efforts to market this manuscript in New York. Eighteen publishers turned it down without comment, but the nineteenth, Devin Garrity, president of Devin Adair Publishing Company, gave me some friendly advice in his office. "I like your book, but we can't print it," he told me. "Neither can anybody else in New York. Why don't you bring in a prospectus for your novel, and I think we can give you an advance. You may as well forget about getting the Federal Reserve book published. I doubt if it could ever be printed."

This was devastating news, coming after two years of intensive work. I reported back to Pound, and we tried to find a publisher in other parts of the country. After two years of fruitless submissions, the book was published in a small edition in 1952 by two of Pound's disciples, John Kasper and David Horton, using their private funds, under the title *Mullins on the Federal Reserve*. In 1954, a second edition, with unauthorized alterations, was published in New Jersey, as *The Federal Reserve Conspiracy*. In 1955, Guido Roeder brought out a German edition in Oberammergau, Germany. The book was seized and the entire edition of 10,000 copies burned by government agents led by Dr. Otto John.

The burning of the book was upheld April 21, 1961 by Judge Israel Katz of the Bavarian Supreme Court. The U.S. Government refused to intervene, because U.S. High Commissioner to Germany, James B. Conant (president of Harvard University 1933 to 1953), had approved the initial book burning order. This is the only book which has been burned in Germany since World War II. In 1968 a pirated edition of this book appeared in California. Both the FBI and the U.S. Postal inspectors refused to act, despite numerous complaints from me during the next decade. In 1980 a new German edition appeared. Because the U.S. Government apparently no longer dictated the internal affairs of Germany, the identical book which had been burned in 1955 now circulates in Germany without interference.

I had collaborated on several books with Mr. H.L. Hunt and he suggested that I should continue my long-delayed research on the Federal Reserve and bring out a more definitive version of this book. I had just signed a contract to write the authorized biography of Ezra Pound, and the Federal Reserve book had to be postponed. Mr. Hunt passed away before I could get back to my research, and once again I faced the problem of financing research for the book.

At a time when it seemed impossible that I could finance the renewal of my research and the revision of the Federal Reserve book, the initial work having been done more than three decades earlier, I was contacted by a patriotic businessman who pledged to finance a year's work on the book. Once again, I was fortunate not merely in finding a patron who could support my research, but also a successful businessman whose incisive understanding of business practices guided me into an entire new realm of secrets of the Federal Reserve System. He has requested for business reasons that he not be identified.

My original book had traced and named the shadowy figures in the United States who planned the Federal Reserve Act. I now discovered that the men whom I exposed in 1952 as the shadowy figures behind the operation of the Federal Reserve System were themselves shadows, the American fronts for the unknown figures who became known as the "London Connection." I found that notwithstanding our successes in the Wars of Independence and 1812 against England, we remained an economic and financial colony of Great Britain. For the first time, we located the original stockholders of the Federal Reserve Banks and traced their parent companies to the London Connection.

This research is substantiated by citations and documentation from hundreds of newspapers, periodicals and books and charts showing blood, marriage, and business relationships. More than a thousand issues of *The New York Times* on microfilm have been checked not only for original information, but verification of statements from other sources.

Eustace Mullins<br>1983

# Introduction

Here are the simple facts of the great betrayal. Wilson and House knew that they were doing something momentous. One cannot fathom men's motives and this pair probably believed in what they were up to. What they did not believe in was representative government. They believed in government by an uncontrolled oligarchy whose acts would only become apparent after an interval so long that the electorate would be forever incapable of doing anything efficient to remedy depredations.

EZRA POUND
(St. Elizabeth's Hospital,
Washington, D.C. 1950)

(AUTHOR'S NOTE: Dr. Pound wrote this introduction for the earliest version of this book, published by Kasper and Horton, New York, 1952. Because he was being held as a political prisoner without trial by the Federal Government, he could not afford to allow his name to appear on the book because of additional reprisals against him. Neither could he allow the book to be dedicated to him, although he had commissioned its writing. The author is gratified to be able to remedy these necessary omissions, thirty-three years after the event.)

CHAPTER ONE
# Jekyll Island

"The matter of a uniform discount rate was discussed and settled at Jekyll Island." —Paul M. Warburg[1]

On the night of November 22, 1910, a group of newspaper reporters stood disconsolately in the railway station at Hoboken, New Jersey. They had just watched a delegation of the nation's leading financiers leave the station on a secret mission. It would be years before they discovered what that mission was, and even then they would not understand that the history of the United States underwent a drastic change after that night in Hoboken.

The delegation had left in a sealed railway car, with blinds drawn, for an undisclosed destination. They were led by Senator Nelson Aldrich, head of the National Monetary Commission. President Theodore Roosevelt had signed into law the bill creating the National Monetary Commission in 1908, after the tragic Panic of 1907 had resulted in a public outcry that the nation's monetary system be stabilized. Aldrich had led the members of the Commission on a two-year tour of Europe, spending some three hundred thousand dollars of public money. He had not yet made a report on the results of this trip, nor had he offered any plan for banking reform.

Accompanying Senator Aldrich at the Hoboken station were his private secretary, Shelton; A. Piatt Andrew, Assistant Secretary of the Treasury, and Special Assistant to the National Monetary Commission; Frank Vanderlip, president of the National City Bank of New York, Henry P. Davison, senior partner of J. P. Morgan Company, and generally regarded as Morgan's personal emissary; and Charles D. Norton, president of the Morgan-dominated First National Bank of New York. Joining the group just before the train left the station were Benjamin Strong, also known as a lieutenant of J.P. Morgan; and Paul Warburg, a recent immigrant from Germany who had joined the banking house of Kuhn, Loeb

---

[1] Prof. Nathaniel Wright Stephenson, Paul Warburg's Memorandum, *Nelson Aldrich A Leader in American Politics*, Scribners, N.Y. 1930

and Company, New York as a partner earning five hundred thousand dollars a year.

Six years later, a financial writer named Bertie Charles Forbes (who later founded the Forbes Magazine; the present editor, Malcolm Forbes, is his son), wrote:

"Picture a party of the nation's greatest bankers stealing out of New York on a private railroad car under cover of darkness, stealthily hieing hundreds of miles South, embarking on a mysterious launch, sneaking onto an island deserted by all but a few servants, living there a full week under such rigid secrecy that the names of not one of them was once mentioned lest the servants learn the identity and disclose to the world this strangest, most secret expedition in the history of American finance. I am not romancing; I am giving to the world, for the first time, the real story of how the famous Aldrich currency report, the foundation of our new currency system, was written . . . . The utmost secrecy was enjoined upon all. The public must not glean a hint of what was to be done. Senator Aldrich notified each one to go quietly into a private car of which the railroad had received orders to draw up on an unfrequented platform. Off the party set. New York's ubiquitous reporters had been foiled . . . Nelson (Aldrich) had confided to Henry, Frank, Paul and Piatt that he was to keep them locked up at Jekyll Island, out of the rest of the world, until they had evolved and compiled a scientific currency system for the United States, the real birth of the present Federal Reserve System, the plan done on Jekyll Island in the conference with Paul, Frank and Henry . . . . Warburg is the link that binds the Aldrich system and the present system together. He more than any one man has made the system possible as a working reality."[2]

The official biography of Senator Nelson Aldrich states:

"In the autumn of 1910, six men went out to shoot ducks, Aldrich, his secretary Shelton, Andrews, Davison, Venderlip and Warburg. Reporters were waiting at the Brunswick (Georgia) station. Mr. Davison went out and talked to them. The reporters dispersed and the secret of the strange journey was not divulged. Mr. Aldrich asked him how he had managed it and he did not volunteer the information."[3]

Davison had an excellent reputation as the person who could conciliate warring factions, a role he had performed for J.P. Morgan during the settling of the Money Panic of 1907. Another Morgan partner, T.W. Lamont, says:

"Henry P. Davison served as arbitrator of the Jekyll Island expedition."[4]

---

[2] "CURRENT OPINION", December, 1916, p. 382
[3] Nathaniel Wright Stephenson, *Nelson W. Aldrich, A Leader in American Politics*, Scribners, N.Y. 1930, Chap. XXIV "Jekyll Island"
[4] T. W. Lamont, Henry P. Davison, Harper, 1933

From these references, it is possible to piece together the story. Aldrich's private car, which had left Hoboken station with its shades drawn, had taken the financiers to Jekyll Island, Georgia. Some years earlier, a very exclusive group of millionaires, led by J.P. Morgan, had purchased the island as a winter retreat. They called themselves the Jekyll Island Hunt Club, and, at first, the island was used only for hunting expeditions, until the millionaires realized that its pleasant climate offered a warm retreat from the rigors of winters in New York, and began to build splendid mansions, which they called "cottages", for their families' winter vacations. The club building itself, being quite isolated, was sometimes in demand for stag parties and other pursuits unrelated to hunting. On such occasions, the club members who were not invited to these specific outings were asked not to appear there for a certain number of days. Before Nelson Aldrich's party had left New York, the club's members had been notified that the club would be occupied for the next two weeks.

The Jekyll Island Club was chosen as the place to draft the plan for control of the money and credit of the people of the United States, not only because of its isolation, but also because it was the private preserve of the people who were drafting the plan. *The New York Times* later noted, on May 3, 1931, in commenting on the death of George F. Baker, one of J.P. Morgan's closest associates, that "Jekyll Island Club has lost one of its most distinguished members. One-sixth of the total wealth of the world was represented by the members of the Jekyll Island Club." Membership was by inheritance only.

The Aldrich group had no interest in hunting. Jekyll Island was chosen for the site of the preparation of the central bank because it offered complete privacy, and because there was not a journalist within fifty miles. Such was the need for secrecy that the members of the party agreed, before arriving at Jekyll Island, that no last names would be used at any time during their two week stay. The group later referred to themselves as the First Name Club, as the last names of Warburg, Strong, Vanderlip and the others were prohibited during their stay. The customary attendants had been given two week vacations from the club, and new servants brought in from the mainland for this occasion who did not know the names of any of those present. Even if they had been interrogated after the Aldrich party went back to New York, they could not have given the names. This arrangement proved to be so satisfactory that the members, limited to those who had actually been present at Jekyll Island, later had a number of informal get-togethers in New York.

Why all this secrecy? Why this thousand mile trip in a closed railway car to a remote hunting club? Ostensibly, it was to carry out a program of public service, to prepare banking reform which would be a boon to the people of the United States, which had been ordered by the National

Monetary Commission. The participants were no strangers to public benefactions. Usually, their names were inscribed on brass plaques, or on the exteriors of buildings which they had donated. This was not the procedure which they followed at Jekyll Island. No brass plaque was ever erected to mark the selfless actions of those who met at their private hunt club in 1910 to improve the lot of every citizen of the United States.

In fact, no benefaction took place at Jekyll Island. The Aldrich group journeyed there in private to write the banking and currency legislation which the National Monetary Commission had been ordered to prepare in public. At stake was the future control of the money and credit of the United States. If any genuine monetary reform had been prepared and presented to Congress, it would have ended the power of the elitist one world money creators. Jekyll Island ensured that a central bank would be established in the United States which would give these bankers everything they had always wanted.

As the most technically proficient of those present, Paul Warburg was charged with doing most of the drafting of the plan. His work would then be discussed and gone over by the rest of the group. Senator Nelson Aldrich was there to see that the completed plan would come out in a form which he could get passed by Congress, and the other bankers were there to include whatever details would be needed to be certain that they got everything they wanted, in a finished draft composed during a one-time stay. After they returned to New York, there could be no second get together to rework their plan. They could not hope to obtain such secrecy for their work on a second journey.

The Jekyll Island group remained at the club for nine days, working furiously to complete their task. Despite the common interests of those present, the work did not proceed without friction. Senator Aldrich, always a domineering person, considered himself the chosen leader of the group, and could not help ordering everyone else about. Aldrich also felt somewhat out of place as the only member who was not a professional banker. He had had substantial banking interests throughout his career, but only as a person who profited from his ownership of bank stock. He knew little about the technical aspects of financial operations. His opposite number, Paul Warburg, believed that every question raised by the group demanded, not merely an answer, but a lecture. He rarely lost an opportunity to give the members a long discourse designed to impress them with the extent of his knowledge of banking. This was resented by the others, and often drew barbed remarks from Aldrich. The natural diplomacy of Henry P. Davison proved to be the catalyst which kept them at their work. Warburg's thick alien accent grated on them, and constantly reminded them that they had to accept his presence if a central bank plan was to be devised which would guarantee them their future profits. Warburg made little effort to smooth over their prejudices, and contested them on every possible occasion on technical banking questions, which he considered his private preserve.

"In all conspiracies there must be great secrecy."[5]

The "monetary reform" plan prepared at Jekyll Island was to be presented to Congress as the completed work of the National Monetary Commission. It was imperative that the real authors of the bill remain hidden. So great was popular resentment against bankers since the Panic of 1907 that no Congressman would dare to vote for a bill bearing the Wall Street taint, no matter who had contributed to his campaign expenses. The Jekyl Island plan was a central bank plan, and in this country there was a long tradition of struggle against inflicting a central bank on the American people. It had begun with Thomas Jefferson's fight against Alexander Hamilton's scheme for the First Bank of the United States, backed by James Rothschild. It had continued with President Andrew Jackson's successful war against Alexander Hamilton's scheme for the Second Bank of the United States, in which Nicholas Biddle was acting as the agent for James Rothschild of Paris. The result of that struggle was the creation of the Independent Sub-Treasury System, which supposedly had served to keep the funds of the United States out of the hands of the financiers. A study of the panics of 1873, 1893, and 1907 indicates that these panics were the result of the international bankers' operations in London. The public was demanding in 1908 that Congress enact legislation to prevent the recurrence of artificially induced money panics. Such monetary reform now seemed inevitable. It was to head off and control such reform that the National Monetary Commission had been set up with Nelson Aldrich at its head, since he was majority leader of the Senate.

The main problem, as Paul Warburg informed his colleagues, was to avoid the name "Central Bank". For that reason, he had decided upon the designation of "Federal Reserve System". This would deceive the people into thinking it was not a central bank. However, the Jekyll Island plan would be a central bank plan, fulfilling the main functions of a central bank; it would be owned by private individuals who would profit from ownership of shares. As a bank of issue, it would control the nation's money and credit.

In the chapter on Jekyll Island in his biography of Aldrich, Stephenson writes of the conference:

"How was the Reserve Bank to be controlled? It must be controlled by Congress. The government was to be represented in the board of directors, it was to have full knowledge of all the Bank's affairs, but a majority

Clarendon, Hist. Reb. 1647

of the directors were to be chosen, directly or indirectly, by the banks of the association."⁶

Thus the proposed Federal Reserve Bank was to be "controlled by Congress" and answerable to the government, but the majority of the directors were to be chosen, "directly or indirectly" by the banks of the association. In the final refinement of Warburg's plan, the Federal Reserve Board of Governors would be appointed by the President of the United States, but the real work of the Board would be controlled by a Federal Advisory Council, meeting with the Governors. The Council would be chosen by the directors of the twelve Federal Reserve Banks, and would remain unknown to the public.

The next consideration was to conceal the fact that the proposed "Federal Reserve System" would be dominated by the masters of the New York money market. The Congressmen from the South and the West could not survive if they voted for a Wall Street plan. Farmers and small businessmen in those areas had suffered most from the money panics. There had been great popular resentment against the Eastern bankers, which during the nineteenth century became a political movement known as "populism". The private papers of Nicholas Biddle, not released until more than a century after his death, show that quite early on the Eastern bankers were fully aware of the widespread public opposition to them.

Paul Warburg advanced at Jekyll Island the primary deception which would prevent the citizens from recognizing that his plan set up a central bank. This was the regional reserve system. He proposed a system of four (later twelve) branch reserve banks located in different sections of the country. Few people outside the banking world would realize that the existing concentration of the nation's money and credit structure in New York made the proposal of a regional reserve system a delusion.

Another proposal advanced by Paul Warburg at Jekyll Island was the manner of selection of administrators for the proposed regional reserve system. Senator Nelson Aldrich had insisted that the officials should be appointive, not elected, and that Congress should have no role in their selection. His Capitol Hill experience had taught him that congressional opinion would often be inimical to the Wall Street interests, as Congressmen from the West and South might wish to demonstrate to their constituents that they were protecting them against the Eastern bankers.

Warburg responded that the administrators of the proposed central banks should be subject to executive approval by the President. This patent removal of the system from Congressional control meant that the

---

⁶Nathaniel Wright Stephenson, *Nelson W. Aldrich, A Leader in American Politics*, Scribners, N.Y. 1930, Chap. XXIV "Jekyll Island" p. 379

Federal Reserve proposal was unconstitutional from its inception, because the Federal Reserve System was to be a bank of issue. Article 1, Sec. 8, Par. 5 of the Constitution expressly charges *Congress* with "the power to coin money and regulate the value thereof". Warburg's plan would deprive Congress of its sovereignty, and the systems of checks and balances of power set up by Thomas Jefferson in the Constitution would now be destroyed. Administrators of the proposed system would control the nation's money and credit, and would themselves be approved by the executive department of the government. The judicial department (the Supreme Court, etc.) was already virtually controlled by the executive department through presidential appointment to the bench.

Paul Warburg later wrote a massive exposition of his plan, *The Federal Reserve System, Its Origin and Growth*[7] of some 1750 pages, but the name "Jekyll Island" appears nowhere in this text. He does state (Vol. 1, p. 58):

> "In November, 1910, I was invited to join a small group of men who, at Senator Aldrich's request, were to take part in a several days' conference with him, to discuss the form that the new banking bill should take. During this conference, I had my first opportunity of studying the Senator carefully, and I was deeply impressed by the earnest devotion with which he approached the subject and the untiring patience with which he applied himself to it."

It is noteworthy that Warburg does not disclose who attended this conference, or where it took place, even though it was a momentous gathering which would decide the future control of the money and credit of the people of the United States. He continues (page 59):

> "But then the conference closed, after a week of earnest deliberation, the rough draft of what later became the Aldrich Bill had been agreed upon, and a plan had been outlined which provided for a 'National Reserve Association,' meaning a central reserve organization with an elastic note issue based on gold and commercial paper."

On page 60, Warburg writes, "The results of the conference were entirely confidential. Even the fact there had been a meeting was not permitted to become public." He adds in a footnote, "Though eighteen [sic] years have since gone by, I do not feel free to give a description of this most interesting conference concerning which Senator Aldrich pledged all participants to secrecy."

B.C. Forbes' revelation[8] of the secret expedition to Jekyll Island, had had surprisingly little impact. It did not appear in print until two years after the Federal Reserve Act had been passed by Congress, hence it was never read during the period when it could have had an effect, that

---

[7] Paul Warburg, *The Federal Reserve System, Its Origin and Growth*, Volume I, p. 58, Macmillan, New York, 1930
[8] *CURRENT OPINION*, December, 1916, p. 382

is, during the Congressional debate on the bill. Forbes' story was also dismissed, by those "in the know," as preposterous, and a mere invention. Stephenson mentions this on page 484 of his book about Aldrich.[9]

"This curious episode of Jekyll Island has been generally regarded as a myth. B.C. Forbes got some information from one of the reporters. It told in vague outline the Jekyll Island story, but made no impression and was generally regarded as a mere yarn."

The coverup of the Jekyll Island conference proceeded along two lines, both of which were successful. The first, as Stephenson mentions, was to dismiss the entire story as a romantic concoction which never actually took place. Although there were brief references to Jekyll Island in later books concerning the Federal Reserve System, these also attracted little public attention. As we have noted, Warburg's massive and supposedly definitive work on the Federal Reserve System does not mention Jekyll Island at all, although he does admit that a conference took place. In none of his voluminous speeches or writings do the words "Jekyll Island" appear, with a single notable exception. He agreed to Professor Stephenson's request that he prepare a brief statement for the Aldrich biography. This appears on page 485 as part of "The Warburg Memorandum". In this excerpt, Warburg writes, "The matter of a uniform discount rate was discussed and settled at Jekyll Island."

Another member of the "First Name Club" was less reticent. Frank Vanderlip later published a few brief references to the conference. In the Saturday Evening Post, February 9, 1935, p. 25, Vanderlip wrote:

"Despite my views about the value to society of greater publicity for the affairs of corporations, there was an occasion near the close of 1910, when I was as secretive, indeed, as furtive, as any conspirator. . . . Since it would have been fatal to Senator Aldrich's plan to have it known that he was calling on anybody from Wall Street to help him in preparing his bill, precautions were taken that would have delighted the heart of James Stillman (a colorful and secretive banker who was President of the National City Bank during the Spanish-American War, and who was thought to have been involved in getting us into that war) . . . I do not feel it is any exaggeration to speak of our secret expedition to Jekyl Island as the occasion of the actual conception of what eventually became the Federal Reserve System."

In a Travel feature in *The Washington Post*, March 27, 1983, "Follow The Rich to Jekyll Island", Roy Hoopes writes:

"In 1910, when Aldrich and four financial experts wanted a place to meet in secret to reform the country's banking system, they faked a hunting trip to Jekyll and for 10 days holed up in the Clubhouse, where they made plans for what eventually would become the Federal Reserve Bank."

---

[9]Nathaniel Wright Stephenson, *Nelson W. Aldrich, A Leader In American Politics*, Scribners, New York, 1930

Vanderlip later wrote in his autobiography, *From Farmboy to Financier:*[10]

"Our secret expedition to Jekyll Island was the occasion of the actual conception of what eventually became the Federal Reserve System. The essential points of the Aldrich Plan were all contained in the Federal Reserve Act as it was passed."

Professor E.R.A. Seligman, a member of the international banking family of J. & W. Seligman, and head of the Department of Economics at Columbia University, wrote in an essay published by the Academy of Political Science, Proceedings, v. 4, No. 4, p. 387-90:

"It is known to a very few how great is the indebtedness of the United States to Mr. Warburg. For it may be said without fear of contradiction that in its fundamental features the Federal Reserve Act is the work of Mr. Warburg more than any other man in the country. The existence of a Federal Reserve Board creates, in everything but in name, a real central bank. In the two fundamentals of command of reserves and of a discount policy, the Federal Reserve Act has frankly accepted the principle of the Aldrich Bill, and these principles, as has been stated, were the creation of Mr. Warburg and Mr. Warburg alone. It must not be forgotten that Mr. Warburg had a practical object in view. In formulating his plans and in advancing in them slightly varying suggestions from time to time, it was incumbent on him to remember that the education of the country must be gradual and that a large part of the task was to break down prejudices and remove suspicion. His plans therefore contained all sorts of elaborate suggestions designed to guard the public against fancied dangers and to persuade the country that the general scheme was at all practicable. It was the hope of Mr. Warburg that with the lapse of time it might be possible to eliminate from the law a few clauses which were inserted largely at his suggestion for educational purposes."

Now that the public debt of the United States has passed a trillion dollars, we may indeed admit "how great is the indebtedness of the United States to Mr. Warburg." At the time he wrote the Federal Reserve Act, the public debt was almost nonexistent.

Professor Seligman points out Warburg's remarkable prescience that the real task of the members of the Jekyll Island conference was to prepare a banking plan which would gradually "educate the country" and "break down prejudices and remove suspicion". The campaign to enact the plan into law succeeded in doing just that.

---

[10]Frank Vanderlip, *From Farmboy to Financier*

## CHAPTER TWO
# THE ALDRICH PLAN

"Finance and the tariff are reserved by Nelson Aldrich as falling within his solo purview and jurisdiction. Mr. Aldrich is endeavoring to devise, through the National Monetary Commission, a banking and currency law. A great many hundred thousand persons are firmly of the opinion that Mr. Aldrich sums up in his personality the greatest and most sinister menace to the popular welfare of the United States. Ernest Newman recently said, 'What the South visits on the Negro in a political way, Aldrich would mete out to the mudsills of the North, if he could devise a safe and practical way to accomplish it.' "—Harper's Weekly, May 7, 1910."

The participants in the Jekyll Island conference returned to New York to direct a nationwide propaganda campaign in favor of the "Aldrich Plan". Three of the leading universities, Princeton, Harvard, and the University of Chicago, were used as the rallying points for this propaganda, and national banks had to contribute to a fund of five million dollars to persuade the American public that this central bank plan should be enacted into law by Congress.

Woodrow Wilson, governor of New Jersey and former president of Princeton University, was enlisted as a spokesman for the Aldrich Plan. During the Panic of 1907, Wilson had declared, "All this trouble could be averted if we appointed a committee of six or seven public-spirited men like J.P. Morgan to handle the affairs of our country."

In his biography of Nelson Aldrich in 1930, Stephenson says:

"A pamphlet was issued January 16, 1911, 'Suggested Plan for Monetary Legislation', by Hon. Nelson Aldrich, based on Jekyll Island conclusions." Stephenson says on page 388, "An organization for financial progress had been formed. Mr. Warburg introduced a resolution authorizing the establishment of the Citizens' League, later the National Citizens League . . . Professor Laughlin of the University of Chicago was given charge of the League's propaganda."[11]

It is notable that Stephenson characterizes the work of the National Citizens League as "propaganda", in line with Seligman's exposition of

---

[11] Nathaniel Wright Stephenson, *Nelson Aldrich, A Leader in American Politics*, Scribners, N.Y. 1930

Warburg's work as "the education of the country" and "to break down prejudices".

Much of the five million dollars of the bankers slush fund was spent under the auspices of the National Citizens' League, which was made up of college professors. The two most tireless propagandists for the Aldrich Plan were Professor O.M. Sprague of Harvard, and J. Laurence Laughlin of the University of Chicago.

Congressman Charles A. Lindbergh, Sr., notes:

> "J. Laurence Laughlin, Chairman of the Executive Committee of the National Citizens' League since its organization, has returned to his position as professor of political economics in the University of Chicago. In June, 1911, Professor Laughlin was given a year's leave from the university, that he might give all of his time to the campaign of education undertaken by the League . . . He has worked indefatigably, and it is largely due to his efforts and his persistence that the campaign enters the final stage with flattering prospects of a successful outcome . . . The reader knows that the University of Chicago is an institution endowed by John D. Rockefeller, with nearly fifty million dollars."[12]

In his biography of Nelson Aldrich, Stephenson reveals that the Citizens' League was also a Jekyll Island product. In chapter 24 we find that: The Aldrich Plan was represented to Congress as the result of three years of work, study and travel by members of the National Monetary Commission, with expenditures of more than three hundred thousand dollars.*

Testifying before the Committee on Rules, December 15, 1911, after the Aldrich plan had been introduced in Congress, Congressman Lindbergh stated,

> "Our financial system is a false one and a huge burden on the people . . . I have alleged that there is a Money Trust. The Aldrich plan is a scheme plainly in the interest of the Trust . . . Why does the Money Trust press so hard for the Aldrich Plan now, before the people know what the money trust has been doing?"

Lindbergh continued in his speech,

> "The Aldrich Plan is the Wall Street Plan. It is a broad challenge to the Government by the champion of the Money Trust. It means another panic, if necessary, to intimidate the people. Aldrich, paid by the Government to represent the people, proposes a plan for the trusts instead. It was by a very clever move that the National Monetary Commission was created. In 1907 nature responded most beautifully and gave this country the most bountiful crop it had ever had. Other industries were busy too, and from a natural standpoint all the conditions were right for a most

---

[12] Charles A. Lindbergh, Sr., *Banking, Currency and the Money Trust*, 1913, p. 131
*In 1911, the Aldrich Plan became part of the official platform of the Republican Party.

prosperous year. Instead, a panic entailed enormous losses upon us. Wall Street knew the American people were demanding a remedy against the recurrence of such a ridiculously unnatural condition. Most Senators and Representatives fell into the Wall Street trap and passed the Aldrich Vreeland Emergency Currency Bill. But the real purpose was to get a monetary commission which would frame a proposition for amendments to our currency and banking laws which would suit the Money Trust. The interests are now busy everywhere educating the people in favor of the Aldrich Plan. It is reported that a large sum of money has been raised for this purpose. Wall Street speculation brought on the Panic of 1907. The depositors' funds were loaned to gamblers and anybody the Money Trust wanted to favour. Then when the depositors wanted their money, the banks did not have it. That made the panic."

Edward Vreeland, co-author of the bill, wrote in the August 25, 1910 Independent (which was owned by Aldrich), "Under the proposed monetary plan of Senator Aldrich, monopolies will disappear, because they will not be able to make more than four percent interest and monopolies cannot continue at such a low rate. Also, this will mark the disappearance of the Government from the banking business."

Vreeland's fantastic claims were typical of the propaganda flood unleashed to pass the Aldrich Plan. Monopolies would disappear, the Government would disappear from the banking business. Pie in the sky.

Nation Magazine, January 19, 1911, noted, "The name of Central Bank is carefully avoided, but the 'Federal Reserve Association', the name given to the proposed central organization, is endowed with the usual powers and responsibilities of a European Central Bank."

After the National Monetary Commission had returned from Europe, it held no official meetings for nearly two years. No records or minutes were ever presented showing who had authored the Aldrich Plan. Since they held no official meetings, the members of the commission could hardly claim the Plan as their own. The sole tangible result of the Commission's three hundred thousand dollar expenditure was a library of thirty massive volumes on European banking. Typical of these works is a thousand page history of the Reichsbank, the central bank which controlled money and credit in Germany, and whose principal stockholders were the Rothschilds and Paul Warburg's family banking house of M.M. Warburg Company. The Commission's records show that it never functioned as a deliberative body. Indeed, its only "meeting" was the secret conference held at Jekyll Island, and this conference is not mentioned in any publication of the Commission. Senator Cummins passed a resolution in Congress ordering the Commission to report on January 8, 1912, and show some constructive result of its three years' work. In the face of this challenge, the National Monetary Commission ceased to exist.

With their five million dollars as a war chest, the Aldrich Plan propagandists waged a no-holds barred war against their opposition. Andrew Frame testified before the House Banking and Currency Committee in 1913 as a member of the Executive Committee of the American Bankers Association. He represented a group of Western bankers who opposed the Aldrich Plan:

CHAIRMAN CARTER GLASS: "Why didn't the Western bankers make themselves heard when the American Bankers Association gave its unqualified and, we are assured, unanimous approval of the scheme proposed by the National Monetary Commission?"

ANDREW FRAME: "I'm glad you called my attention to that. When that monetary bill was given to the country, it was but a few days previous to the meeting of the American Bankers Association in New Orleans in 1911. There was not one banker in a hundred who had read that bill. We had twelve addresses in favor of it. General Hamby of Austin, Texas, wrote a letter to President Watts asking for a hearing against the bill. He did not get a very courteous answer. I refused to vote on it, and a great many other bankers did likewise."

MR. BULKLEY: "Do you mean that no member of the Association could be heard in opposition to the bill?"

ANDREW FRAME: "They throttled all argument."

MR. KINDRED: "But the report was given out that it was practically unanimous."

ANDREW FRAME: "The bill had already been prepared by Senator Aldrich and presented to the executive council of the American Bankers Association in May, 1911. As a member of that council, I received a copy the day before they acted upon it. When the bill came in at New Orleans, the bankers of the United States had not read it."

MR. KINDRED: "Did the presiding officer simply rule out those who wanted to discuss it negatively?"

ANDREW FRAME: "They would not allow anyone on the program who was not in favor of the bill."

CHAIRMAN GLASS: "What significance has the fact that at the next annual meeting of the American Bankers Association held at Detroit in 1912, the Association did not reiterate its endorsement of the plan of the National Monetary Commission, known as the Aldrich scheme?"

ANDREW FRAME: "It did not reiterate the endorsement for the simple fact that the backers of the Aldrich Plan knew that the Association would not endorse it. We were ready for them, but they did not bring it up."

Andrew Frame exposed the collusion which in 1911 procured an endorsement of the Aldrich Plan from the American Bankers Association but which in 1912 did not even dare to repeat its endorsement, for fear of an honest and open discussion of the merits of the plan.

Chairman Glass then called as witness one of the ten most powerful bankers in the United States, George Blumenthal, partner of the international banking house of Lazard Freres and brother-in-law of Eugene Meyer, Jr. Carter Glass effusively welcomed Blumenthal, stating that "Senator O'Gorman of New York was kind enough to suggest your name to us." A year later, O'Gorman prevented a Senate Committee from asking his master, Paul Warburg, any embarrassing questions before approving his nomination as the first Governor of the Federal Reserve Board.

George Blumenthal stated, "Since 1893 my firm of Lazard Freres has been foremost in importations and exportations of gold and has thereby come into contact with everybody who had anything to do with it."

Congressman Taylor asked, "Have you a statement there as to the part you have had in the importation of gold into the United States?" Taylor asked this because the Panic of 1893 is known to economists as a classic example of a money panic caused by gold movements.

"No," replied George Blumenthal, "I have nothing at all on that, because it is not bearing on the question."

A banker from Philadelphia, Leslie Shaw, dissented with other witnesses at these hearings, criticizing the much vaunted "decentralization" of the System. He said, "Under the Aldrich Plan the bankers are to have local associations and district associations, and when you have a local organization, the centered control is assured. Suppose we have a local association in Indianapolis; can you not name the three men who will dominate that association? And then can you not name the one man who will dominate the three? The same is true in Richmond and everywhere else. When you have hooked the banks together, they can have the biggest influence of anything in this country, with the exception of the newspapers."

To promote the Democratic currency bill, Carter Glass made public the sorry record of the Republican efforts of Senator Aldrich's National Monetary Commission. His House Report in 1913 said, "Senator MacVeagh fixes the cost of the National Monetary Commission to May 12, 1911 at $207,130. They have since spent another hundred thousand dollars of the taxpayer's money. The work done at such cost cannot be ignored, but, having examined the extensive literature published by the Commission, the Banking and Currency Committee finds little that bears upon the present state of the credit market of the United States. We object to the Aldrich Bill on the following points:

Its entire lack of adequate government or public control of the banking mechanism it sets up.

Its tendency to throw voting control into the hands of the large banks of the system.

The extreme danger of inflation of currency inherent in the system.

The insincerity of the bond-funding plan provided for by the measure, there being a barefaced pretense that this system was to cost the government nothing.

The dangerous monopolistic aspects of the bill.

Our Committee at the outset of its work was met by a well-defined sentiment in favor of a central bank which was the manifest outgrowth of the work that had been done by the National Monetary Commission."

Glass's denunciation of the Aldrich Bill as a central bank plan ignored the fact that his own Federal Reserve Act would fulfill all the functions of a central bank. Its stock would be owned by private stockholders who could use the credit of the Government for their own profit; it would have control of the nation's money and credit resources; and it would be a bank of issue which would finance the government by "mobilizing" credit in time of war. In "The Rationale of Central Banking," Vera C. Smith (Committee for Monetary Research and Education, June, 1981) writes, "The primary definition of a central bank is a banking system in which a single bank has either a complete or residuary monopoly in the note issue. A central bank is not a natural product of banking development. It is imposed from outside or comes into being as the result of Government favors."

Thus a central bank attains its commanding position from its government granted monopoly of the note issue. This is the key to its power. Also, the act of establishing a central bank has a direct inflationary impact because of the fractional reserve system, which allows the creation of book-entry loans and thereby, money, a number of times the actual "money" which the bank has in its deposits or reserves.

The Aldrich Plan never came to a vote in Congress, because the Republicans lost control of the House in 1910, and subsequently lost the Senate and the Presidency in 1912.

## CHAPTER THREE
# The Federal Reserve Act

"Our financial system is a false one and a huge burden on the people . . . This Act establishes the most gigantic trust on earth."—Congressman Charles Augustus Lindbergh, Sr.

The speeches of Senator LaFollette and Congressman Lindbergh became rallying points of opposition to the Aldrich Plan in 1912. They also aroused popular feeling against the Money Trust. Congressman Lindbergh said, on December 15, 1911, "The government prosecutes other trusts, but supports the money trust. I have been waiting patiently for several years for an opportunity to expose the false money standard, and to show that the greatest of all favoritism is that extended by the government to the money trust."

Senator LaFollette publicly charged that a money trust of fifty men controlled the United States. George F. Baker, partner of J.P. Morgan, on being queried by reporters as to the truth of the charge, replied that it was absolutely in error. He said that he knew from personal knowledge that not more than eight men ran this country.

*The Nation Magazine* replied editorially to Senator LaFollette that "If there is a Money Trust, it will not be practical to establish that it exercises its influence either for good or for bad."

Senator LaFollette remarks in his memoirs that his speech against the Money Trust later cost him the Presidency of the United States, just as Woodrow Wilson's early support of the Aldrich Plan had brought him into consideration for that office.

Congress finally made a gesture to appease popular feeling by appointing a committee to investigate the control of money and credit in the United States. This was the Pujo Committee, a subcommittee of the House Banking and Currency Committee, which conducted the famous "Money Trust" hearings in 1912, under the leadership of Congressman Arsene Pujo of Louisiana, who was regarded as a spokesman for the oil interests. These hearings were deliberately dragged on for five months, and resulted in six-thousand pages of printed testimony in four volumes. Month after month, the bankers made the train trip from New York to Washington, testified before the Committee and returned to New York. The hearings were extremely dull, and no startling information turned up at these sessions. The bankers solemnly admitted that they were indeed bankers, insisted that they always operated in the public interest, and claimed that they were animated only by the highest ideals of public service, like the Congressmen before whom they were testifying.

The paradoxical nature of the Pujo Money Trust Hearings may better be understood if we examine the man who single-handedly carried on these hearings, Samuel Untermyer. He was one of the principal contributors to Woodrow Wilson's Presidential campaign fund, and was one of the wealthiest corporation lawyers in New York. He states in his autobiography in "Who's Who" of 1926 that he once received a $775,000 fee for a single legal transaction, the successful merger of the Utah Copper Company and the Boston Consolidated and Nevada Company, a firm with a market value of one hundred million dollars. He refused to ask either Senator LaFollette or Congressman Lindbergh to testify in the investigation which they alone had forced Congress to hold. As Special Counsel for the Pujo Committee, Untermyer ran the hearings as a one-man operation. The Congressional members, including its chairman, Congressman Arsene Pujo, seemed to have been struck dumb from the commencement of the hearings to their conclusion. One of these silent servants of the public was Congressman James Byrnes, of South Carolina, representing Bernard Baruch's home district, who later achieved fame as "Baruch's man", and was placed by Baruch in charge of the Office of War Mobilization during the Second World War.

Although he was a specialist in such matters, Untermyer did not ask any of the bankers about the system of interlocking directorates through which they controlled industry. He did not go into international gold movements, which were known as a factor in money panics, or the international relationships between American bankers and European bankers. The international banking houses of Eugene Meyer, Lazard Freres, J. & W. Seligman, Ladenburg Thalmann, Speyer Brothers, M. M. Warburg, and the Rothschild Brothers did not arouse Samuel Untermyer's curiosity, although it was well known in the New York financial world that all of these family banking houses either had branches or controlled subsidiary houses in Wall Street. When Jacob Schiff appeared before the Pujo Committee, Mr. Untermyer's adroit questioning allowed Mr. Schiff to talk for many minutes without revealing any information about the operations of the banking house of Kuhn Loeb Company, of which he was senior partner, and which Senator Robert L. Owen had identified as the representative of the European Rothschilds in the United States.

The aging J.P. Morgan, who had only a few more months to live, appeared before the Committee to justify his decades of international financial deals. He stated for Mr. Untermyer's edification that "Money is a commodity." This was a favorite ploy of the money creators, as they wished to make the public believe that the creation of money was a natural occurrence akin to the growing of a field of corn, although it was actually a bounty conferred upon the bankers by governments over which they had gained control.

J.P. Morgan also told the Pujo Committee that, in making a loan, he seriously considered only one factor, a man's character; even the man's ability to repay the loan, or his collateral, were of little importance. This astonishing observation startled even the blasé members of the Committee.

The farce of the Pujo Committee ended without a single well-known opponent of the money creators being allowed to appear or testify. As far as Samuel Untermyer was concerned, Senator LaFollette and Congressman Charles Augustus Lindbergh had never existed. Nevertheless, these Congressmen had managed to convince the people of the United States that the New York bankers did have a monopoly on the nation's money and credit. At the close of the hearings, the bankers and their subsidized newspapers claimed that the only way to break this monopoly was to enact the banking and currency legislation now being proposed to Congress, a bill which would be passed a year later as the Federal Reserve Act. The press seriously demanded that the New York banking monopoly be broken by turning over the administration of the new banking system to the most knowledgeable banker of them all, Paul Warburg.

The Presidential campaign of 1912 records one of the more interesting political upsets in American history. The incumbent, William Howard Taft, was a popular president, and the Republicans, in a period of general prosperity, were firmly in control of the government through a Republican majority in both houses. The Democratic challenger, Woodrow Wilson, Governor of New Jersey, had no national recognition, and was a stiff, austere man who excited little public support. Both parties included a monetary reform bill in their platforms: The Republicans were committed to the Aldrich Plan, which had been denounced as a Wall Street plan, and the Democrats had the Federal Reserve Act. Neither party bothered to inform the public that the bills were almost identical except for the names. In retrospect, it seems obvious that the money creators decided to dump Taft and go with Wilson. How do we know this? Taft seemed certain of reelection, and Wilson would return to obscurity. Suddenly, Theodore Roosevelt "threw his hat into the ring". He announced that he was running as a third party candidate, the "Bull Moose". His candidacy would have been ludicrous had it not been for the fact that he was exceptionally well-financed. Moreover, he was given unlimited press coverage, more than Taft and Wilson combined. As a Republican ex-president, it was obvious that Roosevelt would cut deeply into Taft's vote. This proved the case, and Wilson won the election. To this day, no one can say what Theodore Roosevelt's program was, or why he would sabotage his own party. Since the bankers were financing all three candidates, they would win regardless of the outcome. Later Congressional testimony showed that in the firm of Kuhn Loeb Company, Felix Warburg was supporting Taft, Paul Warburg and Jacob Schiff were supporting Wilson, and Otto Kahn was supporting Roosevelt. The result was that a Democratic Congress and a Democratic President were elected in 1912 to get the central bank legislation passed. It seems probable that the identification of the Aldrich Plan as a Wall Street operation predicted that it would have a difficult passage through Congress, as the Democrats would solidly oppose it, whereas a successful Democratic candidate, supported by a Democratic Congress, would be able to pass the central bank plan. Taft was thrown overboard because the bankers doubted he could deliver on the Aldrich Plan, and Roosevelt was the instrument of his demise.

To further confuse the American people and blind them to the real purpose of the proposed Federal Reserve Act, the architects of the Aldrich Plan, powerful Nelson Aldrich, although no longer a senator, and Frank Vanderlip, president of the National City Bank, set up a hue and cry against the bill. They gave interviews wherever they could find an audience denouncing the proposed Federal Reserve Act as inimical to banking and to good government. The bugaboo of inflation was raised because of the Act's provisions for printing Federal Reserve notes. *The Nation*, on October 23, 1913, pointed out, "Mr. Aldrich himself raised a hue and cry over the issue of government "fiat money", that is, money issued without gold or bullion back of it, although a bill to do precisely that had been passed in 1908 with his own name as author, and he knew besides, that the 'government' had nothing to do with it, that the Federal Reserve Board would have full charge of the issuing of such moneys."

Frank Vanderlip's claims were so bizarre that Senator Robert L. Owen, chairman of the newly formed Senate Banking and Currency Committee, which had been formed on March 18, 1913, accused him of openly carrying on a campaign of misrepresentation about the bill. The interests of the public, so Carter Glass claimed in a speech on September 10, 1913 to Congress, would be protected by an advisory council of bankers. "There can be nothing sinister about its transactions. Meeting with it at least four times a year will be a bankers' advisory council representing every regional reserve district in the system. How could we have exercised greater caution in safeguarding the public interests?"

Glass claimed that the proposed Federal Advisory Council would force the Federal Reserve Board of Governors to act in the best interest of the people.

Senator Root raised the problem of inflation, claiming that under the Federal Reserve Act, note circulation would always expand indefinitely, causing great inflation. However, the later history of the Federal Reserve

System showed that it not only caused inflation, but that the issue of notes could also be restricted, causing deflation, as occurred from 1929 to 1939.

One of the critics of the proposed "decentralized" system was a lawyer from Cleveland, Ohio, Alfred Crozier: Crozier was called to testify for the Senate Committee because he had written a provocative book in 1912, *U.S. Money vs. Corporation Currency*.* He attacked the Aldrich-Vreeland Act of 1908 as a Wall Street instrument, and he pointed out that when our government had to issue money based on privately owned securities, we were no longer a free nation.

Crozier testified before the Senate Committee that, "It should prohibit the granting or calling in of loans for the purpose of influencing quotation prices of securities and the contracting of loans or increasing interest rates in concert by the banks to influence public opinion or the action of any legislative body. Within recent months, William McAdoo, Secretary of the Treasury of the United States was reported in the open press as charging specifically that there was a conspiracy among certain of the large banking interests to put a contraction upon the currency and to raise interest rates for the sake of making the public force Congress into passing currency legislation desired by those interests. The so-called administration currency bill grants just what Wall Street and the big banks for twenty-five years have been striving for, that is, PRIVATE INSTEAD OF PUBLIC CONTROL OF CURRENCY. It does this as completely as the Aldrich Bill. Both measures rob the government and the people of all effective control over the public's money, and vest in the banks exclusively the dangerous power to make money among the people scarce or plenty. The Aldrich Bill puts this power in one central bank. The Administration Bill puts it in twelve regional central banks, all owned exclusively by the identical private interests that would have owned and operated the Aldrich Bank. President Garfield shortly before his assassination declared that whoever controls the supply of currency would control the business and activities of all the people. Thomas Jefferson warned us a hundred years ago that a private central bank issuing the public currency was a greater menace to the liberties of the people than a standing army."

It is interesting to note how many assassinations of Presidents of the United States follow their concern with the issuing of public currency; Lincoln with his Greenback, non-interest-bearing notes, and Garfield, making a pronouncement on currency problems just before he was assassinated.

We now begin to understand why such a lengthy campaign of planned deception was necessary, from the secret conference at Jekyll Island to the identical "reform" plans proposed by the Democratic and

---

*Crozier's book exposed the financiers plan to substitute "corporation currency" for the lawful money of the U.S. as guaranteed by Article I, Sec. 8 Para. 5, of the Constitution.

Republican parties under different names. The bankers could not wrest control of the issuance of money from the citizens of the United States, to whom it had been designated through its Congress by the Constitution, until the Congress granted them their monopoly for a central bank. Therefore, much of the influence exerted to get the Federal Reserve Act passed was done behind the scenes, principally by two shadowy, non-elected persons: The German immigrant, Paul Warburg, and Colonel Edward Mandel House of Texas.

Paul Warburg made an appearance before the House Banking and Currency Committee in 1913, in which he briefly stated his background: "I am a member of the banking house of Kuhn, Loeb Company. I came over to this country in 1902, having been born and educated in the banking business in Hamburg, Germany, and studied banking in London and Paris, and have gone all around the world. In the Panic of 1907, the first suggestion I made was 'Let us get a national clearing house.' The Aldrich Plan contains some things which are simply fundamental rules of banking. Your aim in this plan (the Owen-Glass bill) must be the same—centralizing of reserves, mobilizing commercial credit, and getting an elastic note issue."

Warburg's phrase, "mobilization of credit" was an important one, because the First World War was due to begin shortly, and the first task of the Federal Reserve System would be to finance the World War. The European nations were already bankrupt, because they had maintained large standing armies for almost fifty years, a situation created by their own central banks, and therefore they could not finance a war. A central bank always imposes a tremendous burden on the nation for "rearmament" and "defense", in order to create inextinguishable debt, simultaneously creating a military dictatorship and enslaving the people to pay the "interest" on the debt which the bankers have artificially created.

In the Senate debate on the Federal Reserve Act, Senator Stone said on December 12, 1913,

> "The great banks for years have sought to have and control agents in the Treasury to serve their purposes. Let me quote from this World article, 'Just as soon as Mr. McAdoo came to Washington, a woman whom the National City Bank had installed in the Treasury Department to get advance information on the condition of banks, and other matters of interest to the big Wall Street group, was removed. Immediately the Secretary and the Assistant Secretary, John Skelton Williams, were criticized severely by the agents of the Wall Street group.'"
>
> "I myself have known more than one occasion when bankers refused credit to men who opposed their political views and purposes. When Senator Aldrich and others were going around the country exploiting this scheme, the big banks of New York and Chicago were engaged in

raising a munificent fund to bolster up the Aldrich propaganda. I have been told by bankers of my own state that contributions to this exploitation fund had been demanded of them and that they had contributed because they were afraid of being blacklisted or boycotted. There are bankers of this country who are enemies of the public welfare. In the past, a few great banks have followed policies and projects that have paralized the industrial energies of the country to perpetuate their tremendous power over the financial and business industries of America."

Carter Glass states in his autobiography that he was summoned by Woodrow Wilson to the White House, and that Wilson told him he intended to make the reserve notes obligations of the United States. Glass says, "I was for an instant speechless. I remonstrated. There is not any government obligation here, Mr. President. Wilson said he had had to compromise on this point in order to save the bill."

The term "compromise" on this point came directly from Paul Warburg. Col. Elisha Ely Garrison, in *Roosevelt,\* Wilson and the Federal Reserve Law* wrote,

"In 1911, Lawrence Abbot, Mr. Roosevelt's private office at 'The Outlook' handed me a copy of the so-called Aldrich Plan for currency reform. I said, I could not believe that Mr. Warburg was the author. This plan is nothing more than the Aldrich-Vreeland legislation which provided for currency issue against securities. Warburg knows that as well as I do. I am going to see him at once and ask him about it. All right, good luck, laughed Roosevelt. I went to Warburg and demanded to know the truth. Yes, I wrote it, he said. Why? I asked. It was a compromise, answered Warburg."[13]

Garrison says that Warburg wrote him on February 8, 1912.

"I have no doubt that at the end of a thorough discussion, either you will see it my way or I will see it yours— but I hope you will see it mine."

This was another famous Warburg saying when he secretly lobbied Congressmen to support his interest, the veiled threat that they should "see it his way". Those who did not found large sums contributed to their opponents at the next elections, and usually went down in defeat.

Col. Garrison, an agent of Brown Brothers bankers, later Brown Brothers Harriman, had entree everywhere in the financial community. He writes of Col. House, "Col. House agreed entirely with the early writing of Mr. Warburg." Page 337, he quotes Col. House:

"I am also suggesting that the Central Board be increased from four members to five and their terms lengthened from eight to ten years. This would give stability and would take away the power of a President to change the personnel of the board during a single term of office."

---

\*Theodore Roosevelt
[13] Elisha Ely Garrison, *Roosevelt, Wilson and the Federal Reserve Law*, Christopher Publications, Boston, 1931

House's phrase, "take away the power of a President" is significant, because later Presidents found themselves helpless to change the direction of the government because they did not have the power to change the composition of the Federal Reserve Board to attain a majority on it during that President's term of office. Garrison also wrote in this book,

> "Paul Warburg is the man who got the Federal Reserve Act together after the Aldrich Plan aroused such nationwide resentment and opposition. The mastermind of both plans was Baron Alfred Rothschild of London."

Colonel Edward Mandel House* was referred to by Rabbi Stephen Wise in his autobiography, *Challenging Years* as "the unofficial Secretary of State". House noted that he and Wilson knew that in passing the Federal Reserve Act, they had created an instrument more powerful than the Supreme Court. The Federal Reserve Board of Governors actually comprised a Supreme Court of Finance, and there was no appeal from any of their rulings.

In 1911, prior to Wilson's taking office as President, House had returned to his home in Texas and completed a book called *Philip Dru, Administrator*. Ostensibly a novel, it was actually a detailed plan for the future government of the United States, "which would establish Socialism as dreamed by Karl Marx", according to House. This "novel" predicted the enactment of the graduated income tax, excess profits tax, unemployment insurance, social security, and a flexible currency system. In short, it was the blueprint which was later followed by the Woodrow Wilson and Franklin D. Roosevelt administrations. It was published "anonymously" by B.W. Huebsch of New York, and widely circulated among government officials, who were left in no doubt as to its authorship. George Sylvester Viereck**, who knew House for years, later wrote an account of the Wilson-House relationship, *The Strangest Friendship in History*.[14] In 1955, Westbrook Pegler, the Hearst columnist from 1932 to 1956, heard of the Philip Dru book and called Viereck to ask if he had a copy. Viereck sent Pegler his copy of the book, and Pegler wrote a column about it, stating:

> "One of the institutions outlined in Philip Dru is the Federal Reserve System. The Schiffs, the Warburgs, the Kahns, the Rockefellers and Morgans put their faith in House. The Schiff, Warburg, Rockefeller and Morgan interests were personally represented in the mysterious conference at Jekyll Island. Frankfurter landed on the Harvard law faculty, thanks to a financial contribution to Harvard by Felix Warburg and Paul

---

*See House note in "Biographies"
**See Viereck note in "Biographies"
[14] George Sylvester Viereck, *The Strangest Friendship in History, Woodrow Wilson and Col. House*, Liveright, New York, 1932

Warburg, and so we got Alger and Donald Hiss, Lee Pressman, Harry Dexter White and many other proteges of Little Weenie."*

House's openly Socialistic views were forthrightly expressed in *Philip Dru, Administrator*; on pages 57-58, House wrote:

"In a direct and forceful manner, he pointed out that our civilization was fundamentally wrong, inasmuch, among other things, as it restricted efficiency; that if society were properly organized, there would be none who were not sufficiently clothed and fed. The result, that the laws, habits and ethical training in vogue were alike responsible for the inequalities in opportunity and the consequent wide difference between the few and the many; that the results of such conditions was to render inefficient a large part of the population, the percentage differing in each country in the ratio that education and enlightenment and unselfish laws bore to ignorance, bigotry and selfish laws."[15]

In his book, House (Dru) envisions himself becoming a dictator and forcing on the people his radical views, page 148: "They recognized the fact that Dru dominated the situation and that a master mind had at last risen in the Republic." He now assumes the title of General. "General Dru announced his purpose of assuming the powers of a dictator . . . they were assured that he was free from any personal ambition . . . he proclaimed himself 'Administrator of the Republic.'"*

This pensive dreamer who imagined himself a dictator actually managed to place himself in the position of the confidential advisor to the President of the United States, and then to have many of his desires enacted into law! On page 227, he lists some of the laws he wishes to enact as dictator. Among them are an old age pension law, laborers insurance compensation, cooperative markets, a federal reserve banking system, cooperative loans, national employment bureaus, and other "social legislation", some of which was enacted during Wilson's administration, and others during Franklin D. Roosevelt's administration. The latter was actually a continuation of the Wilson Administration,

---

*The present writer was with Viereck in his suite at the Hotel Belleclaire when Pegler called and asked for the book. Viereck sent it over by his secretary. He grinned and said Pegler seemed very excited. "He ought to get a good column out of that," Viereck told me. Indeed Pegler did get a good column out of it. Unfortunately for him, he had gone too far in mentioning the Warburgs. As long as he confined his attacks to La Grand Bouche (Eleanor Roosevelt), and her spouse, he had been permitted to continue, but now that he had exposed the Warburg connection with the Communist spy ring in Washington, his column was immediately dropped by the big city dailies, and Pegler's long run was over.

[15] Col. Edward M. House, *Philip Dru, Administrator*, B.W. Heubsch, New York, 1912.

*This quotation from *Philip Dru, Administrator*, written by Col. House in 1912, is included here to show his totalitarian Marxist philosophy. House was to become for 8 years with Wilson, the President's closest advisor. Later he continued his influence in the Franklin D. Roosevelt administration. From his home in Magnolia, Mass., House advised FDR through frequent trips of Felix Frankfurter to the White House. Frankfurter was later appointed to the Supreme Court by F.D.R.

with many of the same personnel, and with House guiding the administration from behind the scenes.

Like most of the behind-the-scenes operators in this book, Col. Edward Mandell House had the obligatory "London connection". Originally a Dutch family, "Huis", his ancestors had lived in England for three hundred years, after which his father settled in Texas, where he made a fortune in blockade-running during the Civil War, shipping cotton and other contraband to his British connections, including the Rothschilds, and bringing back supplies for the beleaguered Texans. The senior House, not trusting the volatile Texas situation, prudently deposited all his profits from his blockade-running in gold with Baring banking house in London*. At the close of the Civil War, he was one of the wealthiest men in Texas. He named his son "Mandell" after one of his merchant associates. According to Arthur Howden Smith, when House's father died in 1880, his estate was distributed among his sons as follows: Thomas William got the banking business; John, the sugar plantation; and Edward M. the cotton plantations, which brought him an income of $20,000 a year.[16]

At the age of twelve, the young Edward Mandell House had brain fever, and was later further crippled by sunstroke. He was a semi-invalid, and his ailments gave him an odd Oriental appearance. He never entered any profession, but used his father's money to become the kingmaker of Texas politics, successively electing five governors from 1893 to 1911. In 1911 he began to support Wilson for president, and threw the crucial Texas delegation to him which ensured his nomination. House met Wilson for the first time at the Hotel Gotham, May 31, 1912.

In *The Strangest Friendship In History, Woodrow Wilson and Col. House,* by George Sylvester Viereck, Viereck writes:

> "What," I asked House, "cemented your friendship?" "The identity of our temperaments and our public policies," answered House. "What was your purpose and his?" "To translate into legislation certain liberal and progressive ideas."[17]

House told Viereck that when he went to Wilson at the White

---

*Dope, Inc.*, identifies Barings as follows: "Baring Brothers, the premier merchant bank of the opium trade from 1783 to the present day, also maintained close contact with the Boston families... The group's leading banker became, at the close of the 19th century, the House of Morgan—which also took its cut in the Eastern opium traffic... Morgan's Far Eastern operations were the officially conducted British opium traffic... Morgan's case deserves special scrutiny from American police and regulatory agencies, for the intimate associations of Morgan Guaranty Trust with the identified leadership of the British dope banks."

[16]Arthur Howden Smith, *The Real Col. House,* Doran Company, New York, 1918

[17]George Sylvester Viereck, *The Strangest Friendship In History, Woodrow Wilson and Col. House,* Liveright, New York, 1932

House, he handed him $35,000. This was exceeded only by the $50,000 which Bernard Baruch had given Wilson.

The successful enactment of House's programs did not escape the notice of other Wilson associates. In vol. 1, page 157 of *The Intimate Papers of Col. House*, House notes, "Cabinet members like Mr. Lane and Mr. Bryan commented upon the influence of Dru with the President. 'All that the book has said should be,' wrote Lane, 'comes about. The President comes to 'Philip Dru' in the end.' "[18]

House recorded some of his efforts on behalf of the Federal Reserve Act in *The Intimate Papers of Col. House*,

"December 19, 1912. I talked with Paul Warburg over the phone concerning currency reform. I told of my trip to Washington and what I had done there to get it in working order. I told him that the Senate and the Congressmen seemed anxious to do what he desired, and that President-elect Wilson thought straight concerning the issue."[19]

Thus we have Warburg's agent in Washington, Col. House, assuring him that the Senate and Congressmen will do what he desires, and that the President-elect "thought straight concerning the issue." In this context, representative government seems to have ceased to exist. House continues in his "Papers":

"March 13, 1913. Warburg and I had an intimate discussion concerning currency reform.

March 27, 1913. Mr. J.P. Morgan, Jr. and Mr. Denny of his firm came promptly at five. McAdoo came about ten minutes afterward. Morgan had a currency plan already printed. I suggested he have it typewritten, so it would not seem too prearranged, and send it to Wilson and myself today.

July 23, 1913. I tried to show Mayor Quincy (of Boston) the folly of the Eastern bankers taking an antagonistic attitude towards the Currency Bill. I explained to Major Henry Higginson* with what care the bill had been framed. Just before he arrived, I had finished a review by Professor Sprague of Harvard of Paul Warburg's criticism of the Glass-Owen Bill, and will transmit it to Washington tomorrow. Every banker known to Warburg, who knows the subject practically, has been called up about the making of the bill.

October 13, 1913. Paul Warburg was my first caller today. He came to discuss the currency measure. There are many features of the Owen-Glass Bill that he does not approve. I promised to put him in touch with McAdoo and Senator Owen so that he might discuss it with them.

November 17, 1913. Paul Warburg telephoned about his trip to Washington. Later, he and Mr. Jacob Schiff came over for a few minutes.

---

[18] Col. Edward Mandell House, The Intimate Papers of Col. House, edited by Charles Seymour, Houghton Mifflin Co., 1926-28, Vol. 1, p. 157

[19] *Ibid.* Vol. 1, p. 163

*The most prominent banker in Boston.

Warburg did most of the talking. He had a new suggestion in regard to grouping the regular reserve banks so as to get the units welded together and in easier touch with the Federal Reserve Board."

George Sylvester Viereck in *The Strangest Friendship in History, Woodrow Wilson and Col. House* wrote: "The Schiffs, the Warburgs, the Kahns, the Rockefellers, the Morgans put their faith in House. When the Federal Reserve legislation at last assumed definite shape, House was the intermediary between the White House and the financiers."[20]

On page 45, Viereck notes, "Col. House looks upon the reform of the monetary system as the crowning internal achievement of the Wilson Administration."[21]

The Glass Bill (the House version of the final Federal Reserve Act) had passed the House on September 18, 1913 by 287 to 85. On December 19, 1913, the Senate passed their version by a vote of 54-34. More than forty important differences in the House and Senate versions remained to be settled, and the opponents of the bill in both houses of Congress were led to believe that many weeks would yet elapse before the Conference bill would be ready for consideration. The Congressmen prepared to leave Washington for the annual Christmas recess, assured that the Conference bill would not be brought up until the following year. Now the money creators prepared and executed the most brilliant stroke of their plan. In a single day, they ironed out all forty of the disputed passages in the bill and quickly brought it to a vote. On Monday, December 22, 1913, the bill was passed by the House 282-60 and the Senate 43-23.

On December 21, 1913, *The New York Times* commented editorially on the act, "New York will be on a firmer basis of financial growth, and we shall soon see her the money centre of the world."

*The New York Times* reported on the front page, Monday, December 22, 1913 in headlines: MONEY BILL MAY BE LAW TODAY—CONFEREES HAD ADJUSTED NEARLY ALL DIFFERENCES AT 1:30 THIS MORNING—NO DEPOSIT GUARANTEES—SENATE YIELDS ON THIS POINT BUT PUTS THROUGH MANY OTHER CHANGES "With almost unprecedented speed, the conference to adjust the House and Senate differences on the Currency Bill practically completed its labours early this morning. On Saturday the Conferees did little more than dispose of the preliminaries, leaving forty essential differences to be thrashed out Sunday. . . . No other legislation of importance will be taken up in either House of Congress this week. Members of both houses are already preparing to leave Washington."

---

[20] George Sylvester Viereck, *The Strangest Friendship In History, Woodrow Wilson and Col. House*, Liveright, New York, 1932
[21] Ibid.

"Unprecedented speed", says *The New York Times*. One sees the fine hand of Paul Warburg in this final strategy. Some of the bill's most vocal critics had already left Washington. It was a longstanding political courtesy that important legislation would not be acted upon during the week before Christmas, but this tradition was rudely shattered in order to perpetrate the Federal Reserve Act on the American people.

*The Times* buried a brief quote from Congressman Lindbergh that "the bill would establish the most gigantic trust on earth", and quoted Representative Guernsey of Maine, a Republican on the House Banking and Currency Committee, that "This is an inflation bill, the only question being the extent of the inflation."

Congressman Lindbergh said on that historic day, to the House:

"This Act establishes the most gigantic trust on earth. When the President signs this bill, the invisible government by the Monetary Power will be legalized. The people may not know it immediately, but the day of reckoning is only a few years removed. The trusts will soon realize that they have gone too far even for their own good. The people must make a declaration of independence to relieve themselves from the Monetary Power. This they will be able to do by taking control of Congress. Wall Streeters could not cheat us if you Senators and Representatives did not make a humbug of Congress.... If we had a people's Congress, there would be stability. The greatest crime of Congress is its currency system. The worst legislative crime of the ages is perpetrated by this banking bill. The caucus and the party bosses have again operated and prevented the people from getting the benefit of their own government."

The December 23, 1913 *New York Times* editorially commented, in contrast to Congressman Lindbergh's criticism of the bill, "The Banking and Currency Bill became better and sounder every time it was sent from one end of the Capitol to the other. Congress worked under public supervision in making the bill."

By "public supervision", *The Times* apparently meant Paul Warburg, who for several days had maintained a small office in the Capitol building, where he directed the successful pre-Christmas campaign to pass the bill, and where Senators and Congressmen came hourly at his bidding to carry out his strategy.

The "unprecedented speed" with which the Federal Reserve Act had been passed by Congress during what became known as "the Christmas massacre" had one unforeseen aspect. Woodrow Wilson was taken unaware, as he, like many others, had been assured the bill would not come up for a vote until after Christmas. Now he refused to sign it, because he objected to the provisions for the selection of Class B. Directors. William L. White relates in his biography of Bernard Baruch that Baruch, a principal contributor to Wilson's campaign fund, was stunned when he was informed that Wilson refused to sign the bill. He hurried to the White House and assured Wilson that this was a minor matter, which could be fixed up later through "administrative processes". The important thing was to get the Federal Reserve Act signed into law at once. With this reassurance, Wilson signed the Federal Reserve Act on December 23, 1913. History proved that on that day, the Constitution ceased to be the governing covenant of the American people, and our liberties were handed over to a small group of international bankers.

The December 24, 1913 *New York Times* carried a front page headline "WILSON SIGNS THE CURRENCY BILL!" Below it, also in capital letters, were two further headlines, "PROSPERITY TO BE FREE" and "WILL HELP EVERY CLASS". Who could object to any law which provided benefits to everyone? *The Times* described the festive atmosphere while Wilson's family and government officials watched him sign the bill. "The Christmas spirit pervaded the gathering," exulted *The Times*.

In his biography of Carter Glass, Rixey Smith states that those present at the signing of the bill included Vice President Marshall, Secretary Bryan, Carter Glass, Senator Owen, Secretary McAdoo, Speaker Champ Clark, and other Treasury officials. None of the real writers of the bill, the draftees of Jekyll Island, were present. They had prudently absented themselves from the scene of their victory. Rixey Smith also wrote, "It was as though Christmas had come two days early."On December 24, 1913, Jacob Schiff wrote to Col. House,

"My dear Col. House. I want to say a word to you for the silent, but no doubt effective work you have done in the interest of currency legislation and to congratulate you that the measure thas finally been enacted into law. I am with good wishes, faithfully yours, JACOB SCHIFF."

Representative Moore of Kansas, in commenting on the passage of the Act, said to the House of Representatives:

"The President of the United States now becomes the absolute dictator of all the finances of the country. He appoints a controlling board of seven men, all of whom belong to his political party, even though it is a minority. The Secretary of the Treasury is to rule supreme whenever there is a difference of opinion between himself and the Federal Reserve Board. AND, only one member of the Board is to pass out of office while the President is in office."

The ten year terms of office of the members of the Board were lengthened by the Banking Act of 1935 to fourteen years, which meant that these directors of the nation's finances, although not elected by the people, held office longer than three presidents.

While Col. House, Jacob Schiff and Paul Warburg basked in the glow of a job well done, the other actors in this drama were subject to later afterthoughts. Woodrow Wilson wrote in 1916, National Economy and the Banking System, Sen. Doc. No. 3, No. 223, 76th Congress, 1st session, 1939: "Our system of credit is concentrated (in the Federal Reserve

System). The growth of the nation, therefore, and all our activities, are in the hands of a few men."

When he was asked by Clarence W. Barron whether he approved of the bill as it was finally passed, Warburg remarked, "Well, it hasn't got quite everything we want, but the lack can be adjusted later by administrative processes."

Woodrow Wilson and Carter Glass are given credit for the Act by most contemporary historians, but of all those concerned, Wilson had least to do with Congressional action on the bill. George Creel, a veteran Washington correspondent, wrote in Harper's Weekly, June 26, 1915:

> "As far as the Democratic Party was concerned, Woodrow Wilson was without influence, save for the patronage he possessed. It was Bryan who whipped Congress into line on the tariff bill, on the Panama Canal tolls repeal, and on the currency bill. Mr. Bryan later wrote, "That is the one thing in my public career that I regret—my work to secure the enactment of the Federal Reserve Law."

On December 25, 1913, *The Nation* pointed out that "The New York Stock Market began to rise steadily upon news that the Senate was ready to pass the Federal Reserve Act."

This belies the claim that the Federal Reserve Act was a monetary reform bill. The New York Stock Exchange is generally considered an accurate barometer of the true meaning of any financial legislation passed in Washington. Senator Aldrich also decided that he no longer had misgivings about the Federal Reserve Act. In a magazine which he owned, and which he called The Independent, he wrote in July, 1914: "Before the passage of this Act, the New York bankers could only dominate the reserves of New York. Now we are able to dominate the bank reserves of the entire country."

H.W. Loucks denounced the Federal Reserve Act in *The Great Conspiracy of the House of Morgan*,

> "In the Federal Reserve Law, they have wrested from the people and secured for themselves the constitutional power to issue money and regulate the value thereof." On page 31, Loucks writes, "The House of Morgan is now in supreme control of our industry, commerce and political affairs. They are in complete control of the policy making of the Democratic, Republican and Progressive parties. The present extraordinary propaganda for 'preparedness' is planned more for home coercion than for defense against foreign aggression."[22]

The signing of the Federal Reserve Act by Woodrow Wilson represented the culmination of years of collusion with his intimate friend, Col. House, and Paul Warburg. One of the men with whom House became acquainted in the Wilson Administration was Franklin D.

---

[22] H.W. Loucks, *The Great Conspiracy of the House of Morgan*, Privately printed, 1916

Roosevelt, Assistant Secretary of Navy. As soon as he obtained the Democratic nomination for President, in 1932, Franklin D. Roosevelt made a "pilgrimage" to Col. House's home at Magnolia, Mass. Roosevelt, after the Republican hiatus of the 1920s, filled in the goals of *Philip Dru, Administrator*,[23] which Wilson had not been able to carry out. The late Roosevelt achievements included the enactment of the social security program, excess profits tax, and the expansion of the graduated income tax to 90% of earned income.

House's biographer, Charles Seymour, wrote: "He was wearied by the details of party politics and appointments. Even the share he had taken in constructive domestic legislation (the Federal Reserve Act, tariff revision, and the Income Tax amendment) did not satisfy him. From the beginning of 1914 he game more and more of his time to what he regarded as the highest form of politics and that for which he was particularly suited—international affairs."[24]

In 1938, shortly before he died, House told Charles Seymour, "During the last fifteen years I have been close to the center of things, although few people suspect it. No important foreigner has come to the United States without talking to me. I was close to the movement that nominated Roosevelt. He has given me a free hand in advising him. All the Ambassadors have reported to me frequently."

A comparative print of the Federal Reserve Act of 1913 as passed by the House of Representatives and amended by the Senate shows the following striking change:

The Senate struck out, "To suspend the officials of Federal Reserve banks for cause, stated in writing with opportunity of hearing, require the removal of said officials for incompetency, dereliction of duty, fraud or deceit, such removal to be subject to approval by the President of the United States." This was changed by the Senate to read "To suspend or remove any officer or director of any Federal Reserve Bank, the cause of such removal to be forthwith communicated in writing by the Federal Reserve Board to the removed officer or director and to said bank." This completely altered the conditions under which an officer or director might be removed. We no longer know what the conditions for removal are, or the cause. Apparently incompetency, dereliction of duty, fraud or deceit do not matter to the Federal Reserve Board. Also, the removed officer does not have the opportunity of appeal to the President. In answer to written inquiry, the Assistant Secretary of the Federal Reserve Board replied that only one officer has been removed "for cause" in the thirty-six years, the name and details of this matter being a "private concern" between the individual, the Reserve Bank concerned, and the Federal Reserve Board.

---

[23] E.M. House, *Philip Dru, Administrator*, B.W. Heubsch, N.Y., 1912
[24] Col. E.M. House, *The Intimate Papers of Col. House*, 4 v. 1926-1928, Houghton Mifflin Co.

The Federal Reserve System began its operations in 1914 with the activity of the Organization Committee, appointed by Woodrow Wilson, and composed of Secretary of the Treasury William McAdoo, who was his son-in-law, Secretary of Agriculture Houston and Comptroller of the Currency John Skelton Williams.

On January 6, 1914, *The New York Times* reported that the Organizing Committee of the Federal Reserve System had met in New York, and had conferred with Paul Warburg. "Mr. Warburg is regarded as the leading authority among local bankers on the problems involved in the new banking and currency system. He agreed with the tentative ideas of the committee."

On January 7, 1914, J.P. Morgan met with the Organizing Committee in New York. He informed them that there should not be more than seven regional districts in the new system.

This committee was to select the locations of the "decentralized" reserve banks. They were empowered to select from eight to twelve reserve banks, although J.P. Morgan had testified he thought that not more than four should be selected. Much politicking went into the selection of these sites, as the twelve cities thus favored would become enormously important as centers of finance. New York, of course, was a foregone conclusion. Richmond was the next selection, as a payoff to Carter Glass and Woodrow Wilson, the two Virginians who had been given political credit for the Federal Reserve Act. The other selections of the Committee were Boston, Philadelphia, Cleveland, Chicago, St. Louis, Atlanta, Dallas, Minneapolis, Kansas City, and San Francisco. All of these cities later developed important "financial districts" as the result of this selection.

These local battles, however, paled in view of the complete dominance of the Federal Reserve bank of New York in the system. Ferdinand Lundberg pointed out, in *America's Sixty Families*, that, "In practice, the Federal Reserve Bank of New York became the fountainhead of the system of twelve regional banks, for New York was the money market of the nation. The other eleven banks were so many expensive mausoleums erected to salve the local pride and quell the Jacksonian fears of the hinterland. Benjamin Strong, president of the Bankers Trust (J.P. Morgan) was selected as the first Governor of the New York Federal Reserve Bank. Adept in high finance, Strong for many years manipulated the country's monetary system at the discretion of directors representing the leading New York banks. Under Strong, the Reserve System was brought into interlocking relations with the Bank of England and the Bank of France. Benjamin Strong held his position as Governor of the Federal Reserve Bank of New York until his sudden death in 1928, during a Congressional investigation of the secret meetings between Reserve Governors and heads of European central banks which brought on the Great Depression of 1929-31."[25]

Strong had married the daughter of the President of Bankers Trust, which brought him into the line of succession in the dynastic intrigues which play such an important role in the world of high finance. He also had been a member of the original Jekyll Island group, the First Name Club, and was thus qualified for the highest position in the Federal Reserve System, as the Governor of the Federal Reserve Bank of New York which dominated the entire system.

Paul Warburg also is mentioned in J. Laurence Laughlin's definitive volume, *The Federal Reserve Act, Its Origins and Purposes*,

"Mr. Paul Warburg of Kuhn, Loeb Company offered in March, 1910 a fairly well thought out plan to be known as the United Reserve Bank of the United States. This was published in *The New York Times* of March 24, 1910. The group interested in the purposes of the National Monetary Commission met secretly at Jekyll Island for about two weeks in December, 1910, and concentrated on the preparation of a bill to be presented to Congress by the National Monetary Commission. The men who were present at Jekyll Island were Senator Aldrich, H.P. Davison of J.P. Morgan Company, Paul Warburg of Kuhn, Loeb Company, Frank Vanderlip of the National City Bank, and Charles D. Norton of the First National Bank. No doubt the ablest banking mind in the group was that of Mr. Warburg, who had had a European banking training. Senator Aldrich had no special training in banking."[26]

A mention of Paul Warburg, written by Harold Kelloch, and titled, *"Warburg the Revolutionist"* appeared in the *Century Magazine*, May, 1915. Kelloch writes:

"He imposed his ideas on a nation of a hundred million people . . . Without Mr. Warburg there would have been no Federal Reserve Act. The banking house of Warburg and Warburg in Hamburg has always been strictly a family business. None but a Warburg has been eligible for it, but all Warburgs have been born into it. In 1895 he married the daughter of the late Solomon Loeb of Kuhn Loeb Company. He became a member of Kuhn Loeb Company in 1902. Mr. Warburg's salary from his private business has been approximately a half million a year. Mr. Warburg's motives had been purely those of patriotic self-sacrifice."

The true purposes of the Federal Reserve Act soon began to disillusion many who had at first believe in its claims. W.H. Allen wrote in *Moody's Magazine*, 1916,

"The purpose of the Federal Reserve Act was to prevent concentration of money in the New York banks by making it profitable for country bankers to use their funds at home, but the movement of currency shows

---

[25] Ferdinand Lundberg, *America's Sixty Families*, 1937
[26] J. Laurence Laughlin, *The Federal Reserve Act, It's Origins and Purposes*

that the New York banks gained from the interior in every month except December, 1915, since the Act went into effect. The stabilization of rates has taken place in New York alone. In other parts, high rates continue. The Act, which was to deprive Wall Street of its funds for speculation, has really given the bulls and the bears such a supply as they have never had before. The truth is that far from having clogged the channel to Wall Street, as Mr. Glass so confidently boasted, it actually has widened the old channels and opened up two new ones. The first of these leads directly to Washington and gives Wall Street a string on all the surplus cash in the United States Treasury. Besides, in the power to issue bank-note currency, it furnishes an inexhaustible supply of credit money; the second channel leads to the great central banks of Europe, whereby, through the sale of acceptances, virtually guaranteed by the United States Government, Wall Street is granted immunity from those foreign demands for gold which have precipitated every great crisis in our history."

For many years, there has been considerable mystery about who actually owns the stock of the Federal Reserve Banks. Congressman Wright Patman, leading critic of the System, tried to find out who the stockholders were. The stock in the original twelve regional Federal Reserve Banks was purchased by national banks in those twelve regions. Because the Federal Reserve Bank of New York was to set the interest rates and direct open market operations, thus controlling the daily supply and price of money throughout the United States, it is the stockholders of that bank who are the real directors of the entire system. For the first time, it can be revealed who those stockholders are. This writer has the original organization certificates of the twelve Federal Reserve Banks, giving the ownership of shares by the national banks in each district. The Federal Reserve Bank of New York issued 203,053 shares, and, as filed with the Comptroller of the Currency May 19, 1914, the large New York City banks took more than half of the outstanding shares. The Rockefeller Kuhn, Loeb-controlled National City Bank took the largest number of shares of any bank, 30,000 shares. J.P. Morgan's First National Bank took 15,000 shares. When these two banks merged in 1955, they owned in one block almost one fourth of the shares in the Federal Reserve Bank of New York, which controlled the entire system, and thus they could name Paul Volcker or anyone else they chose to be Chairman of the Federal Reserve Board of Governors. Chase National Bank took 6,000 shares. The Marine National Bank of Buffalo, later known as Marine Midland, took 6,000 shares. This bank was owned by the Schoellkopf family, which controlled Niagara Power Company and other large interests. National Bank of Commerce of New York City took 21,000 shares. The shareholders of these banks which own the stock of the Federal Reserve Bank of New York are the people who have controlled our political and economic destinies since 1914. They are the Rothschilds, of Europe, Lazard Freres (Eugene Meyer), Israel Sieff, Kuhn Loeb Company, Warburg Company, Lehman

Brothers, Goldman Sachs, the Rockefeller family, and the J.P. Morgan interests. These interests have merged and consolidated in recent years, so that the control is much more concentrated. National Bank of Commerce is now Morgan Guaranty Trust Company. Lehman Brothers has merged with Kuhn, Loeb Company, First National Bank has merged with the National City Bank, and in the other eleven Federal Reserve Districts, these same shareholders indirectly own or control shares in those banks, with the other shares owned by the leading families in those areas who own or control the principal industries in these regions.* The "local" families set up regional councils, on orders from New York, of such groups as the Council on Foreign Relations, the Trilateral Commission, and other instruments of control devised by their masters. They finance and control political developments in their area, name candidates, and are seldom successfully opposed in their plans.

With the setting up of the twelve "financial districts" through the Federal Reserve Banks, the traditional division of the United States into the forty-eight states was overthrown, and we entered the era of "regionalism", or twelve regions which had no relation to the traditional state boundaries.

These developments following the passing of the Federal Reserve Act proved every one of the allegations Thomas Jefferson had made against a central bank in 1791: that the subscribers to the Federal Reserve Bank stock had formed a corporation, whose stock could be and was held by aliens; that this stock would be transmitted to a certain line of successors; that it would be placed beyond forfeiture and escheat; that they would receive a monopoly of banking, which was against the laws of monopoly; and that they now had the power to make laws, paramount to the laws of the states. No state legislature can countermand any of the laws laid down by the Federal Reserve Board of Governors for the benefit of their private stockholders. This board issues laws as to what the interest rate shall be, what the quantity of money shall be and what the price of money shall be. All of these powers abrogate the powers of the state legislatures and their responsibility to the citizens of those states.

*The New York Times* stated that the Federal Reserve Banks would be ready for business on August 1, 1914, but they actually began operations on November 16, 1914. At that time, their total assets were listed at $143,000,000, from the sale of shares in the Federal Reserve Banks to stockholders of the national banks which subscribed to it.

The actual part of this $143,000,000 which was paid in for these shares remains shrouded in mystery. Some historians believe that the shareholders only paid about half of the amount in cash; others believe

---
*See charts V through IX

that they paid in no cash at all, but merely sent in checks which they drew on the national banks which they owned. This seems most likely, that from the very outset, the Federal Reserve operations were "paper issued against paper", that bookkeeping entries comprised the only values which changed hands.

The men whom President Woodrow Wilson chose to make up the first Federal Reserve Board of Governors were men drawn from the banking group. He had been nominated for the Presidency by the Democratic Party, which had claimed to represent the "common man" against the "vested interests". According to Wilson himself, he was allowed to choose only one man for the Federal Reserve Board. The others were chosen by the New York bankers. Wilson's choice was Thomas D. Jones, a trustee of Princeton and director of International Harvester and other corporations. The other members were Adolph C. Miller, economist from Rockefeller's University of Chicago and Morgan's Harvard University, and also serving as Assistant Secretary of the Interior; Charles S. Hamlin, who had served previously as an Assistant Secretary of the Treasury for eight years; F.A. Delano, a Roosevelt relative, and railroad operator who took over a number of railroads for Kuhn, Loeb Company, W.P.G. Harding, President of the First National Bank of Atlanta; and Paul Warburg of Kuhn, Loeb Company. According to *The Intimate Papers of Col. House*, Warburg was appointed because "The President accepted (House's) suggestion of Paul Warburg of New York because of his interest and experience in currency problems under both Republican and Democratic Administrations."[27] Like Warburg, Delano had also been born outside the continental limits of the United States, although he was an American citizen. Delano's father, Warren Delano, according to Dr. Josephson and other authorities, was active in Hong Kong in the Chinese opium trade, and Frederick Delano was born in Hong Kong in 1863.

In *The Money Power of Europe*, Paul Emden writes that "The Warburgs reached their outstanding eminence during the last twenty years of the past century, simultaneously with the growth of Kuhn, Loeb Company in New York, with whom they stood in a personal union and family relationship. Paul Warburg with magnificent success carried through in 1913 the reorganization of the American banking system, at which he had with Senator Aldrich been working since 1911, and thus most thoroughly consolidated the currency and finances of the United States."[28]

---

[27] Col. E.M. House, *The Intimate Papers of Col. House*, 4 v. 1926-1928, Houghton Mifflin Co.
[28] Paul Emden, *The Money Power of Europe in the 19th and 20th Century*, S. Low, Marston Co., London, 1937

*The New York Times*\* had noted on May 6, 1914 that Paul Warburg had "retired" from Kuhn, Loeb Company in order to serve on the Federal Reserve Board, although he had not resigned his directorships of American Surety Company, Baltimore and Ohio Railroad, National Railways of Mexico, Wells Fargo, or Westinghouse Electric Corporation, but would continue to serve on these boards of directors. "Who's Who" listed him as holding these directorships and in addition, American I.G. Chemical Company (branch of I.G. Farben), Agfa Ansco Corporation, Westinghouse Acceptance Company, Warburg Company of Amsterdam, chairman of the Board of International Acceptance Bank, and numerous other banks, railways and corporations. "Kuhn Loeb & Co. with Warburg have four votes or the majority of the Federal Reserve Board."[29]

Despite his retirement from Kuhn, Loeb Company in May of 1914 to serve on the Federal Reserve Board of Governors, Warburg was asked to appear before a Senate Subcommittee in June of 1914 and answer some questions about his behind-the-scenes role in getting the Federal Reserve Act through Congress. This might have meant some questions about the secret conference in Jekyll Island, and Warburg refused to appear. On July 7, 1914 he wrote a letter to G.M. Hitchcock, Chairman of the Senate Banking and Currency Committee, stating that it might impair his usefulness on the Board if he were required to answer any questions, and that he would therefore withdraw his name. However, Woodrow Wilson, refused to withdraw his name. It seemed that Warburg was prepared to bluff the Senate Committee into confirming him without any questions asked. On July 10, 1914, *The New York Times* defended Warburg on the editorial page and denounced the "Senatorial Inquisition". Since Warburg had not yet been asked any questions, the term "Inquisition" seemed remarkably inappropriate, nor was there any real danger that the Senators were preparing to use instruments of torture on Mr. Warburg. The imbroglio was resolved when the Senate Committee, in abject surrender, agreed that Mr. Warburg would be given a list of questions in advance of his appearance so that he could go over them, and that he could be excused from answering any questions which might tend to impair his service on the Board of Governors. *The Nation* reported on July 23, 1914 that "Mr. Warburg finally had a conference with Senator O'Gorman and agreed to meet the members of the Senate Subcommittee informally, with a view to coming to an understanding, and to giving them any reasonable information they might desire. The opinion in Washington is that Mr. Warburg's confirmation is assured." *The Nation*

---

\**The New York Times* April 30, 1914, reported that the 12 districts had subscriptions of $74,740,800 and that the subscribing banks would pay one-half of this sum in six months.

[29] Clarence W. Barron, *More They Told Barron*, Arno Press, *New York Times*, 1973, June 12, 1914. p. 204

was correct. Mr. Warburg was confirmed, the way having been smoothed by his "fixer", Senator O'Gorman of New York, more familiarly known as "the Senator from Wall Street". Senator Robert L. Owen had previously charged that Warburg was the American representative of the Rothschild family, but questioning him about this would indeed have smacked of the mediaeval "Inquisition", and his fellow Senators were too civilized to indulge in such barbarity*.

During the Senate Hearings on Paul Warburg before the Senate Banking and Currency Committee, August 1, 1914, Senator Bristow asked, "How many of these partners (of Kuhn, Loeb Company) are American citizens?" WARBURG: "They are all American citizens except Mr. Kahn. He is a British subject." BRISTOW: "He was at one time a candidate for Parliament, was he not?" WARBURG: "There was talk about it, it had been suggested and he had it in his mind."

Paul Warburg also stated to the Committee, "I went to England, where I stayed for two years, first in the banking and discount firm of Samuel Montague & Company. After that I went to France, where I stayed in a French bank."

CHAIRMAN: "What French bank was that?" WARBURG: "It is the Russian bank for foreign trade which has an agency in Paris."

BRISTOW: "I understood you to say that you were a Republican, but when Mr. Theodore Roosevelt came around, you then became a sympathizer with Mr. Wilson and supported him?" WARBURG: "Yes." BRISTOW: "While your brother (Felix Warburg) was supporting Taft?" WARBURG: "Yes." Thus three partners of Kuhn, Loeb Company were supporting three different candidates for President of the United States. Paul Warburg was supporting Wilson, Felix Warburg was supporting Taft, and Otto Kahn was supporting Theodore Roosevelt. Paul Warburg explained this curious situation by telling the Committee that they had no influence over each other's political beliefs, "as finance and politics don't mix."

Questions about Warburg's appointment vanished in a hue and cry with Wilson's sole appointment to the Board of Governors, Thomas B. Jones. Reporters had discovered that Jones, at the time of his appointment, was under indictment by the Attorney General of the United States. Wilson leaped to the defense of his choice, telling reporters that "The majority of the men connected with what we have come to call 'big business' are honest, incorruptible and patriotic." Despite Wilson's protestations, the Senate Banking and Currency Committee scheduled

---

*Warburg was confirmed August 8, 1914, 38-11, and principally opposed by Sen. Bristow of Kansas, who was denounced by *The New York Times* as a "radical Republican", and whose excellent library of rare books on banking were acquired by the present writer in 1983 for research on this work.

hearings on the fitness of Thomas D. Jones to be a member of the Board of Governors. Wilson then wrote a letter to Senator Robert L. Owen, Chairman of that Committee:

White House
June 18, 1914

Dear Senator Owen:

Mr. Jones has always stood for the rights of the people against the rights of privilege. His connection with the Harvester Company was a public service, not a private interest. He is the one man of the whole number who was in a peculiar sense my personal choice.

Sincerely,

Woodrow Wilson

Woodrow Wilson said, "There is no reason to believe that the unfavorable report represents the attitude of the Senate itself." After several weeks, Thomas D. Jones withdrew his name, and the country had to do without his services.

The other members of the first Board of Governors were Secretary of the Treasury, William McAdoo, Wilson's son-in-law, and President of the Hudson-Manhattan Railroad, a Kuhn, Loeb Company controlled enterprise, and Comptroller of the Currency John Skelton Williams.

When the Federal Reserve Banks were opened for business on November 16, 1914, Paul Warburg said, "This date may be considered as the Fourth of July in the economic history of the United States."

CHAPTER FOUR
# The Federal Advisory Council

In steamrolling the Federal Reserve Act through the House of Representatives, Congressman Carter Glass declared on September 30, 1913 on the floor of the House that the interests of the public would be protected by an advisory council of bankers. "There can be nothing sinister about its transactions. Meeting with it at least four times a year will be a bankers' advisory council representing every regional reserve district in the system. How could we have exercised greater caution in safeguarding the public interest?"

Carter Glass neither then nor later gave any substantiation for his belief that a group of bankers would protect the interests of the public, nor is there any evidence in the history of the United States that any group of bankers has ever done so. In fact, the Federal Advisory Council proved to be the "administrative process" which Paul Warburg had inserted into the Federal Reserve Act to provide just the type of remote but unseen control over the System which he desired. When he was asked by financial reporter C.W. Barron, just after the Federal Reserve Act was enacted into law by Congress, whether he approved of the bill as it was finally passed, Warburg replied, "Well, it hasn't got quite everything we want, but the lack can be adjusted later by administrative processes." The council proved to be the ideal vehicle for Warburg's purposes, as it has functioned for seventy years in almost complete anonymity, its members, and their business associations, unnoticed and unknown by the public.

Senator Robert Owen, chairman of the Senate Banking and Currency Committee, had said, as quoted in *The New York Times*, August 3, 1913 before passage of the act:

> "The Federal Reserve Act will furnish the bank and industrial and commercial interests with the discount of qualified commercial paper and thus stablize our commercial and industrial life. The Federal Reserve banks are not intended as money making banks, but to serve a great national purpose of accomodating commerce and businessmen and banks, safeguard a fixed market for manufactured goods, for agricultural products and for labor. There is no reason why the banks should be in control of the Federal Reserve system. Stability will make our commerce expand healthfully in every direction."

Senator Owen's optimism was doomed by the domination of the Jekyll Island promotors over the initial composition of the Federal Reserve System. Not only did the Morgan-Kuhn, Loeb alliance purchase the dominant control of stock in the Federal Reserve Bank of New York, with almost half of the shares owned by the five New York banks under their control, First National Bank, National City Bank, National Bank of Commerce, Chase National Bank and Hanover National Bank, but they also persuaded President Woodrow Wilson to appoint one of the Jekyll Island group, Paul Warburg, to the Federal Reserve Board of Governors.

Each of the twelve regional Federal Reserve Banks was to elect a member of the Federal Advisory Council, which would meet with the Federal Reserve Board of Governors four times a year in Washington, in order to "advise" the Board on future monetary policy. This seemed to assure absolute democracy, as each of the twelve "advisors", representing a different region of the United States, would be expected to speak up for the economic interests of his area, and each of the twelve members would have an equal vote. The theory may have been admirable in its concept, but the hard facts of economic life resulted in a quite different picture. The president of a small bank in St. Louis or Cincinnati, sitting in conference with Paul Warburg and J.P. Morgan to "advise" them on monetary policy, would be unlikely to contradict two of the most powerful international financiers in the world, as a scribbled note from either one of them would be sufficient to plunge his little bank into bankruptcy. In fact, the small banks of the twelve Federal Reserve districts existed only as satellites of the big New York financial interests, and were completely at their mercy. Martin Mayer, in *The Bankers*, points out that "J.P. Morgan maintained correspondent relationships with many small banks all over the country."[30] The big New York banks did not confine themselves to multi-million dollar deals with other great financial interests, but carried on many smaller and more routine dealings with their "correspondent" banks across the United States.

Apparently secure in their belief that their activities would never be exposed to the public, the Morgan-Kuhn, Loeb interests boldly selected the members of the Federal Advisory Council from their correspondent banks and from banks in which they owned stock. No one in the financial community seemed to notice, as nothing was said about it during seventy years of the Federal Reserve System's operation.

To avoid any suspicion that New York interests might control the Federal Advisory Council, its first president, elected in 1914 by the other members, was J.B. Forgan, president of the First National Bank of

---

[30] Martin Mayer, *The Bankers*, Weybright and Talley, New York, 1974, p. 207.

Chicago. Rand McNally Bankers Directory for 1914 lists the principal correspondents of the large banks. The principal correspondent bank of the Baker-Morgan controlled First National Bank of New York is listed as the First National Bank of Chicago. The principal correspondent listed by the First National Bank of Chicago is the Bank of Manhattan in New York, controlled by Jacob Schiff and Paul Warburg of Kuhn, Loeb Company. James B. Forgan also was listed as a director of Equitable Life Insurance Company, also controlled by Morgan. However, the relationship between First National Bank of Chicago and these New York banks was even closer than these listings indicate.

On page 701 of *The Growth of Chicago Banks* by F. Cyril James, we find mention of "the First National Bank of Chicago's profitable connection with the Morgan interests. A goodwill ambassador was hastily sent to New York to invite George F. Baker to become a director of the First National Bank of Chicago."[31] (J.B. Forgan to Ream, January 7, 1903.) In effect, Baker and Morgan had personally chosen the first president of the Federal Advisory Council.

James B. Forgan (1852-1924) also shows the obligatory "London Connection" in the operation of the Federal Reserve System. Born in St. Andrew's, Scotland, he began his banking career there with the Royal Bank of Scotland, a correspondent of the Bank of England. He came to Canada for the Bank of British North America, worked for the Bank of Nova Scotia, which sent him to Chicago in the 1880's, and by 1900 he had become president of the First National Bank of Chicago. He served for six years as president of the Federal Advisory Council, and when he left the council, he was replaced by Frank O. Wetmore, who had also replaced him as president of the First National Bank of Chicago when Forgan was named chairman of the board.

Representing the New York Federal Reserve district on the first Federal Advisory Council was J.P. Morgan. He was named chairman of the Executive Committee. Thus, Paul Warburg and J.P. Morgan sat in conference at the meetings of the Federal Reserve Board during the first four years of its operation, surrounded by the other Governors and members of the council, who could hardly have been unaware that their futures would be guided by these two powerful bankers.

Another member of the Federal Advisory Council in 1914 was Levi L. Rue, representing the Philadelphia district. Rue was president of the Philadelphia National Bank. Rand McNally Bankers Directory of 1914 listed as principal correspondent of the First National Bank of New York,

---

[31] F. Cyril James, *The Growth of Chicago Banks*, Harper, New York, 1938.

the Philadelphia National Bank. First National Bank of Chicago also listed Philadelphia National Bank as its principal correspondent in Philadelphia. The other members of the Federal Advisory Council included Daniel S. Wing, president of the First National Bank of Boston, W.S. Rowe, president of the First National Bank of Cincinnati, and C.T. Jaffray, president of the First National Bank of Minneapolis. These were all correspondent banks of the New York "big five" banks who controlled the money market in the United States.

Jaffray had an even closer connection with the Baker-Morgan interests. In 1908, to reinvest the large annual dividends from their First National Bank of New York stock, Baker and Morgan set up a holding company, First Security Corporation, which bought 500 shares of the First National Bank of Minneapolis. Thus Jaffray was little more than a wage-earning employee of Baker and Morgan, although he had been "selected" by stockholders of the Federal Reserve Bank of Minneapolis to represent their interests. First Security Corporation also owned 50,000 shares of Chase National Bank, 5400 shares of National Bank of Commerce, 2500 shares of Bankers Trust, 928 shares of Liberty National Bank, the bank of which Henry P. Davison had been president when he was tapped to join the J.P. Morgan firm, and shares of New York Trust, Atlantic Trust and Brooklyn Trust. First Security concentrated on bank stocks which rapidly appreciated in value, and paid handsome annual dividends. In 1927, it earned five million dollars, but paid the shareholders eight million, taking the rest from its surplus.

Another member of the initial Federal Advisory Council was E.F. Swinney, president of the First National Bank of Kansas City. He was also a director of Southern Railway, and lists himself in Who's Who as "independent in politics".

Archibald Kains represented the San Francisco district on the Federal Advisory Council, although he maintained his office in New York, as president of the American Foreign Banking Corporation.

After serving as a Governor of the Federal Reserve Board from 1914-1918, Paul Warburg did not request another term. However, he was not ready to sever his connection with the Federal Reserve System which he had done so much to set up and put into operation. J.P. Morgan obligingly gave up his seat on the Federal Advisory Council, and for the next ten years, Paul Warburg continued to represent the Federal Reserve district of New York on the Council. He was vice president of the council 1922-25, and president 1926-27. Thus Warburg remained the dominant presence at Federal Reserve Board meetings throughout the 1920s, when the European central banks were planning the great contraction of credit which precipitated the Crash of 1929 and the Great Depression.

Although most of the Federal Advisory Council's "advice" to the Board of Governors has never been reported, on rare instances a few glimpses into its deliberations were afforded by brief items in *The New York Times*. On November 21, 1916, *The Times* reported that the Federal Advisory Council had met in Washington for its quarterly conference.

"There was talk about absorbing Europe's extension of credit to South America and other countries. Federal Reserve officials said that to maintain a position as one of the world's bankers the United States must expect to be called upon to render a good deal of the service performed largely by England in the past, in extending short term credits necessary in the production and transportation of goods of all kinds in the world's trade, and that acceptances in foreign trade require lowest discounts and the freest and most reliable gold markets." (The First World War was at its zenith in 1916.)

In addition to his service on the Board of Governors and the Federal Advisory Council, Paul Warburg continued to address bankers' groups about the monetary policies they were expected to follow. On October 22, 1915, he addressed the Twin City Bankers Club, St. Paul, Minnesota during which speech he stated,

"It is to your interest to see the Federal Reserve banks as strong as they possibly can be. It staggers the imagaination to think what the future may have in store for the development of American banking. With Europe's foremost powers limited to their own field, with the United States turned into a creditor nation for all the world, the boundaries of the field that lies open for us are determined only by our power of safe expansion. The scope of our banking future will ultimately be limited by the amount of gold that we can muster as the foundation of our banking and credit structure."

The composition of the Federal Reserve Board of Governors and the Federal Reserve Advisory Council, from its initial membership to the present day, shows links to the Jekyll Island conference and the London banking community which offers incontrovertible evidence, acceptable in any court of law, that there was a plan to gain control of the money and credit of the people of the United States, and to use it for the profit of the architects. Old Jekyll Island hands were Frank Vanderlip, president of the National City Bank, which bought a large portion of the shares of the Federal Reserve Bank of New York in 1914; Paul Warburg of Kuhn, Loeb Company; Henry P. Davison, J.P. Morgan's righthand man, and director of the First National Bank of New York and the National Bank of Commerce, which took a large portion of Federal Reserve Bank of New York stock; and Benjamin Strong, also known as a Morgan lieutenant, who served as Governor of the Federal Reserve Bank of New York during the 1920's.*

The selection of the regional members of the Federal Advisory Council from the list of bankers who worked most closely with the "big five" banks of New York, and who were their principal correspondent banks, proves that the much-touted "regional safeguarding of the public interest" by Carter Glass and other Washington proponents of the Federal Reserve Act was from its very inception a deliberate deception. The fact that for seventy years this council was able to meet with the Federal Reserve Board of Governors and to "advise" the Governors on decisions of monetary policy which affected the daily lives of every person in the United States, without the public being aware of their existence, demonstrates that the planners of the central bank operation knew exactly how to achieve their objectives through "administrative processes" of which the public would remain ignorant. The claim that the "advice" of the council members is not binding on the Governors or that it carries no weight is to claim that four times a year, twelve of the most influential bankers in the United States take time from their work to travel to Washington to meet with the Federal Reserve Board merely to drink coffee and exchange pleasantries. It is a claim which anyone familiar with the workings of the business community will find impossible to take seriously. In 1914, it was a four-day trip each way for bankers from the Far West to come to Washington for a council meeting with the Federal Reserve Board. These men had extensive business interests which demanded their time. J.P. Morgan was a director of sixty-three corporations which held annual meetings, and

---

*"The Federal Advisory Council has great influence with the Federal Reserve Board. Conspicuously upon that council is J.P. Morgan, the leading member of J.P. Morgan Company and son of the late J.P. Morgan. Every one of the twelve members of the Advisory Council, as you well know, was educated in the same atmosphere. The Federal Reserve Act is not only a special privilege act but privileged persons have been placed in control and are its advisors in its administration. The Federal Reserve Board and the Federal Advisory Council administer the Federal Reserve System as its head authority, and no one of the lesser officials, even if they wished, would dare to cross swords with them."

(FROM: "Why Is Your Country At War?" by Charles Lindbergh, published in 1917). The above paragraph explains why Woodrow Wilson ordered government agents to seize and destroy the printing plates and copies of this book in the spring of 1918.

could hardly be exected to travel to Washington to attend meetings of the Federal Reserve Board if his advice was to be considered of no importance.**

---

**The J.P. Morgan connection has remained predominant on the Federal Advisory Council. For the past several years, the prestigious Federal Reserve District No. 2, the New York District, has been represented on the Federal Advisory Council by Lewis Preston. Preston is Chairman of J.P. Morgan Company and also Chairman and Chief Executive Officer of Morgan Guaranty Trust, New York. An heir to the Baldwin fortune (a company controlled by Morgan), Preston married the heiress to the Pulitzer newspaper fortune. On February 26, 1929, *The New York Times* noted that a merger had been effected between National Bank of Commerce and Guaranty Trust, making them the largest bank in the United States, with a capital of two billion dollars. The merger was negotiated by Myron C. Taylor, president of U.S. Steel, a Morgan firm. The banks occupied adjoining buildings on Wall Street, and, as *The New York Times* noted, "The Guaranty Trust Company long has been known as one of 'the Morgan group' of banks." The National Bank of Commerce has also been identified with Morgan interests.

CHAPTER FIVE
# The House of Rothschild

The success of the Federal Reserve Conspiracy will raise many questions in the minds of readers who are unfamiliar with the history of the United States and finance capital. How could the Kuhn, Loeb-Morgan alliance, powerful though it might be, believe that it would be capable, first, of devising a plan which would bring the entire money and credit of the people of the United States into their hands, and second, of getting such a plan enacted into law?

The capability of devising and enacting the "National Reserve Plan", as the immediate result of the Jekyll Island expedition was called, was easily within the powers of the Kuhn, Loeb-Morgan alliance, according to the following from *McClure's Magazine*, August 1911, "The Seven Men" by John Moody:

"Seven men in Wall Street now control a great share of the fundamental industry and resources of the United States. Three of the seven men, J.P. Morgan, James J. Hill, and George F. Baker, head of the First National Bank of New York belong to the so-called Morgan group; four of them, John D. and William Rockefeller, James Stillman, head of the National City Bank, and Jacob H. Schiff of the private banking firm of Kuhn, Loeb Company, to the so-called Standard Oil City Bank group... the central machine of capital extends its control over the United States... The process is not only economically logical; it is now practically automatic."[32]

Thus we see that the 1910 plot to seize control of the money and credit of the people of the United States was planned by men who already controlled most of the country's resources. It seemed to John Moody "practically automatic" that they should continue with their operations.

What John Moody did not know, or did not tell his readers, was that the most powerful men in the United States were themselves answerable to another power, a foreign power, and a power which had been steadfastly seeking to extend its control over the young republic of the United States since its very inception. This power was the financial power of England, centered in the London Branch of the House of Rothschild. The fact was that in 1910, the United States was for all practical purposes being ruled

---
[32]John Moody, "The Seven Men", McClure's Magazine, August, 1911, p. 418

from England, and so it is today. The ten largest bank holding companies in the United States are firmly in the hands of certain banking houses, all of which have branches in London. They are J.P. Morgan Company, Brown Brothers Harriman, Warburg, Kuhn, Loeb and J. Henry Schroder. All of them maintain close relationships with the House of Rothschild, principally through the Rothschild control of international money markets through its manipulation of the price of gold. Each day, the world price of gold is set in the London office of N.M. Rothschild and Company.

Although these firms are ostensibly American firms, which merely maintain branches in London, the fact is that these banking houses actually take their direction from London. Their history is a fascinating one, and unknown to the American public, originating as it did in the international traffic in gold, slaves, diamonds, and other contraband. There are no moral considerations in any business decision made by these firms. They are interested solely in money and power.

Tourists today gape at the magnificent mansions of the very rich in Newport, Rhode Island, without realizing that not only do these "cottages" stand as a memorial to the baronial desires of our Victorian millionaires, but that their erection in Newport represented a nostalgic memorialization of the great American fortunes, which had their beginnings in Newport when it was the capital of the slave trade.

The slave trade for centuries had its headquarters in Venice, until Seventeenth Century Britain, the new master of the seas, used its control of the oceans to gain a monopoly. As the American colonies were settled, its fiercely independent people, most of whom did not want slaves, found to their surprise that slaves were being sent to our ports in great numbers.

For many years, Newport was the capital of this unsavory trade. William Ellery, the Collector of the Port of Newport, said in 1791:

"... an Ethiopian cld as soon change his skin as a Newport merchant cld be induced to change so lucrative a trade.... for the slow profits of any manufactory."

John Quincy Adams remarked in his Diary, page 459, "Newport's former prosperity was chiefly owing to its extensive employment in the African slave trade."

The pre-eminence of J.P. Morgan and the Brown firm in American finance can be dated to the development of Baltimore as the nineteenth century capital of the slave trade. Both of these firms originated in Baltimore, opened branches in London, came under the aegis of the House of Rothschild, and returned to the United States to open branches in New York and to become the dominant power, not only in finance, but also in government. In recent years, key posts such as Secretary of Defense have been held by Robert Lovett, partner of Brown Brothers Harriman, and Thomas S. Gates, partner of Drexel and Company, a J.P. Morgan subsidiary firm. The present Vice President, George Bush, is the son of Prescott Bush, a partner of Brown Brothers Harriman, for many years the senator from Connecticut, and the financial organizer of Columbia Broadcasting System of which he also was a director for many years.

To understand why these firms operate as they do, it is necessary to give a brief history of their origins. Few Americans know that J.P. Morgan Company began as George Peabody and Company. George Peabody (1795-1869), born at South Danvers, Massachusetts, began business in Georgetown, D.C. in 1814 as Peabody, Riggs and Company, dealing in wholesale dry goods, and in operating the Georgetown Slave Market. In 1815, to be closer to their source of supply, they moved to Baltimore, where they operated as Peabody and Riggs, from 1815 to 1835. Peabody found himself increasingly involved with business originating from London, and in 1835, he established the firm of George Peabody and Company in London. He had excellent entree in London business through another Baltimore firm established in Liverpool, the Brown Brothers. Alexander Brown came to Baltimore in 1801, and established what is now known as the oldest banking house in the United States, still operating as Brown Brothers Harriman of New York; Brown, Shipley and Company of England; and Alex Brown and Son of Baltimore. The behind the scenes power wielded by this firm is indicated by the fact that Sir Montagu Norman, Governor of the Bank of England for many years, was a partner of Brown, Shipley and Company.* Considered the single most influential banker in the world, Sir Montagu Norman was organizer of "informal talks" between heads of central banks in 1927, which led directly to the Great Stockmarket Crash of 1929.

Soon after he arrived in London, George Peabody was surprised to be summoned to an audience with the gruff Baron Nathan Mayer Rothschild. Without mincing words, Rothschild revealed to Peabody, that much of the London aristocracy openly disliked Rothschild and refused his invitations. He proposed that Peabody, a man of modest means, be established as a lavish host whose entertainments would soon be the talk of London. Rothschild would, of course, pay all the bills. Peabody accepted the offer, and soon became known as the most popular host in London. His annual Fourth of July dinner, celebrating American Independence, became extremely popular with the English aristocracy, many of whom, while drinking Peabody's wine, regaled each other with jokes about Rothschild's crudities and bad manners, without realizing that every drop they drank had been paid for by Rothschild.

---

*"There is an informal understanding that a director of Brown, Shipley should be on the Board of the Bank of England, and Norman was elected to it in 1907." Montagu Norman, Current Biography, 1940.

It is hardly surprising that the most popular host in London would also become a very successful businessman, particularly with the House of Rothschild supporting him behind the scenes. Peabody often operated with a capital of 500,000 pounds on hand, and became very astute in his buying and selling on both sides of the Atlantic. His American agent was the Boston firm of Beebe, Morgan and Company, headed by Junius S. Morgan, father of John Pierpont Morgan. Peabody, who never married, had no one to succeed him, and he was very favorably impressed by the tall, handsome Junius Morgan. He persuaded Morgan to join him in London as a partner in George Peabody and Company in 1854. In 1860, John Pierpoint Morgan had been taken on as an apprentice by the firm of Duncan, Sherman in New York. He was not very attentive to business, and in 1864, Morgan's father was outraged when Duncan, Sherman refused to make his son a partner. He promptly extended an arrangment whereby one of the chief employees of Duncan, Sherman, Charles H. Dabney, was persuaded to join John Pierpont Morgan in a new firm, Dabney, Morgan and Company. *Bankers Magazine*, December, 1864, noted that Peabody had withdrawn his account from Duncan, Sherman, and that other firms were expected to do so. The Peabody account, of course, went to Dabney, Morgan Company.

John Pierpont Morgan was born in 1837, during the first money panic in the United States. Significantly, it had been caused by the House of Rothschild, with whom Morgan was later to become associated.

In 1836, President Andrew Jackson, infuriated by the tactics of the bankers who were attempting to persuade him to renew the charter of the Second Bank of the United States, said, "You are a den of vipers. I intend to rout you out and by the Eternal God I will rout you out. If the people only understood the rank injustice of our money and banking system, there would be a revolution before morning."

Although Nicholas Biddle was President of the Bank of the United States, it was well known that Baron James de Rothschild of Paris was the principal investor in this central bank. Although Jackson had vetoed the renewal of the charter of the Bank of the United States, he probably was unaware that a few months earlier, in 1835, the House of Rothschild had cemented a relationship with the United States Government by superseding the firm of Baring as financial agent of the Department of State on January 1, 1835.

Henry Clews, the famous banker, in his book, *Twenty-Eight Years in Wall Street*[33], states that the Panic of 1837 was engineered because the charter of the Second Bank of the United States had run out in 1836. Not only did President Jackson promptly withdraw government funds

---

[33] Henry Clews, *Twenty Eight Years in Wall Street*, Irving Company, New York, 1888, page 157

from the Second Bank of the United States, but he deposited these funds, $10 million, in state banks. The immediate result, Clews tell us, is that the country began to enjoy great prosperity. This sudden flow of cash caused an immediate expansion of the national economy, and the government paid off the entire national debt, leaving a surplus of $50 million in the Treasury.

The European financiers had the answer to this situation. Clews further states, "The Panic of 1837 was aggravated by the Bank of England when it in one day threw out all the paper connected with the United States."

The Bank of England, of course, was synonymous with the name of Baron Nathan Mayer Rothschild. Why did the Bank of England in one day "throw out" all paper connected with the United States, that is, refuse to accept or discount any securities, bonds or other financial paper based in the United States? The purpose of this action was to create an immediate financial panic in the United States, cause a complete contraction of credit, halt further issues of stocks and bonds, and ruin those seeking to turn United States securities into cash. In this atmosphere of financial panic, John Pierpont Morgan came into the world. His grandfather, Joseph Morgan, was a well to do farmer who owned 106 acres in Hartford, Connecticut. He later opened the City Hotel, and the Exchange Coffee Shop, and in 1819, was one of the founders of the Aetna Insurance Company.

George Peabody found that he had chosen well in selecting Junius S. Morgan as his successor. Morgan agreed to continue the sub rosa relationship with N.M. Rothschild Company, and soon expanded the firm's activities by shipping large quantities of railroad iron to the United States. It was Peabody iron which was the foundation for much of American railroad tracks from 1860 to 1890. In 1864, content to retire and leave his firm in the hands of Morgan, Peabody allowed the name to be changed to Junius S. Morgan Company. The Morgan firm then and since has always been directed from London. John Pierpont Morgan spent much of his time at his magnificent London mansion, Prince's Gate.

One of the high water marks of the successful Rothschild-Peabody-Morgan business venture was the Panic of 1857. It had been twenty years since the Panic of 1837: its lessons had been forgotten by hordes of eager investors who were anxious to invest the profits of a developing America. It was time to fleece them again. The stock market operates like a wave washing up on the beach. It sweeps with it many minuscule creatures who derive all of their life support from the oxygen and water of the wave. They coast along at the crest of the "Tide of Prosperity". Suddenly the wave, having reached the high water mark on the beach, recede, leaving all of the creatures gasping on the sand. Another wave may come in time to save them, but in all likelihood it will not come as far, and some of the sea creatures are doomed, In the same manner, waves of prosperity, fed by newly created money, through an artificial contraction of credit, recedes, leaving those it had borne high to gasp and die without hope of salvation.

*Corsair, the Life of J.P. Morgan*,[34] tells us that the Panic of 1857 was caused by the collapse of the grain market and by the sudden collapse of Ohio Life and Trust, for a loss of five million dollars. With this collapse, nine hundred other American companies failed. Significantly, one not only survived, but prospered from the crash. In *Corsair*, we learn that the Bank of England lent George Peabody and Company five million pounds during the panic of 1857. Winkler, in *Morgan the Magnificent*[35] says that the Bank of England advanced Peabody one million pounds, an enormous sum at that time, and the equivalent of one hundred million dollars today, to save the firm. However, no other firm received such beneficence during this Panic. The reason is revealed by Matthew Josephson, in *The Robber Barons*. He says on page 60:

"For such qualities of conservatism and purity, George Peabody and Company, the old tree out of which the House of Morgan grew, was famous. In the panic of 1857, when depreciated securities had been thrown on the market by distressed investors in America, Peabody and the elder Morgan, being in possession of cash, had purchased such bonds as possessed real value freely, and then resold them at a large advance when sanity was restored."[36]

Thus, from a number of biographies of Morgan, the story can be pieced together. After the panic had been engineered, one firm came into the market with one million pounds in cash, purchased securities from distressed investors at panic prices, and later resold them at an enormous profit. That firm was the Morgan firm, and behind it was the clever maneuvering of Baron Nathan Mayer Rothschild. The association remained secret from the most knowledgeable financial minds in London and New York, although Morgan occasionally appeared as the financial agent in a Rothschild operation. As the Morgan firm grew rapidly during the late nineteenth century, until it dominated the finances of the nation, many observers were puzzled that the Rothschilds seemed so little interested in profiting by investing in the rapidly advancing American economy. John Moody notes, in *The Masters of Capital*, page 27, "The Rothschilds were content to remain a close ally of Morgan... as far as the American field was concerned."[37] Secrecy was more profitable than valor.

---

[34]Corsair, *The Life of J.P. Morgan*
[35]John K. Winkler, *Morgan the Magnificent*, Vanguard, N.Y. 1930
[36]Matthew Josephson, *The Robber Barons*, Harcourt Brace, N.Y. 1934
[37]John Moody, *The Masters of Capital*

The reason that the European Rothschilds preferred to operate anonymously in the United States behind the facade of J.P. Morgan and Company is explained by George Wheeler, in *Pierpont Morgan and Friends, the Anatomy of a Myth*, page 17:

"But there were steps being taken even now to bring him out of the financial backwaters—and they were not being taken by Pierpont Morgan himself. The first suggestion of his name for a role in the recharging of the reserve originated with the London branch of the House of Rothschild, Belmont's employers."[38]

Wheeler goes on to explain that a considerable anti-Rothschild movement had developed in Europe and the United States which focused on the banking activities of the Rothschild family. Even though they had a registered agent in the United States, August Schoenberg, who had changed his name to Belmont when he came to the United States as the representative of the Rothschilds in 1837, it was extremely advantageous to them to have an American representative who was not known as a Rothschild agent.

Although the London house of Junius S. Morgan and Company continued to be the dominant branch of the Morgan enterprises, with the death of the senior Morgan in 1890 in a carriage accident on the Riviera, John Pierpont Morgan became the head of the firm. After operating as the American representative of the London firm from 1864-1871 as Dabney Morgan Company, Morgan took on a new partner in 1871, Anthony Drexel of Philadelphia and operated as Drexel Morgan and Company until 1895. Drexel died in that year, and Morgan changed the name of the American branch to J.P. Morgan and Company.

LaRouche[39] tells us that on February 5, 1891, a secret association known as the Round Table Group was formed in London by Cecil Rhodes, his banker, Lord Rothschild, the Rothschild in-law, Lord Rosebery, and Lord Curzon. He states that in the United States the Round Table was represented by the Morgan group. Dr. Carrol Quigley refers to this group as "The British-American Secret Society" in *Tragedy and Hope*, stating that "The chief backbone of this organization grew up along the already existing financial cooperation running from the Morgan Bank in New York to a group of international financiers in London led by Lazard Brothers (in 1901)."[40]

William Guy Carr, in *Pawns In The Game* states that, "In 1899, J.P. Morgan and Drexel went to England to attend the International Bankers

---

[38]George Wheeler, *Pierpont Morgan and Friends, the Anatomy of a Myth*, Prentice Hall, N.J. 1973

[39]Lyndon H. LaRouche, Jr., *Dope, Inc.*, The New Benjamin Franklin House Publishing Company, N.Y. 1978

[40]Dr. Carrol Quigley, *Tragedy and Hope*, Macmillan Co., N.Y.

Convention. When they returned, J.P. Morgan had been appointed head representative of the Rothschild interests in the United States. As the result of the London Conference, J.P. Morgan and Company of New York, Drexel and Company of Philadelphia, Grenfell and Company of London, and Morgan Harjes Cie of Paris, M.M. Warburg Company of Germany and America, and the House of Rothschild were all affiliated."[41]

Apparently unaware of the Peabody connection with the Rothschilds and the fact that the Morgans had always been affiliated with the House of Rothschild, Carr supposed that he had uncovered this relationship as of 1899, when in fact it went back to 1835.*

After World War I, the Round Table became known as the Council on Foreign Relations in the United States, and the Royal Institute of International Affairs in London. The leading government officials of both England and the United States were chosen from its members. In the 1960s, as growing attention centered on the surreptitious governmental acitivities of the Council on Foreign Relations, subsidiary groups, known as the Trilateral Commission and the Bilderbergers, representing the identical financial interests, began operations, with the more important officials, such as Robert Roosa, being members of all three groups.

---

[41]William Guy Carr, *Pawns In The Game*, privately printed, 1956, pg. 60

*July 30, 1930 McFadden *Basis of Control of Economic Conditions*. This control of the world business structure and of human happiness and progress by a small group is a matter of the most intense public interest. In analyzing it, we must begin with the internal group which centers itself around J.P. Morgan Company. Never before had there been such a powerful centralized control over finance, industrial production, credit and wages as is at this time vested in the Morgan group...The Morgan control of the Federal Reserve System is exercised through control of the management of the Federal Reserve Bank of New York.

George F. Peabody *History of the Great American Fortunes*, Gustavus Myers, Mod. Lib. 537, notes that J.P. Morgan's father, Junius S. Morgan, had become a partner of George Peabody in the banking business. "When the Civil War came on, George Peabody and Company were appointed the financial representatives in England of the U.S. Government.... with this appointment their wealth suddenly began to pile up; where hitherto they had amassed riches by stages not remarkably rapid, they now added many millions within a very few years." According to writers of the day, the methods of George Peabody & Company were not only unreasonable but double treason, in that, while in the act of giving inside aid to the enemy, George Peabody & Company were the potentiaries of the U.S. Government and were being well paid to advance its interests. "Springfield Republic", 1866: "For all who know anything on the subject know very well that Peabody and his partners gave us no faith and no help in our struggle for national existence. They participated to the fullest in the common English distrust of our cause and our success, and talked and acted for the South rather than for our nation. No individuals contributed so much to flooding our money markets and weakening financial confidence in our nationality than George Peabody & Company, and none made more money by the operation. All the money that Mr. Peabody is giving away so lavishly among our institutions of learning was gained by the speculations of his house in our misfortunes." Also, *New York Times*, Oct. 31, 1866: Reconstruction Carpetbaggers Money Fund.

*Lightning over the Treasury Building*, John Elson, Meador Publishing Co., Boston 41, pg. 53, "The Bank of England with its subsidiary banks in America (under the domination of J.P. Morgan) the Bank of France, and the Reichsbank of Germany, composed an interlocking and cooperative banking system, the main objective of which was the exploitation of the people."

According to William Guy Carr, in *Pawns In The Game*,[42] the initial meeting of these ex officio planners took place in Mayer Amschel Bauer's Goldsmith Shop in Frankfurt in 1773. Bauer, who adopted the name of "Rothschild" or Red Shield, from the red shield which he hung over his door to advertise his business (the red shield today is the official coat of arms of the City of Frankfurt), (See Cover) "was only thirty years of age when he invited twelve other wealthy and influential men to meet him in Frankfurt. His purpose was to convince them that if they agreed to pool their resources they could then finance and control the World Revolutionary Movement and use it as their Manual of Action to win ultimate control of the wealth, natural resources, and manpower of the entire world. This agreement reached, Mayer unfolded his revolutionary plan. The project would be backed by all the power that could be purchased with their pooled resources. By clever manipulation of their combined wealth it would be possible to create such adverse economic conditions that the masses would be reduced to a state bordering on starvation by unemployment... Their paid propagandists would arouse feelings of hatred and revenge against the ruling classes by exposing all real and alleged cases of extravagance, licentious conduct, injustice, oppression, and persecution. They would also invent infamies to bring into disrepute others who might, if left alone, interfere with their overall plans... Rothschild turned to a manuscript and proceeded to read a carefully prepared plan of action. 1. He argued that LAW was FORCE only in disguise. He reasoned it was logical to conclude 'By the laws of nature right lies in force.' 2. Political freedom is an idea, not a fact. In order to usurp political power all that was necessary was to preach 'Liberalism' so that the electorate, for the sake of an idea, would yield some of their power and prerogatives which the plotters could then gather into their own hands. 3. The speaker asserted that the Power of Gold had usurped the power of Liberal rulers.... He pointed out that it was immaterial to the success of his plan whether the established governments were destroyed by external or internal foes because the victor had to of necessity ask the aid of 'Capital' which 'Is entirely in our hands'. 4. He argued that the use of any and all means to reach their final goal was justified on the grounds that the ruler who governed by the moral code was not a skilled politician because he left himself vulnerable and in an unstable position. 5. He asserted that 'Our right lies in force. The word RIGHT is an abstract thought and proves nothing. I find a new RIGHT... to attack by the Right of the Strong, to reconstruct all existing institutions, and to become the sovereign Lord of all those who left to us the Rights to their powers by laying them down to us in their liberalism. 6. The power of our resources must remain invisible until the very moment when it has gained such

---

[42] William Guy Carr, *Pawns In The Game*, privately printed, 1956

strength that no cunning or force can undermine it. He went on to outline twenty-five points. Number 8 dealt with the use of alcoholic liquors, drugs, moral corruption, and all vice to systematically corrupt youth of all nations. 9. They had the right to seize property by any means, and without hesitation, if by doing so they secured submission and sovereignty. 10. We were the first to put the slogans Liberty, Equality, and Fraternity into the mouths of the masses, which set up a new aristocracy. The qualification for this aristocracy is WEALTH which is dependent on us. 11. Wars should be directed so that the nations engaged on both sides should be further in our debt. 12. Candidates for public office should be servile and obedient to our commands, so that they may readily be used. 13. Propaganda—their combined wealth would control all outlets of public information. 14. Panics and financial depressions would ultimately result in World Government, a new order of one world government."

The Rothschild family has played a crucial role in international finance for two centuries, as Frederick Morton, in *The Rothschilds* writes:

"For the last one hundred and fifty years the history of the House of Rothschild has been to an amazing extent the backstage history of Western Europe."[38] (Preface)... Because of their success in making loans not to individuals, but to nations, they reaped huge profits, although as Morton writes, p.36, "Someone once said that the wealth of Rothschild consists of the bankruptcy of nations."[43]

E.C. Knuth writes, in *The Empire of the City*, "The fact that the House of Rothschild made its money in the great crashes of history and the great wars of history, the very periods when others lost their money, is beyond question."[44]

The Great Soviet Encyclopaedia, states, "The clearest example of a personal linkup (international directorates) on a Western European scale is the Rothschild family. The London and Paris branches of the Rothschilds are bound not just by family ties but also by personal link-ups in jointly controlled companies."[45] The encyclopaedia further described these companies as international monopolies.

The sire of the family, Mayer Amschel Rothschild, established a small business as a coin dealer in Frankfurt in 1743. Although previously known as Bauer*, he advertised his profession by putting up a sign depicting an eagle on a red shield, an adaptation of the coat of arms of the City of Frankfurt, to which he added five golden arrows extending from the talons, signifying his five sons. Because of this sign, he took the

---

[43]Frederick Morton, *The Rothchilds*, Fawcett Publishing Company, N.Y., 1961
[44]E.C. Knuth, *Empire of the City*, p. 71,
[45]Great Soviet Encyclopaedia, Edition 3, 1973, Macmillan, London, Vol. 14, pg. 691
*"The original name of Rothschild was Bauer." p. 397, Henry Clews, *Twenty-eight years in Wall Street*.

name 'Rothschild" or "Red Shield". When the Elector of Hesse earned a fortune by renting Hessian mercenaries to the British to put down the rebellion in the American colonies, Rothschild was entrusted with this money to invest. He made an excellent profit both for himself and the Elector, and attracted other accounts. In 1785 he moved to a larger house, 148 Judengasse, a five story house known as "The Green Shield" which he shared with the Schiff family.

The five sons established branches in the principal cities of Europe, the most successful being James in Paris and Nathan Mayer in London. Ignatius Balla in *The Romance of the Rothschilds*[46] tells us how the London Rothschild established his fortune. He went to Waterloo, where the fate of Europe hung in the balance, saw that Napoleon was losing the battle, and rushed back to Brussels. At Ostend, he tried to hire a boat to England, but because of a raging storm, no one was willing to go out. Rothschild offered 500 francs, then 700, and finally 1,000 francs for a boat. One sailor said, "I will take you for 2000 francs; then at least my widow will have something if we are drowned." Despite the storm, they crossed the Channel.

The next morning, Rothschild was at his usual post in the London Exchange. Everyone noticed how pale and exhausted he looked. Suddenly, he started selling, dumping large quantities of securities. Panic immediately swept the Exchange. Rothschild is selling; he knows we have lost the Battle of Waterloo. Rothschild and all of his known agents continued to throw securities onto the market. Balla says, "Nothing could arrest the disaster. At the same time he was quietly buying up all securities by means of secret agents whom no one knew. In a single day, he had gained nearly a million sterling, giving rise to the saying, 'The Allies won the Battle of Waterloo, but it was really Rothschild who won.'"*

In *The Profits of War*, Richard Lewinsohn says, "Rothschild's war profits from the Napoleonic Wars financed their later stock speculations. Under Metternich, Austria after long hestitation, finally agreed to accept financial direction from the House of Rothschild."[47]

---

[46]Ignatius Balla, *The Romance of the Rothschilds*, Everleigh Nash, London, 1913

*The New York Times, April 1, 1915 reported that in 1914, Baron Nathan Mayer de Rothschild went to court to suppress Ignatius Balla's book on the grounds that the Waterloo story about his grandfather was untrue and libelous. The court ruled that the story was true, dismissed Rothschild's suit, and ordered him to pay all costs. *The New York Times* noted in this story that "The total Rothschild wealth has been estimated at $2 billion." A previous story in *The New York Times* (May 27, 1905) noted that Baron Alphonse de Rothschild, head of the French house of Rothschild, possessed $60 million in American securities in his fortune, although the Rothschilds reputedly were not active in the American field. This explains why their agent, J.P. Morgan, had only $19 million in securities in his estate when he died in 1913, and owed $7 million of that to the dealer Duveen! The tremendous amounts of American securities handled by Morgan were actually owned by his employer, Rothschild."

[47]Richard Lewinsohn, *The Profits of War*, E.P. Dutton, 1937

After the success of his Waterloo exploit, Nathan Mayer Rothschild gained control of the Bank of England through his near monopoly of "Consols" and other shares. Several "central" banks, or banks which had the power to issue currency, had been started in Europe: The Bank of Sweden, in 1656, which began to issue notes in 1661, the earliest being the Bank of Amsterdam, which had started in 1609, and the Bank of Hamburg in 1619. The establishment of the Bank of England had been made possible by the Bank of Amsterdam, which financed Oliver Cromwell's seizure of power in England in 1649, ostensibly because of religious differences. Cromwell died in 1657 and the throne of England was re-established when Charles II was crowned in 1660. He died in 1685. In 1689, the same group of bankers regained power in England by putting King William of Orange on the throne. He soon repaid his backers by ordering the British Treasury to borrow 1,250,000 pounds from these bankers. He also issued them a Royal Charter for the Bank of England, which permitted them to consolidate the National debt (which had just been created by this loan) and to secure payments of interest and principal by direct taxation of the people. The Charter forbade private goldsmiths to store gold and to issue receipts, which gave the stockholders of the Bank of England a money monopoly. The goldsmiths also were required to store their gold in the Bank of England vaults. Not only had their privilege of issuing circulating medium been taken away by government decree, but their fortunes were now turned over to those who had supplanted them.*

In his "Cantos", 46; 27, Ezra Pound refers to the unique privileges which William Paterson advertised in his prospectus for the Charter of the Bank of England:

"Said Paterson
Hath benefit of interest on all
the moneys which it, the bank, creates out of nothing."

The "nothing" which is referred to, of course, is the bookkeeping operation of the bank, which "creates" money by entering a notation that it has "lent" you one thousand dollars, money which did not exist until the bank made the entry.

By 1698, the British Treasury owed 16 million pounds sterling to the Bank of England. By 1815, principally due to the compounding of interest, the debt had risen to 885 million pounds sterling. Some of this increase was due to the wars which had flourished during that period, including the Napoleonic Wars and the wars which England had fought to retain its American Colony.

---

*NOTE: In the United States, after the stockholders of the Federal Reserve System had consolidated their power in 1934, our government also issued orders that private citizens could not store or hold gold.

William Paterson (1658-1719) himself benefited little from "the moneys which the bank creates out of nothing", as he withdrew, after a policy disagreement, from the Bank of England a year after it was founded. A later William Paterson became one of the framers of the United States Constitution, while the name lingers on, like the pernicious central bank itself.

Paterson had found himself unable to work with the Bank of England's stockholders. Many of them remained anonymous, but an early description of the Bank of England stated it was "A society of about 1330 persons, including the King and Queen of England, who had 10,000 pounds of stock, the Duke of Leeds, Duke of Devonshire, Earl of Pembroke, and the Earl of Bradford."

Because of his success in his speculations, Baron Nathan Mayer de Rothschild, as he now called himself, reigned as the supreme financial power in London. He arrogantly exclaimed, during a party in his mansion, "I care not what puppet is placed upon the throne of England to rule the Empire on which the sun never sets. The man that controls Britain's money supply controls the British Empire, and I control the British money supply."

His brother James in Paris had also achieved dominance in French finance. In *Baron Edmond de Rothschild*, David Druck writes, "(James) Rothschild's wealth had reached the 600 million mark. Only one man in France possessed more. That was the King, whose wealth was 800 million The aggregate wealth of all the bankers in France was 150 million less than that of James Rothschild. This naturally gave him untold powers, even to the extent of unseating governments whenever he chose to do so. It is well known, for example, that he overthrew the Cabinet of Prime Minister Thiers."[48]

The expansion of Germany under Bismarck was accompanied by his dependence on Samuel Bleichroder, Court Bankers of the Prussian Emperor, who had been known as an agent of the Rothschilds since 1828. The later Chancellor of Germany, Dr. von Bethmann Hollweg, was the son of Moritz Bethmann of Frankfort, who had intermarried with the Rothschilds. Emperor Wilhelm I also relied heavily on Bischoffsheim, Goldschmidt, and Sir Ernest Cassel of Frankfort, who emigrated to England and became personal banker to the Prince of Wales, later Edward VII. Cassel's daughter married Lord Mountbatten, giving the family a direct relationship to the present British Crown.

---

[48]David Druck, *Baron Edmond de Rothschild*, (Privately printed), N.Y. 1850
[49]E.M. Josephson, *The Strange Death of Franklin D. Roosevelt*, pg. 39, Chedney Press, N.Y. 1948

Josephson[49] states that Philip Mountbatten was related through the Cassels to the Meyer Rothschilds of Frankfurt. Thus, the English royal House of Windsor has a direct family relationship to the Rothschilds. In 1901, when Queen Victoria's son, Edward, became King Edward VII, he re-established the Rothschild ties.

Paul Emden in *Behind The Throne* says,

"Edward's preparation for his metier was quite different from that of his mother, hence he 'ruled' less than she did. Gratefully, he retained around him men who had been with him in the age of the building of the Bagdad Railway...there were added to the advisory staff Leopold and Alfred de Rothschild, various members of the Sassoon family, and above all his private financial advisor Sir Ernest Cassel."[50]

The enormous fortune which Cassel made in a relatively short time gave him an immense power which he never misused. He amalgamated the firm of Vickers Sons with the Naval Construction Company and the Maxim-Nordenfeldt Guns and Ammunition Company, a fusion from which there arose the worldwide firm of Vickers Sons and Maxim. On an entirely different capacity from Cassel were businessmen like the Rothschilds. The firm was run on democratic principles, and the various partners all had to be members of the family. With great hospitality and in a princely manner they led the lives of grand seigneurs, and it was natural that Edward VII should find them congenial. Thanks to their international family relationships and still more extended business connections, they knew the whole world, were well informed about everybody, and had reliable knowledge of matters which did not appear on the surface. This combination of finance and politics had been a trademark of the Rothschilds from the very beginning. The House of Rothschild always knew more than could be found in the papers and even more than could be read in the reports which arrived at the Foreign Office. In other countries also the relations of the Rothschilds extended behind the throne. Not until numerous diplomatic publications appeared in the years after the war did a wider public learn how strongly Alfred de Rothschild's hand affected the politics of Central Europe during the twenty years before the war (World War I)."

With the control of the money came the control of the news media. Kent Cooper, head of the Associated Press, writes in his autobiography, *Barriers Down*,

"International bankers under the House of Rothschild acquired an interest in the three leading European agencies."[51]

Thus the Rothschilds bought control of Reuters International News Agency, based in London, Havas of France, and Wolf in Germany, which controlled the dissemination of all news in Europe.

---

[50] Paul Emden, *Behind The Throne*, Hoddard Stoughton, London, 1934
[51] Kent Cooper, *Barriers Down*, pg. 21

In *Inside Europe*[52], John Gunther wrote in 1936 that any French prime minister, at the end of 1935, was a creature of the financial oligarchy, and that this financial oligarchy was dominated by twelve regents, of whom six were bankers, and were headed by Baron Edmond de Rothchild.

The iron grip of the "London Connection" on the media was exposed in a recent book by Ben J. Bagdikian *The Media Monopoly*, described as "A startling report on the 50 corporations that control what America sees, hears, reads".[53] Bagdikian, who edited the nation's most influential magazine the *Saturday Evening Post* until the monopoly suddenly closed it down, reveals the interlocking directorates among the fifty corporations which control the news, but fails to trace them back to the five London banking houses which control them. He mentions that CBS interlocks with the *Washington Post*, Allied Chemical, Wells Fargo Bank, and others, but does not tell the reader that Brown Brothers Harriman controls CBS, or that the Eugene Meyer family (Lazard Freres) controls Allied Chemical and the *Washington Post*, and Kuhn Loeb Co. the Wells Fargo Bank. He shows the *New York Times* interlocked with Morgan Guaranty Trust, American Express, First Boston Corporation and others, but does show the banking interlocks. He does not mention the Federal Reserve System in his entire book, which is conspicuous by its absence.

Bagdikian documents that the media monopoly is steadily closing down more newspapers and magazines. Washington, D.C., with one paper, *The Post*, is unique among world capitols. London has eleven daily newspapers, Paris fourteen, Rome eighteen, Tokyo seventeen, and Moscow nine. He cites a study from the 1982 World Press Encyclopaedia that the United States is at the bottom of industrial nations in the number of daily newspapers sold per 1,000 population. Sweden leads the list with 572, the United States is at the bottom with 287. There is universal distrust of the media by Americans, because of their notorious monopoly and bias. The media unanimously urge higher taxes on working people, more government spending, a welfare state with totalitarian powers, closer relations with Russia, and a rabid denunciation of anyone who opposes Communism. This is the program of "the London Connection." It flaunts a maniacal racism, and has as its motto the dictum of its currently high priestess, Susan Sontag, that "The white race is the cancer of history." Everyone should be against cancer. The media monopoly deals with its opponents in one of two ways; either frontal assault of libel which the average person cannot afford to litigate, or an iron curtain of silence, the standard treatment for any work which exposes its clandestine activities.

---

[52]John Gunthere, *Inside Europe*, 1936
[53]Ben H. Bagdikian, *The Media Monopoly*, Beacon Press, Boston 1983

Although the Rothschild plan does not match any single political or economic movement since it was enunciated in 1773, vital parts of it can be discerned in all political evolution since that date. LaRouche[54] points out that the Round Tables sponsored Fabian Socialism in England, while backing the Nazi regime through a Round Table member in Germany, Dr. Hjalmar Schacht, and that they used the Nazi Government throughout World War II through Round Table member Admiral Canaris, while Allen Dulles ran a collaborating intelligence operation in Switzerland for the Allies.

---

[54]Lyndon H. LaRouche, Jr., *Dope, Inc.*, New Benjamin Franklin House Publishing Co., New York, 1978

CHAPTER SIX
# The London Connection

"So you see, my dear Coningsby, that the world is governed by very different personages from what is imagined by those who are not behind the scenes."[55]—Disraeli, Prime Minister of England during Queen Victoria's reign.

In 1775, the colonists of America declared their independence from Great Britain, and subsequently won their freedom by the American Revolution. Although they achieved political freedom, financial independence proved to be a more difficult matter. In 1791, Alexander Hamilton, at the behest of European bankers, formed the first Bank of the United States, a central bank with much the same powers as the Bank of England. The foreign influences behind this bank, more than a century later, were able to get the Federal Reserve Act through Congress, giving them at last the central bank of issue for our economy. Although the Federal Reserve Bank was neither Federal, being owned by private stockholders, nor a Reserve, because it was intended to create money, instead of to hold it in reserve, it did achieve enormous financial power, so much so that it has gradually superseded the popular elected government of the United States. Through the Federal Reserve System, American independence was stealthily but invincibly absorbed back into the British sphere of influence. Thus the London Connection became the actual arbiter of policy of the United States.

Because of England's loss of her colonial empire after the Second World War, it seemed that her influence as a world political power was waning. Essentially, this was true. The England of 1980 is not the England of 1880. She no longer rules the waves; she is a second rate, perhaps third rate, military power, but paradoxically, as her political and military power waned, her financial power grew. In *Capital City* we find, "On almost any measure you care to take, London is the world's leading financial centre . . . In the 1960s London dominance increased . . . "[56]

A partial explanation of this fact is given:

"Daniel Davison, head of London's Morgan Grenfell, said, 'The American banks have brought the necessary money, customers, capital

---

[55]Coningsby, by Disraeli, Longmans Co., London, 1881, p. 252
[56]McRae and Cairncross, *Capital City*, Eyre Methuen, London, 1963, p. 1

and skills which have established London in its present preeminence .... only the American banks have a lender of last resort. The Federal Reserve Board of the United States can, and does, create dollars when necessary. Without the Americans, the big dollar deals cannot be put together. Without them, London would not be credible as an international financial centre.' "[57]

Thus London is the world's financial center, because it can command enormous amounts of capital, created at its command by the Federal Reserve Board of the United States. But how is this possible? We have already established that the monetary policies of the United States, the interest rates, the volume and value of money, and sales of bonds, are decided, not by the figurehead of the Federal Reserve Board of Governors, but by the Federal Reserve Bank of New York. The pretended decentralization of the Federal Reserve System and its twelve, equally autonomous "regional" banks, is and has been a deception since the Federal Reserve Act became law in 1913. That United States monetary policy stems solely from the Federal Reserve Bank of New York is yet another fallacy. That the Federal Reserve Bank of New York is itself autonomous, and free to set monetary policy for the entire United States without any outside interference is especially untrue.

We might believe in this autonomy if we did not know that the majority stock of the Federal Reserve Bank of New York was purchased by three New York City banks: First National Bank, National City Bank, and the National Bank of Commerce. An examination of the principal stockholders in these banks, in 1914, and today, reveals a direct London connection.

In 1812, the National City Bank began business as the City Bank, in the same room in which the defunct Bank of the United States, whose charter had expired, had been doing business. It represented many of the same stockholders, who were now functioning under a legitimate American charter. During the early 1800s, the most famous name associated with City Bank was Moses Taylor (1806-1882). Taylor's father had been a confidential agent employed in buying property for the Astor interests while concealing the fact that Astor was the purchaser. Through this tactic, Astor succeeded in buying many farms, and also a great deal of potentially valuable real estate in Manhattan. Although Astor's capital was reputed to come from his fur trading, a number of sources indicate that he also represented foreign interests. LaRouche[58] states that Astor, in exchange for providing intelligence to the British during the years before and after the Revolutionary War, and for inciting Indians to attack

---

[57] *Ibid*, p. 225

[58] Lyndon H. LaRouche, *Dope, Inc.*, New Benjamin Franklin House Publishing Co., NY 1978

and kill American settlers along the frontier, received a handsome reward. He was not paid in cash, but was given a percentage of the British opium trade with China. It was the income from this lucrative concession which provided the basis for the Astor fortune.

With his father's connection with the Astors, young Moses Taylor had no difficulty in finding a place as apprentice in a banking house at the age of 15. Like so many others in these pages, he found his greatest opportunities when many other Americans were going bankrupt during an abrupt contraction of credit. During the Panic of 1837, when more than half the business firms in New York failed, he doubled his fortune. In 1855, he became president of City Bank. During the Panic of 1857, the City Bank profited by the failure of many of its competitors. Like George Peabody and Junius Morgan, Taylor seemed to have an ample supply of cash for buying up distressed stocks. He purchased nearly all the stock of Delaware Lackawanna Railroad for $5 a share. Seven years later, it was selling for $240 a share. Moses Taylor was now worth fifty million dollars.

In August, 1861, Taylor was named Chairman of the Loan Committee to finance the Union Government in the Civil War. The Committee shocked Lincoln by offering the government $5,000,000 at 12% to finance the war. Lincoln refused and financed the war by issuing the famous "Greenbacks" through the U.S. Treasury, which were backed by gold. Taylor continued to increase his fortune throughout the war, and in his later years, the youthful James Stillman became his protege. In 1882, when Moses Taylor died, he left seventy million dollars.* His son-in-law, Percy Pyne, succeeded him as president of City Bank, which had now become National City Bank. Pyne was paralyzed, and was barely able to function at the bank. For nine years, the bank stagnated, nearly all its capital being the estate of Moses Taylor. William Rockefeller, brother of John D. Rockefeller, had bought into the bank, and was anxious to see it progress. He persuaded Pyne to step aside in 1891 in favor of James Stillman, and soon the National City Bank became the principal repository of the Rockefeller oil income. William Rockefeller's son, William, married Elsie, James Stillman's daughter, and his other son, Percy, married Stillman's other daughter, Isabel. Like so many others in New York banking, James Stillman also had a British connection. His father, Don Carlos Stillman, had come to Brownsville, Texas, as a British agent and blockade runner during the Civil War. Through his banking connections in New York, Don Carlos had been able to find a place for

---

*The New York Times* noted on May 24, 1882 that Moses Taylor was chairman of the Loan Committee of the Associated Banks of New York City in 1861. Two hundred million dollars worth of securities were entrusted to him. It is probably due to him more than to any other one man that the goverment in 1861 found itself with the means to prosecute the war.

his son as apprentice in a banking house. In 1914, when National City Bank purchased almost ten per cent of the shares of the newly organized Federal Reserve Bank of New York, two of Moses Taylor's grandsons, Moses Taylor Pyne and Percy Pyne, owned 15,000 shares of National City stock. Moses Taylor's son, H.A.C. Taylor, owned 7699 shares of National City Bank. The bank's attorney, John W. Sterling, of the firm of Shearman and Sterling, also owned 6000 shares of National City Bank. However, James Stillman owned 47,498 shares, or almost twenty percent of the banks's total shares of 250,000. [See Chart I]

The second largest purchaser of Federal Reserve Bank of New York shares in 1914, First National Bank, was generally known as "the Morgan Bank", because of the Morgan representation on the board, although the bank's founder, George F. Baker held 20,000 shares, and his son G.F. Baker, Jr., had 5,000 shares, for twenty-five percent of the bank's total stock of 100,000 shares. George F. Baker Sr.'s daughter married George F. St. George of London. The St. George later settled in the United States, where their daughter, Katherine St. George, became a prominent Congresswoman for a number of years. Dr. E.M. Josephson wrote of her, "Mrs. St. George, a first cousin of FDR and New Dealer, said, 'Democracy is a failure.'"[59] George Baker, Jr.'s daughter, Edith Brevoort Baker, married Jacob Schiff's grandson, John M. Schiff, in 1934. John M. Schiff is now honorary chairman of Lehman Brothers Kuhn Loeb Company.

The third large purchaser of Federal Reserve Bank of New York stock in 1914 was the National Bank of Commerce which issued 250,000 shares. J.P. Morgan, through his controlling interest in Equitable Life, which held 24,700 shares and Mutual Life, which held 17,294 shares of National Bank of Commerce, also held another 10,000 shares of National Bank of Commerce through J.P. Morgan and Company (7800 shares), J.P. Morgan, Jr. (1100 shares), and Morgan partner H.P. Davison (1100 shares). Paul Warburg, a Governor of the Federal Reserve Board of Governors, also held 3000 shares of National Bank of Commerce. His partner, Jacob Schiff had 1,000 shares of National Bank of Commerce. This bank was clearly controlled by Morgan, who was really a subsidiary of Junius S. Morgan Company in London and the N.M. Rothschild Company of London, and Kuhn, Loeb Company, which was also known as a principal agent of the Rothschilds.

The financier Thomas Fortune Ryan also held 5100 shares of National Bank of Commerce stock in 1914. His son, John Barry Ryan, married Otto Kahn's daughter. Kahn was a partner of Warburg and Schiff in Kuhn, Loeb Company. Ryan's granddaughter, Virginia Fortune Ryan,

---

[59]E.M. Josephson, *The Strange Death of Franklin D. Roosevelt*, Chedney Press, N.Y. 1948

married Lord Airlie, the present head of J. Henry Schroder Banking Corporation in London and New York.

Another director of National Bank of Commerce in 1914, A.D. Juillard, was president of A.D. Juillard Company, a trustee of New York Life, and Guaranty Trust, all of which were controlled by J.P. Morgan. Juillard also had a British connection, being a director of the North British and Mercantile Insurance Company. Juillard owned 2000 shares of National Bank of Commerce stock, and was also a director of Chemical Bank.

In *The Robber Barons*, by Matthew Josephson, Josephson tells us that Morgan dominated New York Life, Equitable Life and Mutual Life by 1900, which had one billion dollars in assets, and which had fifty million dollars a year to invest. He says,

> "In this campaign of secret alliances he (Morgan) acquired direct control of the National Bank of Commerce; then a part ownership in the First National Bank, allying himself to the very strong and conservative financier, George F. Baker, who headed it; then by means of stock ownership and interlocking directorates he linked to the first named banks other leading banks, the Hanover, the Liberty, and Chase."[60]

Mary W. Harriman, widow of E.H. Harriman, also owned 5,000 shares of National Bank of Commerce in 1914. E.H. Harriman's railroad empire had been entirely financed by Jacob Schiff of Kuhn, Loeb Company. Levi P. Morton also owned 1500 shares of National Bank of Commerce stock in 1914. He had been the twenty-second vice-president of the United States, was an ex-Minister from the U.S. to France, and president of L.P. Morton Company, New York, Morton-Rose and Company and Morton Chaplin Company of London. He was a director of Equitable Life Insurance Company, Home Insurance Company, Guaranty Trust, and Newport Trust.

The astounding idea that the Federal Reserve System of the United States is actually operated from London will probably be rejected at first hearing by most Americans. However, Minsky has become famous for his theory of the "dominant frame". He states that in any particular situation, there is a "dominant frame" to which everything in that situation is related and through which it can be interpreted. The "dominant frame" in the monetary policy decisions of the Federal Reserve System is that these decisions are made by those who stand to benefit most from them. At first glance, this would seem to be the principal stockholders of the Federal Reserve Bank of New York. However, we have seen that these stockholders all have a "London Connection". The "London Connection" becomes more obvious as the dominant power when we find in *The*

---

[60] Matthew Josephson, *The Robber Barons*, p. 409

*Capital City*[61] that only seventeen firms are allowed to operate as merchant bankers in the City of London, England's financial district. All of them must be approved by the Bank of England. In fact, most of the Governors of the Bank of England come from the partners of these seventeen firms. Clarke ranks the seventeen in order of their capitalization. Number 2 is the Schroder Bank. Number 6 is Morgan Grenfell, the London branch of the House of Morgan and actually its dominant branch. Lazard Brothers is Number 8. N.M. Rothschild is Number 9. Brown Shipley Company, the London branch of Brown Brothers Harriman, is Number 14. These five merchant banking firms of London actually control the New York banks which own the controlling interest in the Federal Reserve Bank of New York.

The control over Federal Reserve System decisions is also founded in another unique situation. Each day, representatives of four other London banking firms meet in the offices of N.M. Rothschild Company in London to fix the price of gold for that day. The other four bankers are from Samuel Montagu Company, which ranks Number 5 on the list of seventeen London merchant banking firms, Sharps Pixley, Johnson Matheson, and Mocatta and Goldsmid. Despite the huge tide of paper pyramided currency and notes which are now flooding the world, at some point, every credit extension must return to be based, in however minuscule a fashion, on some deposit of gold in some bank somewhere in the world. Because of this factor, the London merchant bankers, with their power to set the price of gold each day, become the final arbiters of the volume of money and the price of money in those countries which must bow to their power. Not the least of these is the United States. No official of the Federal Reserve Bank of New York, or of the Federal Reserve Board of Governors, can command the power over the money of the world which is held by these London merchant bankers. Great Britain, while waning in political and military power, today exercises the greatest financial power. It is for this reason that London is the present financial center of the world.

---

[61]McRae and Cairncross, *Capital City*, Eyre Methuen, London, 1963

CHAPTER SEVEN
# The Hitler Connection

J. Henry Schroder Banking Company is listed as Number 2 in capitalization in *Capital City*[62] on the list of the seventeen merchant bankers who make up the exclusive Accepting Houses Committee in London. Although it is almost unknown in the United States, it has played a large part in our history. Like the others on this list, it had first to be approved by the Bank of England. And, like the Warburg family, the von Schroders began their banking operations in Hamburg, Germany. At the turn of the century, in 1900, Baron Bruno von Schroder established the London branch of the firm. He was soon joined by Frank Cyril Tiarks, in 1902. Tiarks married Emma Franziska of Hamburg, and was a director of the Bank of England from 1912 to 1945.

During World War I, J. Henry Schroder Banking Company played an important role behind the scenes. No historian has a reasonable explanation of how World War I started. Archduke Ferdinand was assassinated at Sarajevo by Gavril Princeps, Austria demanded an apology from Serbia, and Serbia sent the note of apology. Despite this, Austria declared war, and soon the other nations of Europe joined the fray. Once the war had gotten started, it was found that it wasn't easy to keep it going. The principal problem was that Germany was desperately short of food and coal, and without Germany, the war could not go on. John Hamill in *The Strange Career of Mr. Hoover*[63] explains how the problem was solved.\*
He quotes from *Nordeutsche Allgemeine Zeitung*, March 4, 1915, "Justice, however, demands that publicity should be given to the preeminent part taken by the German authorities in Belgium in the solution of this problem. The initiative came from them and it was only due to their continuous relations with the American Relief Committee that the provisioning question was solved." Hamill points out "That is what the Belgian Relief Committee was organized for—to keep Germany in food." (from page 308)

The Belgian Relief Commission was organized by Emile Francqui, director of a large Belgian bank, Societe Generale, and a London mining

---

[62]McRae and Cairncross, *Capital City*, Eyre Methuen, London, 1963
[63]John Hamill, *The Strange Career of Mr. Hoover*, William Faro, New York, 1931
\*Copies of Hamill's book were systematically located and destroyed by government agents, because it was published on the eve of President Hoover's re-election campaign.

promoter, an American named Herbert Hoover, who had been associated with Francqui in a number of scandals which had become celebrated court cases, notably the Kaiping Coal Company scandal in China, said to have set off the Boxer Rebellion, which had as its goal the expulsion of all foreign businessmen from China. Hoover had been barred from dealing on the London Stock Exchange because of one judgement against him, and his associate, Stanley Rowe, had been sent to prison for ten years. With this background, Hoover was called an ideal choice for a career in humanitarian work.

Although his name is unknown in the United States, Emile Francqui was the guiding spirit behind Herbert Hoover's rise to fortune. Hamill (on page 156) identifies Francqui as the director of many atrocities committed against natives in the Congo. "For every cartridge they spent, they had to bring in a man's hand". Francqui's frightful record may have been the source for the charge later leveled against German soldiers in Belgium, that they chopped off the hands of women and children, a claim which proved to be groundless. Hamill also says that Francqui "tricked the Americans out of the Hankow-Canton railroad concession in China in 1901, and at the same time had "stood by' in case Hoover needed any further help in the 'taking' of the Kaiping coal mines. This is the humanitarian who had sole charge of the distribution of the Belgian 'relief' during the World War, for which Hoover did the buying and shipping. Francqui was a director with Hoover, in the Chinese Engineering and Mining Company (the Kaiping mines), through which Hoover transported 200,000 Chinese slave workers to the Congo to work Francqui's copper mines."

Hamill says on page 311 that "Francqui opened the offices of the Belgian Relief in his bank, Societe Generale, as a one-man show, with a letter of permission from the German Governor General von der Goltz dated October 16, 1914.

*The New York Herald Tribune* of February 18, 1930, quoted by Congressman Louis McFadden in the House on February 26, 1930, said, "One of Belgium's two directors on the Bank for International Settlements will be Emile Francqui of the Societe Generale, a member of both the Young and Dawes Plan Committees. The board of directors of the international bank will have no more colorful character than Emile Francqui, former Minister of Finance, veteran of the Congo and China . . . he is rated as the richest man in Belgium, and among the twelve richest men in Europe."

Despite his prominence, *The New York Times* Index mentions Francqui only a few times during two decades before his death. On October 3, 1931, *The New York Times* quoted *Le Peuple* of Brussels that Francqui would visit the United States. "As a friend of President Hoover, Monsieur Francqui will not fail to pay a visit to the President."

On October 30, 1931, *The New York Times* reported this visit with the headline, "Hoover-Francqui Talk was Unofficial". "It was stated that Mr. Francqui spent Tuesday night as a personal guest of the President, and that they talked of world financial problems in general, strictly unofficial. Mr. Francqui was an associate of President Hoover during the latters ministrations in Belgium during the war. Their visit had no official significance. Mr. Francqui is a private citizen and not engaged in any official mission."

No reference is made to the Hoover-Francqui business associations which were the subject of huge lawsuits in London. The Francqui visit probably involved Hoover's Moratorium on German War Debts, which stunned the financial world. On December 15, 1931, Chairman McFadden informed the House of a dispatch in the *Public Ledger* of Philadelphia, October 24, 1931, "GERMAN REVEALS HOOVER'S SECRET. The American President was in intimate negotiations with the German government regarding a year's debt holiday as early as December, 1930." McFadden continued, "Behind the Hoover announcement there were many months of hurried and furtive preparations both in Germany and in Wall Street offices of German bankers. Germany, like a sponge, had to be saturated with American money. Mr. Hoover himself had to be elected, because this scheme began before he became President. If the German international bankers of Wall Street—that is Kuhn Loeb Company, J. & W. Seligman, Paul Warburg, J. Henry Schroder—and their satellites had not had this job waiting to be done, Herbert Hoover would never have been elected President of the United States. The election of Mr. Hoover to the Presidency was through the influence of the Warburg Brothers, directors of the great bank of Kuhn Loeb Company, who carried the cost of his election. In exchange for this collaboration Mr. Hoover promised to impose the moratorium of German debts. Hoover sought to exempt Kreuger's loan to Germany of $125 million from the operation of the Hoover Moratorium. The nature of Kreuger's swindle was known here in January when he visited his friend, Mr. Hoover, in the White House."

Not only did Hoover entertain Francqui in the White House, but also Ivar Kreuger, the most famous swindler of the twentieth century.

When Francqui died on November 13, 1935, *The New York Times* memorialized him as "the copper king of the Congo . . . Mr. Francqui, last year having gained dictatorial powers over the belga, maintained it on the gold standard during a crisis. In 1891 he led an expedition into the Congo and gained it for King Leopold. A man of great wealth, rated among the twelve richest men in Europe, he secured enormous copper deposits. He was Minister of State in 1926 and Minister of Finance in 1934. It was his pride that he never accepted a centime of remuneration for his services to the government. While consul general at Shanghai, he secured valuable concessions, notably the Kaiping coal mines and the railway concession for the Tientsin Railroad. He was governor of the Societe Generale de Belgique, Lloyd Royal Belge, and regent of La Banque Nationale de Belgique."

*The Times* does not mention Francqui's business partnerships with Hoover. Like Francqui, Hoover also refused remuneration for "government service", and as Secretary of Commerce and as President of the United States, he turned his salary back to the government.

On December 13, 1932, Chairman McFadden introduced a resolution of impeachment against President Hoover for high crimes and misdemeanours, which covers many pages, including violation of contracts, unlawful dissipation of the financial resources of the United States, and his appointment of Eugene Meyer to the Federal Reserve Board. The resolution was tabled and never acted upon by the House.

In criticizing Hoover's Moratorium of German War Debts, McFadden had referred to Hoover's "German" backers. Although all of the principals of "the London Connection" did originate in Germany, most of them in Frankfurt, at the time they sponsored Hoover's candidacy for the Presidency of the United States, they were operating from London, as Hoover himself had done for most of his career.

Also, the Hoover Moratorium was not intended to "help" Germany, as Hoover had never been "pro-German". The Moratorium on Germany's war debts was necessary so that Germany would have funds for rearming. In 1931, the truly forward-looking diplomats were anticipating the Second World War, and there could be no war without an "aggressor".

Hoover had also carried out a number of mining promotions in various parts of the world as a secret agent for the Rothschilds, and had been rewarded with a directorship in one of the principal Rothschild enterprises, the Rio Tinto Mines in Spain and Bolivia. Francqui and Hoover threw themselves into the seemingly impossible task of provisioning Germany during the First World War. Their success was noted in *Nordeutsche Allgemeine Zeitung,* March 13, 1915, which noted that large quantities of food were now arriving from Belgium by rail. Schmoller's *Yearbook for Legislation, Administration and Political Economy* for 1916, shows that one billion pounds of meat, one and a half billion pounds of potatoes, one and a half billion pounds of bread, and one hundred twenty-one million pounds of butter had been shipped from Belgium to Germany in that year. A patriotic British woman who had operated a small hospital in Belgium for several years, Edith Cavell, wrote to the *Nursing Mirror* in London, April 15, 1915, complaining that the "Belgian Relief" supplies were being shipped to Germany to feed the German army. The Germans considered Miss Cavell to be of no importance, and paid no attention to her, but the British Intelligence Service in London was appalled by Miss Cavell's discovery, and demanded that the Germans arrest her as a spy.

Sir William Wiseman, head of British Intelligence, and partner of Kuhn Loeb Company, feared that the continuance of the war was at stake, and secretly notified the Germans that Miss Cavell must be executed. The Germans reluctantly arrested her and charged her with aiding prisoners of war to escape. The usual penalty for this offense was three months imprisonment, but the Germans bowed to Sir William Wiseman's demands, and shot Edith Cavell, thus creating one of the principal martyrs of the First World War.

With Edith Cavell out of the way, the "Belgian Relief" operation continued, although in 1916, German emissaries again approached London officials with the information that they did not believe Germany could continue military operations, not only because of food shortages, but because of financial problems. More "emergency relief" was sent, and Germany continued in the war until November, 1918. Two of Hoover's principal assistants were a former lumber shipping clerk from the West Coast, Prentiss Gray, and Julius H. Barnes, a grain salesman from Duluth. Both men became partners in J. Henry Schroder Banking Corporation in New York after the war, and amassed large fortunes, principally in grain and sugar.

With the entry of the United States into the war, Barnes and Gray were given important posts in the newly created U.S. Food Administration, which also was placed under Herbert Hoover's direction. Barnes became President of the Grain Corporation of the U.S. Food Administration from 1917 to 1918, and Gray was chief of Marine Transportation. Another J. Henry Schroder partner, G. A. Zabriskie, was named head of the U.S. Sugar Equalization Board. Thus the London Connection controlled all food in the United States through its grain and sugar "Czars" during the First World War. Despite many complaints of corruption and scandal in the U.S. Food Administration, no one was ever indicted. After the war, the partners of J. Henry Schroder Company found that they now owned most of Cuba's sugar industry. One partner, M.E. Rionda, was president of Cuba Cane Corporation, and director of Manati Sugar and many other Cuban sugar firms. Barnes was also a director of Manati Sugar, Chairman of the Board of Pitney Bowes Corporation, and had stock in many other firms. Prentiss Gray was a director of Manati Sugar Company, American British and Continental Corporation, and other firms. Baron Bruno von Schroder, senior partner of the firm, was a director of North British and Mercantile Insurance Company. His father, Baron Rudolph von Schroder of Hamburg, was a director of Sao Paulo Coffee Ltd., one of the largest Brazilian coffee companies, with F.C. Tiarks, also of the Schroder firm.*

---

*The New York Times noted on October 11, 1923: "Frank C. Tiarks, Governor of the Bank of England, will spend two weeks here to set up the opening of the banking house branch of J. Henry Schroder of London."

After the war, Zabriskie, who had been sugar Czar of the United States by presiding over the U.S. Sugar Equalization Board, became the president of several of the largest baking corporations in the United States: Empire Biscuit, Southern Baking Corporation, Columbia Baking, and other firms.

As his principal assistant in the U.S. Food Administration, Hoover chose Lewis Lichtenstein Strauss, who was soon to become a partner in Kuhn Loeb Company, marrying the daughter of Jerome Hanauer of Kuhn Loeb. Throughout his distinguished humanitarian service with the Belgian Relief Commission, the U.S. Food Administration, and, after the war, the American Relief Administration, Hoover's closest associate was one Edgar Rickard, born in Pontgibaud, France. In Who's Who, he states that he was "World War administrative assistant to Herbert Hoover in all war and post-war organizations including the Commission For Relief in Belgium. He also served on the U.S. Food Administration from 1914-1924." He remained one of Hoover's closest friends, and usually the Rickards and Hoovers took their vacations together. After Hoover became Secretary of Commerce under Coolidge, Hamill tells us that Hoover awarded his friend the Hazeltine Radio patents, which paid him one million dollars a year in royalties.

In 1928, "the London Connection" decided to run Herbert Hoover for president of the United States. There was only one problem; although Herbert Hoover had been born in the United States, and was thus eligible for the office of the presidency, according to the Constitution, he had never had a business address or a home address in the United States, as he had gone abroad just after completing college at Stanford. The result was that during his campaign for the presidency, Herbert Hoover listed as his American address Suite 2000, 42 Broadway, New York, which was the office of Edgar Rickard. Suite 2000 was also shared by the grain tycoon and partner of J. Henry Schroder Banking Corporation, Julius H. Barnes.

After Herbert Hoover was elected president of the United States, he insisted on appointing one of the old London crowd, Eugene Meyer, as Governor of the Federal Reserve Board. Meyer's father had been one of the partners of Lazard Freres of Paris, and Lazard Brothers of London. Meyer, with Baruch, had been one of the most powerful men in the United States during World War I, a member of the famous Triumvirate which exercised unequalled power; Meyer as Chairman of the War Finance Corporation, Bernard Baruch as Chairman of the War Industries Board, and Paul Warburg as Governor of the Federal Reserve System.

A longtime critic of Eugene Meyer, Chairman Louis McFadden of the House Banking and Currency Committee, was quoted in *The New York Times*, December 17, 1930, as having made a speech on the floor of the House attacking Hoover's appointment of Meyer, and charging that "He represents the Rothschild interest and is liason officer between the French Government and J.P. Morgan." On December 18, *The Times* reported that "Herbert Hoover is deeply concerned" and that McFadden's speech was "an unfortunate occurrence." On December 20, *The Times* commented on the editorial page, under the headline, "McFadden Again", "The speech ought to insure the Senate ratification of Mr. Meyer as head of the Federal Reserve. The speech was incoherent, as Mr. McFadden's speeches usually are." As *The Times* predicted, Meyer was duly approved by the Senate.

Not content with having a friend in the White House, J. Henry Schroder Corporation was soon embarked on further international adventures, nothing less than a plan to set up World War II. This was to be done by providing, at a crucial juncture, the financing for Adolf Hitler's assumption of power in Germany. Although any number of magnates have been given credit for the financing of Hitler, including Fritz Thyssen, Henry Ford, and J.P. Morgan, they, as well as others, did provide millions of dollars for his political campaigns during the 1920s, just as they did for others who also had a chance of winning, but who disappeared and were never heard from again. In December of 1932, it seemed inevitable to many observers of the German scene that Hitler was also ready for a toboggan slide into oblivion. Despite the fact that he had done well in national campaigns, he had spent all the money from his usual sources and now faced heavy debts. In his book *Aggression*, Otto Lehmann-Russbeldt tells us that "Hitler was invited to a meeting at the Schroder Bank in Berlin on January 4, 1933. The leading industrialists and bankers of Germany tided Hitler over his financial difficulties and enabled him to meet the enormous debt he had incurred in connection with the maintenance of his private army. In return, he promised to break the power of the trade unions. On May 2, 1933, he fulfilled his promise."[64]

Present at the January 4, 1933 meeting were the Dulles brothers, John Foster Dulles and Allen W. Dulles of the New York law firm, Sullivan and Cromwell, which represented the Schroder Bank. The Dulles brothers often turned up at important meetings. They had represented the United States at the Paris Peace Conference (1919); John Foster Dulles would die in harness as Eisenhower's Secretary of State, while Allen Dulles headed the Central Intelligence Agency for many years. Their apologists have seldom attempted to defend the Dulles brothers appearance at the meeting which installed Hitler as the Chancellor of Germany, preferring to pretend that it never happened. Obliquely, one biographer Leonard Mosley, bypasses it in *Dulles* when he states,

---

[64]Otto Lehmann-Russbeldt, *Aggression*, Hutchinson & Co., Ltd., London, 1934, p. 44

"Both brothers had spent large amounts of time in Germany, where Sullivan and Cromwell had considerable interests during the early 1930's, having represented several provincial governments, some large industrial combines, a number of big American companies with interests in the Reich, and some rich individuals."[65]

Allen Dulles later became a director of J. Henry Schroder Company. Neither he nor J. Henry Schroder were to be suspected of being pro-Nazi or pro-Hitler; the inescapable fact was that if Hitler did not become Chancellor of Germany, there was little likelihood of getting a Second World War going, the war which would double their profits.*

The Great Soviet Encyclopaedia states "The banking house Schroeder Bros. (it was Hitler's banker) was established in 1846; its partners today are the barons von Schroeder, related to branches in the United States and England."[66]**

The financial editor of "The Daily Herald" of London wrote on Sept. 30, 1933 of "Mr. Norman's decision to give the Nazis the backing of the Bank (of England.)" John Hargrave, in his biography of Montagu Norman, says,

> "It is quite certain that Norman did all he could to assist Hitlerism to gain and maintain political power, operating on the financial plane from his stronghold in Treadneedle Street." [i.e. Bank of England.—Ed.]

Baron Wilhelm de Ropp, a journalist whose closest friend was Major F.W. Winterbotham, chief of Air Intelligence of the British Secret Service, brought the Nazi philosopher, Alfred Rosenberg, to London and introduced him to Lord Hailsham, Secretary for War, Geoffrey Dawson, editor of *The Times*, and Norman, Governor of the Bank of England. After talking with Norman, Rosenberg met with the representative of the Schroder Bank of London. The managing director of the Schroder Bank, F.C. Tiarks, was also a director of the Bank of England. Hargrave says (p. 217), "Early in 1934 a select group of City financiers gathered in Norman's room behind the windowless walls, Sir Robert Kindersley, partner of Lazard Brothers, Charles Hambro, F.C. Tiarks, Sir Josiah Stamp, (also a director of the Bank of England). Governor Norman spoke of the political situation in Europe. A new power had established itself, a great 'stabilizing

---

[65]Leonard Mosely, *Dulles*, Dial Publishing Co., New York 1978, p. 88

*Ezra Pound, in an April 18, 1943 broadcast over Radio Rome stated, "...and men in America, not content with this war are already aiming at the next one. The time to object is now."

[66]The Great Soviet Encyclopaedia, Macmillan, London, 1973, v. 2, p. 620

**The New York Times noted on October 11, 1944: "Senator Claude Pepper criticized John Foster Dulles, Gov. Dewey's foreign relations advisor for his connection with the law firm of Sullivan and Cromwell and having aided Hitler financially in 1933. Pepper described the January 4, 1933 meeting of Franz von Papen and Hitler in Baron Schroder's home in Cologne, and from that time on the Nazis were able to continue their march to power."

force', namely, Nazi Germany. Norman advised his co-workers to include Hitler in their plans for financing Europe. There was no opposition."

In *Wall Street and the Rise of Hitler*, Antony C. Sutton writes "The Nazi Baron Kurt von Schroeder acted as the conduit for I.T.T. money funnelled to Heinrich Himmler's S.S. organization in 1944, while World War II was in progress, and the United States was at war with Germany."[67] Kurt von Schroeder, born in 1889, was partner in the Cologne Bankhaus, J.H. Stein & Co., which had been founded in 1788. After the Nazis gained power in 1933, Schroeder was appointed the German representative at the Bank for International Settlements. The Kilgore Committee in 1940 stated that Schroeder's influence with the Hitler Administration was so great that he had Pierre Laval appointed head of the French Government during the Nazi Occupation. The Kilgore Committee listed more than a dozen important titles held by Kurt von Schroeder in the 1940's, including President of Deutsche Reichsbahn, Reich Board of Economic Affairs, SS Senior Group Leader, Council of Reich Post Office, Deutsche Reichsbank and other leading banks and industrial groups. Schroeder served on the board of all International Telephone and Telegraph subsidiaries in Germany.

In 1938, the London Schroder Bank became the German financial agent in Great Britain. The New York branch of Schroder had been merged in 1936 with the Rockefellers, as Schroder, Rockefeller, Inc. at 48 Wall Street. Carlton P. Fuller of Schroder was president of this firm, and Avery Rockefeller was vice-president. He had been a behind the scenes partner of J. Henry Schroder for years, and had set up the construction firm of Bechtel Corporation, whose employees (on leave) now play a leading role in the Reagan Administration, as Secretary of Defense and Secretary of State.

Ladislas Farago, in *The Game of the Foxes*,[68] reported that Baron William de Ropp, a double agent, had penetrated the highest echelons in pre-World War II days, and Hitler relied upon de Ropp as his confidential consultant about British affairs. It was de Ropp's advice which Hitler followed when he refused to invade England.

Victor Perlo writes, in *The Empire of High Finance:*

"The Hitler government made the London Schroder Bank their financial agent in Britain and America. Hitler's personal banking account was with J.M. Stein Bankhaus, the German subsidiary of the Schroder Bank. F.C. Tiarks of the British J. Henry Schroder Company

---

[67]Antony C. Sutton, *WALL STREET AND THE RISE OF HITLER*, 76 Press, Seal Beach, California, 1976, p. 79
[68]Ladislas Farago, *The Game of the Foxes*, 1973

was a member of the Anglo-German Fellowship, with two other partners as members, and a corporate membership."[69]

The story goes much further than Perlo suspects. J. Henry Schroder WAS the Anglo-German Fellowship, the English equivalent of the America First movement, and also attracting patriots who did not wish to see their nation involved in a needless war with Germany. During the 1930s, until the outbreak of World War II, the Schroders poured money into the Anglo-German Fellowship, with the result that Hitler was convinced he had a large pro-German fifth column in England composed of many prominent politicians and financiers. The two divergent political groups in the 1930s in England were the War Party, led by Winston Churchill, who furiously demanded that England go to war against Germany, and the Appeasement Party, led by Neville Chamberlain. After Munich, Hitler believed the Chamberlain group to be the dominant party in England, and Churchill a minor rabble-rouser. Because his own financial backers, the Schroders, were sponsoring the Appeasement Party, Hitler believed there would be no war. He did not suspect that the backers of the Appeasement Party, now that Chamberlain had served his purpose in duping Hitler, would cast Chamberlain aside and make Churchill the Prime Minister. It was not only Chamberlain, but also Hitler, who came away from Munich believing that it would be "Peace in our time."

The success of the Schroders in duping Hitler into this belief explains several of the most puzzling questions of World War II. Why did Hitler allow the British Army to decamp from Dunkirk and return home, when he could have wiped them out? Against the frantic advice of his generals, who wished to deliver the coup de grace to the English Army, Hitler held back because he did not wish to alienate his supposed vast following in England. For the same reason, he refused to invade England during a period when he had military superiority, believing that it would not be necessary, as the Anglo-German Fellowship group was ready to make peace with him. The Rudolf Hess flight to England was an attempt to confirm that the Schroder group was ready to make peace and form a common bond against the Soviets. Rudolf Hess continues to languish in prison today, many years after the war, because he would, if released,

---

[69]Victor Perlo, *The Empire of High Finance*, International Publishers, 1957, p. 177

testify that he had gone to England to contact the members of the Anglo-German Fellowship, that is, the Schroder group, about ending the war.*

If anyone supposes this is all ancient history, with no application to the present political scene, we introduce the name of John Lowery Simpson of Sacramento, California. Although he appears for the first time in Who's Who in America for 1952, Mr. Simpson states that he served under Herbert Hoover on the Commission for Relief in Belgium from 1915 to 1917; U.S. Food Administration, 1917 to 1918, American Relief Commission, 1919, and with P.N. Gray Company, Vienna, 1919 to 1921. Gray was the Chief of Maritime Transportation for the U.S. Food Administration, which enabled him to set up his own shipping company after the war. Like other Hoover humanitarians, Simpson also joined the J. Henry Schroder Banking Company (Adolf Hitler's personal bankers) and the J. Henry Schroder Trust Company. He also became a partner of Schroder-Rockefeller Company when that investment trust backed a construction company which became the world's largest, the firm of Bechtel Incorporated. Simpson was chairman of the finance committee of Bechtel Company, Bechtel International, and Canadian Bechtel. Simpson states he was consultant to the Bechtel-McCone interests in war production during World War II. He served on the Allied Control Commission in Italy 1943-44. He married Margaret Mandel, of the merchant family for whom Col. Edward Mandel House was named, and he backed a California personality, first for Governor, then for President. As a result, Simpson and J. Henry Schroder Company now have serving them as Secretary of Defense, former Bechtel employee Caspar Weinberger. As Secretary of State they have serving them George Pratt Schultz, also a Bechtel employee, who happens to be a Standard Oil heir, reaffirming the Schroder-Rockefeller company ties. Thus the "conservative" Reagan Administration has a Secretary of Defense from Schroder Company, a Secretary of State from Schroder Rockefeller, and a vice president whose father was senior partner of Brown Brothers Harriman.

---

*The following accounts are from The New York Times: October 21, 1945, "A broadcast over the Luxembourg radio said tonight that Baron Kurt von Schroder, former banker who helped finance the rise of the Nazi party, had been recognized in an American prison camp and arrested." November 1, 1945, "British Army Headquarters: Baron Kurt von Schroder, 55 year old banker and friend of Heinrich Himmler is being held in Dusseldorf pending decision on his indictment as a war criminal, the Military Government official announcement said today." February 29, 1948, "An immediate investigation was demanded yesterday by the Society for the Prevention of World War III as to why the German Nazi banker, Kurt von Schroder, was not tried as a war criminal by an allied military tribunal. Noting that von Schroder was sentenced last November to three months imprisonment and fined 1500 Reichsmarks by a German denazification court in Bielefeld, in the British Zone, C. Monteith Gilpin, secretary for the society said the question should be asked why von Schroder was allowed to escape allied justice, and why our own officials have not demanded that von Schroder be tried by an Allied military tribunal. 'Von Schroder is as guilty as Hitler or Goering.'"

The Heritage Foundation has also been an important factor in the policy-making of the Reagan Administration. Now we find that the Heritage Foundation is part of the Tavistock Institute network, directed by British Intelligence. The financial decisions are still made at the Bank of England, and who is head of the Bank of England? Sir Gordon Richardson, chairman of J. Henry Schroder Co. of London and New York from 1962 to 1972, when he became Governor of the Bank of England. The "London Connection" has never been more firmly in the saddle of the United States Government.

On July 3, 1983, *The New York Times* announced that Gordon Richardson, Governor of the Bank of England for the past ten years, had been replaced by Robert Leigh-Pemberton, Chairman of the National Westminster Bank. The list of directors of National Westminster Bank reads like a Who's Who of the British ruling class. They include the Chairman, Lord Aldenham, who is also Chairman of Antony Gibbs & Son, merchant bankers, one of the seventeen privileged firms chartered by the Bank of England; Sir Walter Barrie, Chairman of the British Broadcasting System; F.E. Harmer, Governor of the London School of Economics, the training school for the international bankers, and chairman of New Zealand Shipping Company; Sir E.C. Mieville, private secretary to the King of England 1937-45; Marquess of Salisbury, Lord Cecil, Lord Privy Seal (the Cecils have been considered one of England's three ruling families since the Middle Ages); Lord Leathers, Baron of Purfleet, Minister of War Transport 1941-45, chairman of William Cory group of companies; Sir W.H. Coates and W.J. Worboys of Imperial Chemical Industries (the English DuPont); Earl of Dudley, chairman British Iron & Steel and many other steel companies; Sir W. Benton Jones, chairman United Steel and many other steel and many other steel companies; Sir G.E. Schuster, Bank of New Zealand; East India Coal Company; A. d'A. Willis, Ashanti Goldfields and many banks, tea companies and other firms; V.W. Yorke, chairman of Mexican Railways Ltd.

Richardson, former chairman of Schroders with a New York subsidiary holding Federal Reserve Bank of New York stock, was replaced by the chairman of National Westminster, with a subsidiary in New York holding Federal Reserve Bank of New York stock. Robert Leigh Pemberton, a director of Equitable Life Assurance Society (J.P. Morgan), married the daughter of the Marchioness of Exeter, (the Cecil Burghley family). Thereby, the control of the London Connection remains constantly in effect.

The list of the present directors of J. Henry Schroder Bank and Trust shows the continuing international influence since the First World War. George A. Braga is also director of Czarnikow-Rionda Company, vice-president of Francisco Sugar Company, president of Manati Sugar Company, and vice-president of New Tuinicui Sugar Company. His relative,

Rionda B. Braga, is president of Francisco Sugar Company and vice president of Manati Sugar Company. The Schroder control of sugar goes back to the U.S. Food Administration under Herbert Hoover and Lewis L. Strauss of Kuhn, Loeb, Company during World War I. Schroder's attorneys are the firm of Sullivan and Cromwell. John Foster Dulles of this firm was present during the historic agreement to finance Hitler, and was later Secretary of State in the Eisenhower administration. Alfred Jaretzki, Jr., of Sullivan and Cromwell is also a director of Manati Sugar Company and Francisco Sugar Company.

Another director of J. Henry Schroder is Norris Darrell, Jr., born in Berlin, Germany, partner of Sullivan and Cromwell, and a director of Schroder Trust Company. Bayless Manning, partner of the Wall Street law firm of Paul, Weiss, Rifkind and Wharton, is also a director of J. Henry Schroder. He was president of the Council on Foreign Relations from 1971-1977, and is editor in chief of the Yale Law Review.

Paul H. Nitze, the prominent "disarmament negotiator" for the United States government, is a director of Schroder's Inc. He married Phyllis Pratt, of the Standard Oil fortune, whose father gave the Pratt family mansion as the building which houses the Council on Foreign Relations.

## CHAPTER EIGHT
# World War One

"Money is the worst of all contraband."—William Jennings Bryan

It is now apparent that there might have been no World War without the Federal Reserve System. A strange sequence of events, none of which were accidental, had occurred. Without Theodore Roosevelt's "Bull Moose" candidacy, the popular President Taft would have been reelected, and Woodrow Wilson would have returned to obscurity.* If Wilson had not been elected, we might have had no Federal Reserve Act, and World War One could have been avoided. The European nations had been led to maintain large standing armies as the policy of the central banks which dictated their governmental decisions. In April, 1887, the *Quarterly Journal of Economics* had pointed out:

> "A detailed revue of the public debts of Europe shows interest and sinking fund payments of $5,343 million annually (five and one-third billion). M. Neymarck's conclusion is much like Mr. Atkinson's. The finances of Europe are so involved that the governments may ask whether war, with all its terrible chances, is not preferable to the maintenance of such a precarious and costly peace. If the military preparations of Europe do not end in war, they may well end in the bankruptcy of the States. Or, if such follies lead neither to war nor to ruin, then they assuredly point to industrial and economic revolution."

From 1887 to 1914, this precarious system of heavily armed but bankrupt European nations endured, while the United States continued to be a debtor nation, borrowing money from abroad, but making few international loans, because we did not have a central bank or "mobilization of credit". The system of national loans developed by the Rothschilds served to finance European struggles during the nineteenth century, because they were spread out over Rothschild branches in several countries. By 1900, it was obvious that the European countries could not afford a major war. They had large standing armies, universal military service, and modern weapons, but their economies could not support the enormous expenditures. The Federal Reserve System began operations in

---

*NOTE: P. 34. House revealed to me in a confidential moment, 'Wilson was elected by Teddy Roosevelt.'" *The Strangest Friendship in History, Woodrow Wilson and Col. House*, George Sylvester Viereck, Liveright, NY 1932

1914, forcing the American people to lend the Allies twenty-five billion dollars which was not repaid, although considerable interest was paid to New York bankers. The American people were driven to make war on the German people, with whom we had no conceivable political or economic quarrel. Moreover, the United States comprised the largest nation in the world composed of Germans; almost half of its citizens were of German descent, and by a narrow margin, German had been voted down as the national language.* The German Ambassador to Turkey, baron Wangeheim asked the American Ambassador to Turkey, Henry Morgenthau, why the United States intended to make war in Germany. "We Americans," replied Morgenthau, speaking for the group of Harlem real estate operators of which he was the head, "are going to war for a moral principle." J.P. Morgan received the proceeds of the First Liberty Loan to pay off $400,000,000 which he advanced to Great Britain at the outset of the war. To cover this loan, $68,000,000 in notes had been issued under the provisions of the Aldrich-Vreeland Act for issuing notes against securities, the only time this provision was employed. The notes were retired as soon as the Federal Reserve Banks began operations, and replaced by Federal Reserve Notes.

During 1915 and 1916, Wilson kept faith with the bankers who had purchased the White House for him, by continuing to make loans to the Allies. His Secretary of State, William Jennings Bryan, protested constantly, stating that "Money is the worst of all contraband." By 1917, the Morgans and Kuhn, Loeb Company had floated a billion and a half dollars in loans to the Allies. The bankers also financed a host of "peace" organizations which worked to get us involved in the World War. The Commission for Relief in Belgium manufactured atrocity stories against the Germans, while a Carnegie organization, The League to *Enforce Peace*, agitated in Washington for our entry into war. This later became the Carnegie Endowment for International Peace, which during the 1940s was headed by Alger Hiss. One writer* claimed that he had never seen any "peace movement" which did not end in war.

The U.S. Ambassador to Britain, Walter Hines Page, complained that he could not afford the position, and was given twenty-five thousand dollars a year spending money by Cleveland H. Dodge, president of the National City Bank. H.L. Mencken openly accused Page in 1916 of being a British agent, which was unfair. Page was merely a bankers' agent.

On March 5, 1917, Page sent a confidential letter to Wilson. "I think that the pressure of this approaching crisis has gone beyond the ability of the Morgan Financial Agency for the British and French Govern-

---

*1787 Constitutional Convention
*NOTE: Emmett Tyrell, Jr., *Richmond Times Dispatch*, Feb. 15, 1983 "Every peace movement of this century has been followed by war."

ments . . . The greatest help we could give the Allies would be a credit. Unless we go to war with Germany, our Government, of course, cannot make such a direct grant of credit."

The Rothschilds were wary of Germany's ability to continue in the war, despite the financial chaos caused by their agents, the Warburgs, who were financing the Kaiser, and Paul Warburg's brother, Max, who, as head of the German Secret Service, authorized Lenin's train to pass through the lines and execute the Bolshevik Revolution in Russia. According to Under Secretary of the Navy, Franklin D. Roosevelt, America's heavy industry had been preparing for war for a year. Both the Army and Navy Departments had been purchasing war supplies in large amounts since early in 1916. Cordell Hull remarks in his Memoirs:

"The conflict forced the further development of the income-tax principle. Aiming, as it did, at the one great untaxed source of revenue, the income-tax law had been enacted in the nick of time to meet the demands of war. And the conflict also assisted the putting into effect of the Federal Reserve System, likewise in the nick of time."[70]

One may ask, in the nick of time for whom? Certainly not for the American people, who had no need for "mobilization of credit" for a European war, or to enact an income tax to finance a war. Hull's statement affords a rare glimpse into the machinations of our "public servants".

The Notes of the Journal of Political Economy, October, 1917, state:

"The effect of the war upon the business of the Federal Reserve Banks has required an immense development of the staffs of these banks, with a corresponding increase in expenses. Without, of course, being able to anticipate so early and extensive a demand for their services in this connection, the framers of the Federal Reserve Act had provided that the Federal Reserve Banks should act as fiscal agents of the Government."

The bankers had been waiting since 1887 for the United States to enact a central bank plan so that they could finance a European war among the nations whom they had already bankrupted with armament and "defense" programs. The most demanding function of the central bank mechanism is war finance.

On October 13, 1917, Woodrow Wilson made a major address, stating:

"It is manifestly imperative that there should be a complete mobilization of the banking reserves of the United States. The burden and the privilege (of the Allied loans) must be shared by every banking institution in the country. I believe that cooperation on the part of the banks is a patriotic duty at this time, and that membership in the Federal Reserve System is a distinct and significant evidence of patriotism."

---

[70]Cordell Hull, *Memoirs*, Macmillan, New York, 1948, v. 1, page 76

E.W. Kemmerer writes that "As fiscal agents of the Government, the federal reserve banks rendered the nation services of incalculable value after our entrance into the war. They aided greatly in the conservation of our gold resources, in the regulation of our foreign exchanges, and in the centralization of our financial energies. One shudders when he thinks what might have happened if the war had found us with our former decentralized and antiquated banking system."

Mr. Kemmerer's shudders ignore the fact that if we had kept "our antiquated banking system" we would not have been able to finance the World War or to enter as a participant ourselves.

Woodrow Wilson himself did not believe in his crusade to save the world for democracy. He later wrote that "The World War was a matter of economic rivalry."

On being questioned by Senator McCumber about the circumstances of our entry into the war, Wilson was asked, "Do you think if Germany had committed no act of war or no act of injustice against our citizens that we would have gotten into this war?"

"I do think so," Wilson replied.

"You think we would have gotten in anyway?" pursued McCumber.

"I do," said Wilson.

In Wilson's War Message in 1917, he included an incredible tribute to the Communists in Russia who were busily slaughtering the middle class in that unfortunate country.

> "Assurance has been added to our hope for the future peace of the world by the wonderful and heartening things that have been happening in the last few weeks in Russia. Here is a fit partner for a League of Honor."[71]

Wilson's paean to a bloodthirsty regime which has since murdered sixty-six million of its inhabitants in the most barbarous manner exposes his true sympathies and his true backers, the bankers who had financed the blood purge in Russia. When the Communist Revolution seemed in doubt, Wilson sent his personal emissary, Elihu Root, to Russia with one hundred million dollars from his Special Emergency War Fund to save the toppling Bolshevik regime.

The documentation of Kuhn, Loeb Company's involvement in the establishment of Communism in Russia is much too extensive to be quoted here, but we include one brief mention, typical of the literature on this subject. In his book, *Czarism and the Revolution*, Gen. Arsene de Goulevitch writes,

---

[71] *Public Papers of Woodrow Wilson*, Dodd & Baker, v. 5, p. 12-13

"Mr. Bakmetiev, the late Russian Imperial Ambassador to the United States, tells us that the Bolsheviks, after victory, transferred 600 million roubles in gold between the years 1918-1922 to Kuhn, Loeb Company."

After our entry into World War I, Woodrow Wilson turned the government of the United States over to a triumvirate of his campaign backers, Paul Warburg, Bernard Baruch and Eugene Meyer. Baruch was appointed head of the War Industries Board, with life and death powers over every factory in the United States. Eugene Meyer was appointed head of the War Finance Corporation, in charge of the loan program which financed the war. Paul Warburg was in control of the nation's banking system*.

Knowing that the overwhelming sentiment of the American people during 1915 and 1916 had been anti-British and pro-German, our British allies viewed with some trepidation the prominence of Paul Warburg and Kuhn, Loeb Company in the prosecution of the war. They were uneasy about his high position in the Administration because his brother, Max Warburg, was at that time serving as head of the German Secret Service. On December 12, 1918, the United States Naval Secret Service Report on Mr. Warburg was as follows:

"WARBURG, PAUL: New York City. German, naturalized citizen, 1911. was decorated by the Kaiser in 1912, was vice chairman of the Federal Reserve Board. handled large sums furnished by Germany for Lenin and Trotsky. Has a brother who is leader of the espionage system of Germany."

Strangely enough, this report, which must have been compiled much earlier, while we were at war with Germany, is not dated until December 12, 1918. AFTER the Armistice had been signed. Also, it does not contain the information that Paul Warburg resigned from the Federal Reserve Board in May, 1918, which indicates that it was compiled before May, 1918, when Paul Warburg would theoretically have been open to a charge of treason because of his brother's control of Germany's Secret Service.

Paul Warburg's brother Felix in New York was a director of the Prussian Life Insurance Company of Berlin, and presumably would not have liked to see too many of his policyholders killed in the war. On September 26, 1920, *The New York Times* mentioned in its obituary of Jacob Schiff in reference to Kuhn, Loeb and Company, "During the World War certain of its members were in constant contact with the Government in an advisory capacity. It shared in the conferences which were held regarding the organization and formation of the Federal Reserve System."

---

*NOTE: *New York Times*, August 10, 1918; "Mr. (Paul) Warburg was the author of the plan organizing the War Finance Corporation."

The 1920 Schiff obituary revealed for the first time that Jacob Schiff, like the Warburgs, also had two brothers in Germany during World War I, Philip and Ludwig Schiff, of Frankfurt-on-Main, who also were active as bankers to the German Government! This was not a circumstance to be taken lightly, as on neither side of the Atlantic were the said bankers obscure individuals who had no influence in the conduct of the war. On the contrary, the Kuhn, Loeb partners held the highest governmental posts in the United States during World War I, while in Germany, Max and Fritz Warburg, and Philip and Ludwig Schiff, moved in the highest councils of government. From *Memoirs of Max Warburg*, "The Kaiser thumped the table violently and shouted, 'Must you always be right?' but then listened carefully to Max's view on financial matters."[72]

In June, 1918, Paul Warburg wrote a private note to Woodrow Wilson, "I have two brothers in Germany who are bankers. They naturally now serve their country to their utmost ability, as I serve mine."[73]

Neither Wilson nor Warburg viewed the situation as one of concern, and Paul Warburg served out his term on the Federal Reserve Board of Governors, while World War I continued to rage.

The background of Kuhn, Loeb & Company had been exposed in "Truth Magazine", edited by George Conroy:

"Mr. Schiff is head of the great private banking house of Kuhn, Loeb & Co. which represents the Rothschild interest on this side of the Atlantic. He has been described as a financial strategist and has been for years the financial minister to the great impersonal power known as Standard Oil. He was hand-in-glove with the Harrimans, the Goulds and the Rockefellers, in all their railroad enterprises and has become the dominant power in the railroad and financial world in America. Louis Brandeis, because of his great ability as a lawyer and for other reasons which will appear later, was selected by Schiff as the instrument through which Schiff hoped to achieve his ambition in New England. His job was to carry on an agitation which would undermine public confidence in the New Haven system and cause a decrease in the price of its securities, thus forcing them on the market for the wreckers to buy."[74]

We mention Schiff's lawyer, Brandeis, here because the first available appointment on the Supreme Court of the United States which Woodrow Wilson was allowed to fill was given to the Kuhn, Loeb lawyer, Brandeis.

Not only was the U.S. Food Administration managed by Hoover's director, Lewis Lichtenstein Strauss, who married into the Kuhn Loeb Company by marrying Alice Hanauer, daughter of partner Jerome

---

[72]Max Warburg, *Memoirs of Max Warburg*, Berlin, 1936

[73]David Farrar, *The Warburgs*, Michael Joseph, Ltd., London, 1974

[74]"Truth Magazine", George Conroy, editor, Boston, issue of December 16, 1912

Hanauer, but in the most critical field, military intelligence, Sir William Wiseman, chief of the British Secret Service, was a partner of Kuhn, Loeb & Company. He worked most closely with Wilson's alter ego, Col. House. "Between House and Wiseman there were soon to be few political secrets, and from their mutual comprehension resulted in large measure our close cooperation with the British."[75]

One example of House's cooperation with Wiseman was a confidential agreement which House negotiated pledging the United States to enter into World War I on the side of the Allies. Ten months before the election which returned Wilson to the White House in 1916 'because he kept us out of war'. Col. House negotiated a secret agreement with England and France on behalf of Wilson which pledged the United States to intervene on behalf of the Allies. On March 9, 1916, Wilson formally sanctioned the undertaking.[76]

Nothing could more forcefully illustrate the duplicity of Woodrow Wilson's nature than his nationwide campaign on the slogan, "He kept us out of war", when he had pledged ten months earlier to involve us in the war on the side of England and France. This explains why he was regarded with such contempt by those who learned the facts of his career. H.L. Mencken wrote that Wilson was "the perfect model of the Christian cad", and that we ought "to dig up his bones and make dice of them."

According to *The New York Times*, Paul Warburg's letter of resignation stated that some objection had been made because he had a brother in the Swiss Secret Service. *The New York Times* has never corrected this blatent falsehood, perhaps because Kuhn, Loeb Company owned a controlling interest in its stock. Max Warburg was not Swiss, and although he had probably come into contact with the Swiss Secret Service during his term of office as head of the German Secret Service, no responsible editor at *The New York Times* could have been unaware of the fact that Max Warburg was German, and that his family banking house was in Hamburg, and that he held a number of high positions in the German Government. He represented Germany at the Versailles Peace Conference, and remained peacefully in Germany until 1939, during a period when persons of his religion were being persecuted. To avoid injury during the approaching war, when bombs would rain on Germany, Max Warburg was allowed to sail to New York, his funds intact.

At the outset of World War I, Kuhn, Loeb Company had figured in the transfer of German shipping interests to other control. Sir Cecil

---

[75]Edward M. House, *The Intimate Papers of Col. House*, edited by Charles Seymour, Vol. II, p. 399. Houghton, Mifflin Co.

[76]George Sylvester Viereck, *The Strangest Friendship in History, Woodrow Wilson and Col. House*, p. 106

Spring-Rice, British Ambassador to the United States, in a letter to Lord Grey wrote:

"Another matter is the question of the transfer of the flag to the Hamburg Amerika ships. The company is practically a German Government affair. The ships are used for Government purposes, the Emperor himself is a large shareholder, and so is the great banking house of Kuhn, Loeb Company. A member of that house (Warburg) has been appointed to a very responsible position in New York, although only just naturalized. He is connected in business with the Secretary of the Treasury, who is the President's son-in-law. It is he who is negotiating on behalf of the Hamburg Amerika Shipping Company."[77]

On November 13, 1914, in a letter to Sir Valentine Chirol, Spring-Rice wrote, (p. 241, v. 2)

"I was told today that *The New York Times* has been practically acquired by Kuhn, Loeb and Schiff, special protege of the (German) Emperor. Warburg, nearly related to Kuhn Loeb and Schiff is a brother of the well known Warburg of Hamburg, the associate of Ballin (Hamburg Amerika line), is a member of the Federal Reserve Board or rather THE member. He practically controls the financial policy of the Administration, and Paish & Blackett (England) had mainly to negotiate with him. Of course, it was exactly like negotiating with Germany. Everything that was said was German property."

Col. Garrison wrote in *Roosevelt, Wilson and the Federal Reserve Law*, that "Through the banking House of the Kuhn Loeb Company, a powerful weapon would have been placed in the hands of the German Kaiser over the destiny of American business and American citizens."[78]

Garrison was referring to the Hamburg Amerika affair.

It seemed strange that Woodrow Wilson felt it necessary to place the nation in the hands of three men whose personal history was one of ruthless speculation and the quest for personal gain, or that during war with Germany, he found as persons of supreme trust a German immigrant naturalized in 1911, the son of an immigrant from Poland, and the son of an immigrant from France. Bernard Baruch first attracted attention on Wall Street in 1890 while working for A.A. Housman & Co. He was at the age of twenty, but stock speculators such as Thomas Fortune Ryan and Henry H. Rogers recognized his ability to organize.

In 1896 he merged the six principal tobacco companies of the United States into the Consolidated Tobacco Company, forcing James Duke and the American Tobacco Trust to enter into this combination. The second great trust set up by Baruch brought the copper industry into the hands

---

[77] Letters and Friendships of Sir Cecil Spring-Rice, p. 219-220

[78] Col. Elish Garrison, *Roosevelt, Wilson and the Federal Reserve Law*, Christopher Publishing House, Boston, 1931, p. 260

of the Guggenheim family, who have controlled it ever since. Baruch worked with Edward H. Harriman, who was Schiff's front man in controlling America's railway system for the Rothschild family. Baruch and Harriman also combined their talents to gain control over the New York City transit system, which has been in perilous financial condition ever since.

In 1901, Baruch formed the firm of Baruch Brothers, bankers, with his brother Herman, in New York. In 1917, when Baruch was appointed Chairman of the War Industries Board, the name was changed to Hentz Brothers.

Testifying before the Nye Committee on September 13, 1937, Bernard Baruch stated that "All wars are economic in their origin." So much for religious and political disagreements, which had been specially touted as the causes of wars.*

A profile in the "New Yorker" magazine reported that Baruch made a profit of seven hundred and fifty thousand dollars in one day during World War I, after a phony peace rumor was planted in Washington. In "Who's Who" which handled all purchasing for the Allies during World War I. In fact, Baruch WAS the Commission. He spent the American taxpayers' money at the rate of ten billion dollars a year, and was also the dominant member of the Munitions Price-Fixing Committee. He set the prices at which the Government bought war materials. It would be naive to presume that the orders did not go to firms in which he and his associates had more than a polite interest.

As Chairman of the War Industries Board, Baruch was a virtual dictator over American manufacturers.* At the Nye Committee hearings in 1935, Baruch testified,

"President Wilson gave me a letter authorizing me to take over any industry or plant. There was Judge Gary, President of United States Steel, whom we were having trouble with, and when I showed him that letter, he said, 'I guess we will have to fix this up', and he did fix it up."

Some members of Congress were curious about Baruch's qualifications to exercise life and death powers over American industry in time of war. He was not a manufacturer, and had never been in a factory. When he was called before a Congressional Committee, Bernard Baruch stated that his profession was "Speculator". A Wall Street gambler had been made Czar of American Industry.

---

*NOTE: Baruch also stated in this testimony, "I carried through the war three major investments, Alaska Juneau Gold Mining Company (with partner Eugene Meyer), Texas Gulf Sulphur, and Atolia Mining Company (tungsten)." Rep. Mason, Illinois, told the House on February 21, 1921 that Baruch made more than $50 million in copper during the war.

*Baruch chose as Assistant Chairman of the War Industries Board of Fellow Wall Street speculator, Clarence Dillon (Lapowitz). See biographies.

## THE NEW YORK TIMES.
## WEDNESDAY, SEPTEMBER 23, 1914.

# BANKS' STOCK LIST FULL OF SURPRISES

**Many Names Associated by Public with Big Stockholdings Not Found.**

**HETTY GREEN'S 30 SHARES**

**Frank Vanderlip Missing from Among Large Interests in National City.**

Publication yesterday of lists of stockholders in some of New York City's largest banks aroused considerable interest in the financial district, as much because of the absences of expected names as of the amounts of the principal holdings. The date at which the lists were compiled was not made known, and important changes may have taken place since, although as a rule there is little activity in bank shares and the controlling interests in most institutions have been in the same hands for many years.

Among the surprises in the lists, as published by Dow, Jones & Co., was the discovery that Hetty Green, often spoken of as a very important factor in the conduct of the Chemical National, owns only 31 of the 30,000 shares of that institution. Frank Vanderlip, President of the National City Bank, is not down among the principal shareholders, while James Stillman, Chairman of the Board of Directors, holds 47,498 shares of the total of 250,000. Mr. Stillman is also a large holder in the Hanover and the Citizens' Central. J. P. Morgan & Co. have the biggest holdings of any firm.

The shareholders, capitalization, number of shares, dividends, and book value, follow:

National City Bank—Capital, $25,000; total stockholders, 1,013; book value, $230; par value, $100; annual dividend, 10 per cent. Stock also includes $10,000,000 capital of National City Company, which pays annual dividend of 6 per cent.

| | | | |
|---|---|---|---|
| James Stillman.. | 47,498 | W. A. Rockefeller | 10 |
| J. P. Morgan & Co. | 14,000 | A. T. Russell... | 8,287 |
| W. Rockefeller.. | 10,000 | *A. C. Taylor | 7,599 |
| M. T. Pyne... | 8,267 | J. W. Sterling.. | 6,087 |
| Percy Pyne... | 8,267 | U. S. Trust Co... | |
| J. D. Rockefeller | 1,750 | New York.... | 4,500 |
| J. S. Rockefeller | 100 | J. P. Morgan, Jr. | 1,000 |
| *Trustee. | | | |

National Bank of Commerce—Capital, $25,000,000; total stockholders, 3,013; book value, $166; par value, $100; annual dividend, 8 per cent.

| | | | |
|---|---|---|---|
| Equitable Life.. | 24,700 | A. D. Juilliard. | 2,000 |
| Mutual Life... | 17,294 | J. J. Gerdan... | 1,696 |
| G. F. Baker... | 10,000 | J. P. Goodhart & Co. | |
| North. Finance Corporation. | 9,300 | J. N. Jarvine... | 1,287 |
| J. P. Morgan & Co. | 7,800 | F. A. V. Twombly | 1,285 |
| Mary W. Harriman | | Kidder, Peabody & Co. | 1,250 |
| E. J. Berwind.. | 5,650 | J. P. Morgan, Jr. | 1,125 |
| T. F. Ryan.... | 5,100 | L. P. Morton... | 1,100 |
| R. W. Winthrop Co. agents.. | 4,900 | H. B. Davison.. | 1,500 |
| S. J. Saltus.... | 4,757 | W. Astor... | 1,100 |
| T. A. Reynolds. | 3,175 | H. Schiff..... | 1,000 |
| *P. M. Warburg. | 3,000 | V. P. Snyder... | 1,000 |
| A. J. Hemphill. | 2,000 | G. Whittell .... | 1,000 |
| *Since sold his holdings. | | E. T. Nichols... | 1,000 |

First National—Capital, $10,000,000; total stockholders, 626; book value, $329; par value, $100; annual dividend, 40 per cent. Of this 28 per cent. is paid on bank's stock and 12 per cent. on stock of First Security Company.

| | | | |
|---|---|---|---|
| G. F. Baker.... | 20,000 | G. F. Baker, Jr. | 5,000 |
| J. P. Morgan & Co. | 13,900 | J. J. Hill..... | 4,000 |
| H. C. Fahnestock | 10,000 | North'n Fin. Co. | 1,700 |
| Garland, Doison & Emmer, Tr. of est. of J. A Garland | | P. L. Hine..... | 1,400 |
| | | H. B. Davison.. | 1,010 |
| | | Mary C. Thompson | 9,000 |
| | 6,980 | | |

Chase National—Capital, $5,000,000; total shareholders, 309; book value, $299; par value, $100; annual dividend, 20 per cent.

| | | | |
|---|---|---|---|
| G. F. Baker... | 13,408 | H. W. Cannon... | 1,400 |
| A. H. Wiggin.. | 6,492 | G. B. Schley.... | 500 |
| C. A. Edwards.. | 3,500 | S. Miller | 500 |
| A. B. Hepburn.. | 2,878 | J. J. Mitchell... | 500 |
| J. J. Hill..... | 1,500 | Faith Moore ... | 500 |
| L. G. Thompson. | 1,500 | W. H. Porter... | 500 |
| E. Tuck...... | 1,500 | F. N. Thompson, | |
| Trustees Princeton Univ..... | 1,000 | U. S. T. Co.,Tr. | 1,000 |

Hanover National—Capital, $3,000,000; total stockholders, 404; book value, $579; par value, $100; annual dividend, 16 per cent.

| | | | |
|---|---|---|---|
| Wm. Woodward, | 6,600 | Bessemer Invest. | |
| James Stillman.. | 4,000 | Co. | 325 |
| Wm. Rockefeller | 1,540 | Wm. J. Clark... | 423 |
| Wm. Barbour... | 1,200 | Wm. J. Halls... | 419 |
| Jas. M. Donald.. | 1,025 | C. Wodawörth... | 750 |
| | | Robt. M. Goelet. | 400 |

*Facsimile of an article which appeared in The New York Times dated September 23, 1914. Listed are major stockholders of the five New York City banks which purchased 40% of the 203,053 shares of the Federal Reserve Bank of New York when the System was organized in 1914. They thus obtained control of that Federal Reserve Bank and have held it ever since. As of Tuesday, July 26, 1983, the top five surviving New York City banks have increased their ownership of the Federal Reserve Bank of New York to 53% of the shares.*

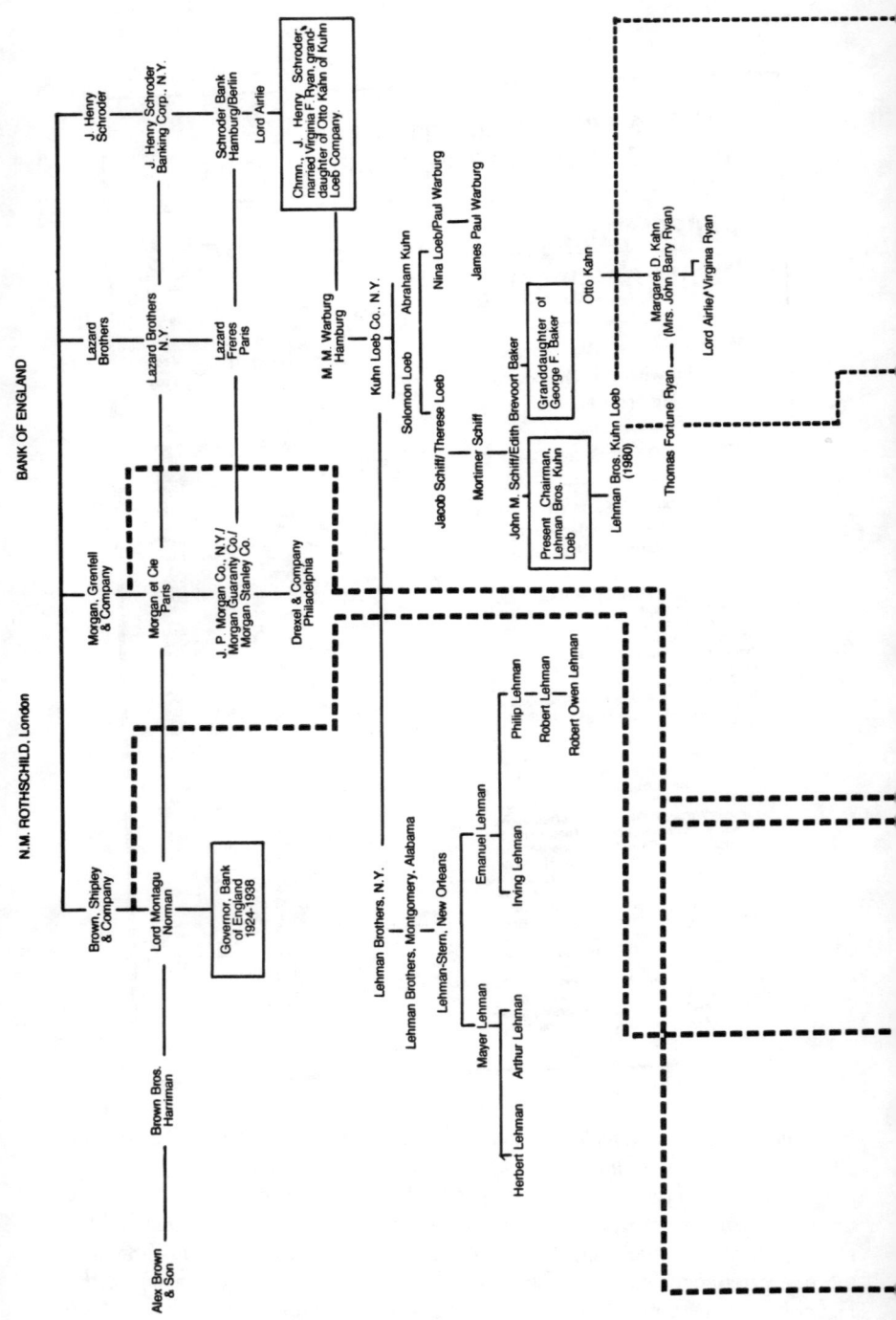

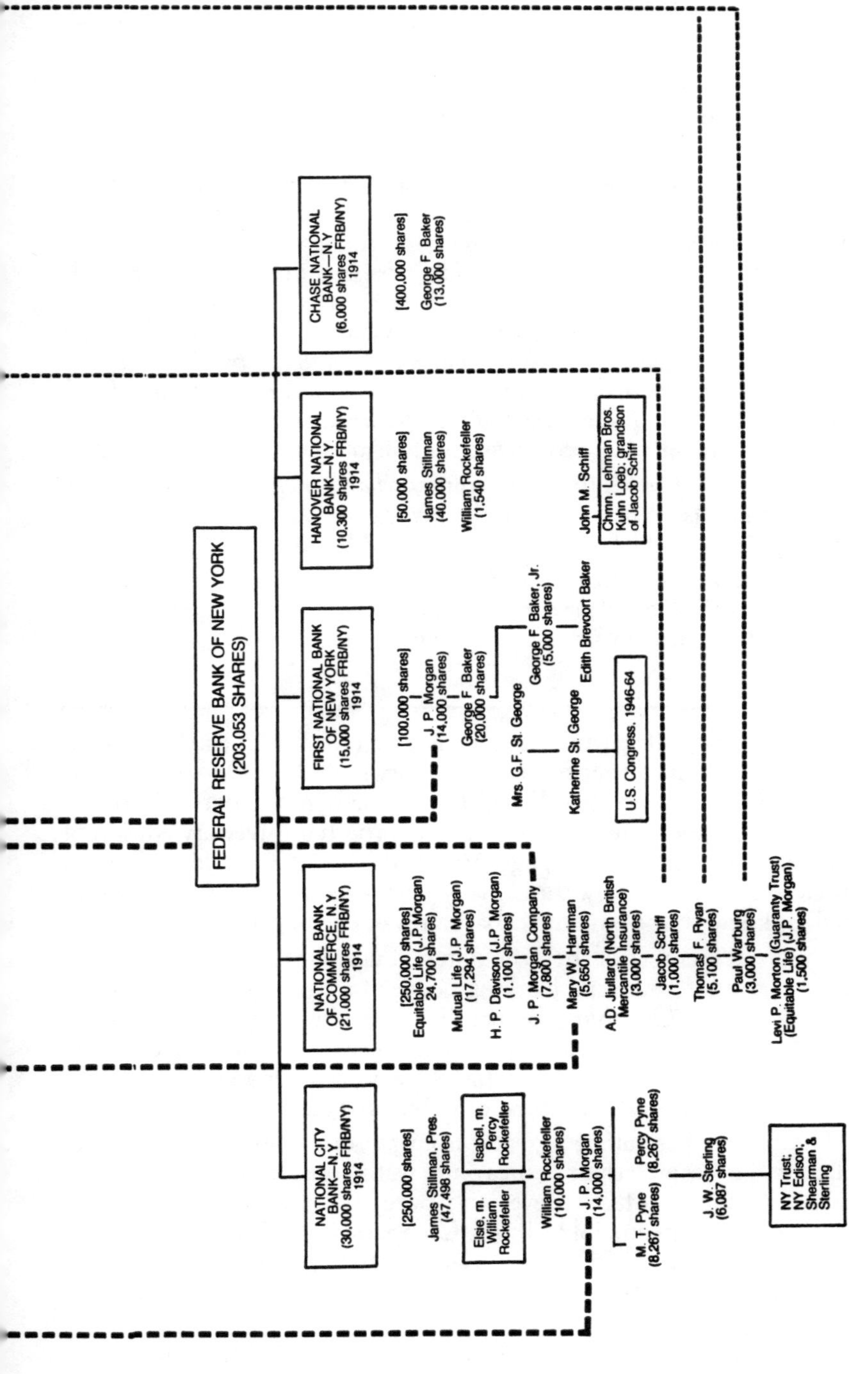

## CHART I

**FEDERAL RESERVE BANK OF NEW YORK**
(203,053 SHARES)

### NATIONAL CITY BANK—N.Y.
(30,000 shares FRB/NY) 1914

[250,000 shares]
James Stillman, Pres. (47,498 shares)

Isabel, m. Percy Rockefeller

Elsie, m. William Rockefeller

William Rockefeller (10,000 shares)

J.P. Morgan (14,000 shares)

M.T. Pyne (8,267 shares) — Percy Pyne (8,267 shares)

J.W. Sterling (6,087 shares)

**NY Trust; NY Edison; Shearman & Sterling**

### NATIONAL BANK OF COMMERCE, N.Y.
(21,000 shares FRB/NY) 1914

[250,000 shares]
Equitable Life (J.P. Morgan) 24,700 shares

Mutual Life (J.P. Morgan) 17,294 shares

H.P. Davison (J.P. Morgan) (1,100 shares)

J.P. Morgan Company (7,800 shares)

Mary W. Harriman (5,650 shares)

A.D. Jiullard (North British Mercantile Insurance) (3,000 shares)

Jacob Schiff (1,000 shares)

Thomas F. Ryan (5,100 shares)

Paul Warburg (3,000 shares)

Levi P. Morton (Guaranty Trust) (Equitable Life) (J.P. Morgan) (1,500 shares)

### FIRST NATIONAL BANK OF NEW YORK
(15,000 shares FRB/NY) 1914

[100,000 shares]
J.P. Morgan (14,000 shares)

George F. Baker (20,000 shares)

George F. Baker, Jr. (5,000 shares)

Mrs. G.F. St. George — Edith Brevoort Baker

Katherine St. George

U.S. Congress, 1946-64

### HANOVER NATIONAL BANK—N.Y.
(10,300 shares FRB/NY) 1914

[50,000 shares]
James Stillman (40,000 shares)

William Rockefeller (1,540 shares)

John M. Schiff
Chmn. Lehman Bros.
Kuhn Loeb, grandson of Jacob Schiff

### CHASE NATIONAL BANK—N.Y.
(6,000 shares FRB/NY) 1914

[400,000 shares]
George F. Baker (13,000 shares)

93

# CHART I

    *Chart I reveals the linear connection between the Rothschilds and the Bank of England, and the London banking houses which ultimately control the Federal Reserve Banks through their stockholdings of bank stock and their subsidiary firms in New York. The two principal Rothschild representatives in New York, J.P. Morgan Co., and Kuhn, Loeb & Co. were the firms which set up the Jekyll Island Conference at which the Federal Reserve Act was drafted, who directed the subsequent successful campaign to have the plan enacted into law by Congress, and who purchased the controlling amounts of stock in the Federal Reserve Bank of New York in 1914. These firms had their principal officers appointed to the Federal Reserve Board of Governors and the Federal Advisory Council in 1914.*

    *In 1914 a few families (blood or business related) owning controlling stock in existing banks (such as in New York City) caused those banks to purchase controlling shares in the Federal Reserve regional banks.*

    *Examination of the charts and text in the House Banking Committee Staff Report of August, 1976 and the current stockholders list of the 12 regional Federal Reserve Banks shows this same family control.*

---

    Baruch's erstwhile partner, Eugene Meyer, (Alaska-Juneau Gold Mining Co.), later claimed that Baruch was a nitwit, and that Meyer, with his family banking connections (Lazard Freres), had guided Baruch's investment career. These claims appeared in the fiftieth anniversary edition of *The Washington Post*, editorial page, June 4, 1983, with a parting shot from Meyer's editor, Al Friendly, that "Every journalist in Washington, Meyer included, knew that Bernard M. Baruch was a self-aggrandizing phony."

    The third member of the Triumvirate, Eugene Meyer, was son of the partner in the international banking house of Lazard Freres, of Paris and New York. In *My Own Story* Baruch explains how Meyer became head of the War Finance Corporation. "At the outset of World War One," he says, "I sought out Eugene Meyer, Jr. . . . who was a man of the highest integrity with a keen desire to be of public service."[79]

    The nation has suffered greatly from persons who desired to be of public service, because their desires often went considerably beyond their passion for office. In fact, Meyer and Baruch had operated an Alaska venture, Alaska-Juneau Gold Mining Company in 1915, and had worked together on other financial schemes. Meyer's family house of Lazard Freres specialized in international gold movements.

---

[79] Bernard Baruch, *My Own Story*, Henry-Holt Company, New York, 1957, p. 194

Eugene Meyer's stewardship of the War Finance Corporation comprises one of the most amazing financial operations ever partially recorded in this country. We say "partially recorded", because subsequent Congressional investigations revealed that each night, the books were being altered before being brought in for the next day's investigation. Louis McFadden, Chairman of the House Banking and Currency Committee, figured in two investigations of Meyer, in 1925, and again in 1930, when Meyer was proposed as Governor of the Federal Reserve Board. The Select Committee to Investigate the Destruction of Government Bonds, submitted, on March 2, 1925, *"Preparation and Destruction of Government Bonds—68th Congress, 2d Session, Report No. 1635:*

p.2. "Duplicate bonds amounting to 2314 pairs and duplicate coupons amounting to 4698 pairs ranging in denominations from $50 to $10,000 have been redeemed to July 1, 1924. Some of these duplications have resulted from error and some from fraud."

These investigations may explain why, at the end of World War One, Eugene Meyer was able to buy control of Allied Chemical and Dye Corporation, and later on, the nation's most influential newspaper, *The Washington Post*. The duplication of bonds, "one for the government, one for me" in denominations to the amount of $10,000 each, resulted in a tidy sum.

p. 6 of these Hearings. "These transactions of the Treasury prior to June 20, 1920 (including settlements for purchases and sales), executed by the War Finance Corporation (Eugene Meyer, managing director), were largely directed by the managing director of the War Finance Corporation, and settlements with the Treasury were made principally by him with the Assistant Secretary of the Treasury, and the books show that the basis of the price paid by the Government for over $1,894 millions worth of bonds ($1,894,000,000.00), which the Treasury purchased through the War Finance Corporation was not the market price and was not the cost of the bond plus interest, and the elements entering into the settlement are not disclosed by the correspondence. The managing director of the War Finance Corporation stated that he had and an Assistant Secretary of the Treasury (Jerome J. Hanauer, partner of Kuhn, Loeb Co. whose daughter married Lewis L. Strauss) agreed to the price, and it was simply an arbitrary figure set by an Assistant Secretary of the Treasury as to the bonds so purchased by the War Finance Corporation. During the period of these transactions and up until quite a recent date the managing director of the War Finance Corporation, Eugene Meyer, Jr., in his private capacity maintained an office at No. 14 Wall Street, New York City, and through the War Finance Corporation sold about $70 millions in bonds to the Government, and also bought through the War Finance Corporation about $10 millions in bonds, and approved the bills for most, if not all, of these bonds in his official capacity as managing director of the War Finance Corporation. When these transactions, just referred to, were disclosed to the committee in open hearing, the managing director

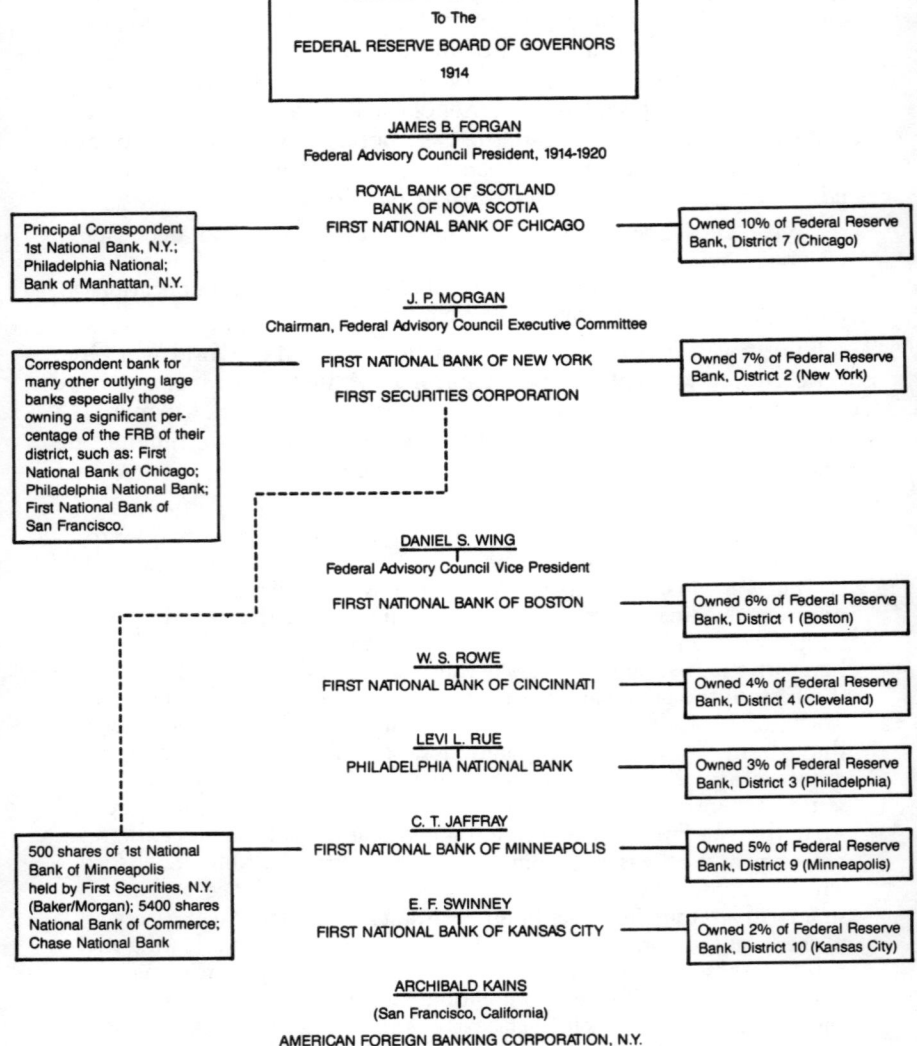

**CHART II**

## CHART II

*This chart shows the interlocking banking directorates which were revealed by the backgrounds of the officials selected to be the original members of the Federal Advisory Council in 1914. The principals were the same bankers who had been present or represented at the Jekyll Island Conference in 1910, and during the campaign to have the Federal Reserve Act enacted into law by Congress in 1913. These officials represented the largest stock holdings in the New York banks which bought the controlling stock in the Federal Reserve Bank of New York, and also were the principal correspondent banks of the banks in other Federal Reserve districts who, in turn, selected their officials to represent them on the Federal Advisory Council.*

appeared before the committee and stated the fact that commissions were paid on these transactions, they were in turn paid over to the brokers, selected by the managing director, who executed the orders issued by his brokerage house, and immediately after this disclosure to the committee, the managing director employed Ernst and Ernst, certified public accountants, to audit the books of the War Finance Corporation, who did, upon completion of the examination of these books, report to the committee that all moneys received by the brokerage house of the managing director had been accounted for. While simultaneously with the examination being made by the committee, the certified public accountants, heretofore referred to, were nightly carrying on their examination, it was discovered by your committee that alterations and changes were being made in the books of record covering these transactions, and when the same was called to the attention of the treasurer of the War Finance Corporation, he admitted to the committee that changes were being made. To what extent these books have been altered during the process the committee have not been able to determine. After June, 1921, about $10 billions worth of securities were destroyed."

It was Eugene Meyer's *Washington Post*, (under the direction of his daughter, Katherine Graham) which was later to drive a President of the United States from the White House on the grounds that he had knowledge of a burglary. What are we to think of the revelations of duplications of hundreds of millions of dollars worth of bonds during

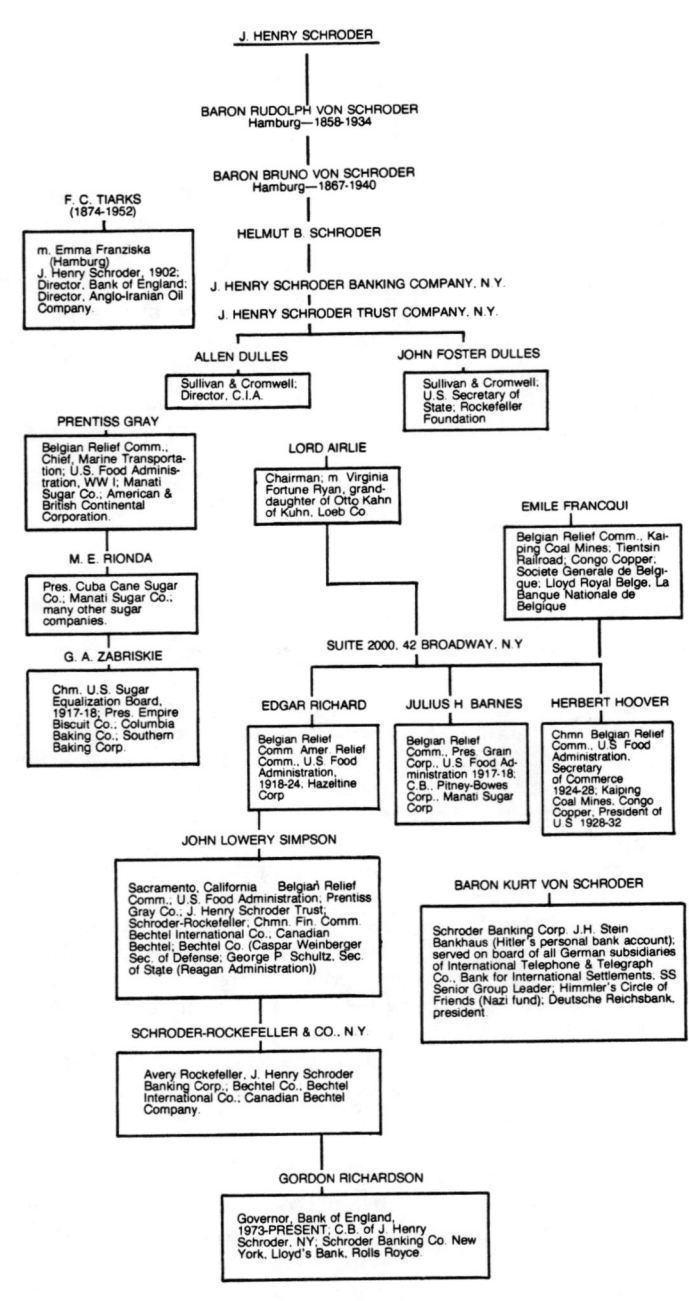

**CHART III**

# CHART III

The J. Henry Schroder Banking Company chart encompasses the entire history of the twentieth century, embracing as it does the program (Belgian Relief Commission) which provisioned Germany from 1915-1918 and dissuaded Germany from seeking peace in 1916; financing Hitler in 1933 so as to make a Second World War possible; backing the Presidential campaign of Herbert Hoover; and even at the present time, having two of its major executives of its subsidiary firm, Bechtel Corporation serving as Secretary of Defense and Secretary of State in the Reagan Administration.

The head of the Bank of England since 1973, Sir Gordon Richardson, Governor of the Bank of England (controlled by the House of Rothschild), was chairman of J. Henry Schroder Wagg and Company of London from 1963-72, and director of J. Henry Schroder, New York, and Schroder Banking Corporation, New York, as well as Lloyd's Bank of London, and Rolls Royce. He maintains a residence on Sutton Place in New York City, and as head of "The London Connection", can be said to be the single most influential banker in the world.

---

Meyer's directorship of the War Finance Corporation, the alteration of the books during a Congressional investigation, and the fact that Meyer came out of this situation with many millions of dollars with which he proceeded to buy Allied Chemical Corporation, The Washington Post, and other properties? Incidentally, Lazard Brothers, Meyer's family banking house, personally manages the fortunes of many of our political luminaries, including the Kennedy family fortune.

Besides these men, Warburg, Baruch, and Meyer, a host of J.P. Morgan Co., and Kuhn, Loeb Co., partners, employees, and satellites came to Washington after 1917 to administer the fate of the American people.

The Liberty Loans, which sold bonds to our citizens, were nominally in the jurisdiction of the United States Treasury, under the leadership of Wilson's Secretary of the Treasury, William G. McAdoo, whom Kuhn, Loeb Co. had placed in charge of the Hudson-Manhattan Railway Co. in 1902. Paul Warburg had most of the Kuhn Loeb Co. firm with him in Washington during the War. Jerome Hanauer, partner in Kuhn, Loeb Co., was Assistant Secretary of the Treasury in charge of Liberty Loans. The two Under-secretaries of the Treasury during the War were S. Parker Gilbert and Roscoe C. Leffingwell. Both Gilbert and Leffingwell came to the Treasury from the law firm of Cravath and Henderson, and returned

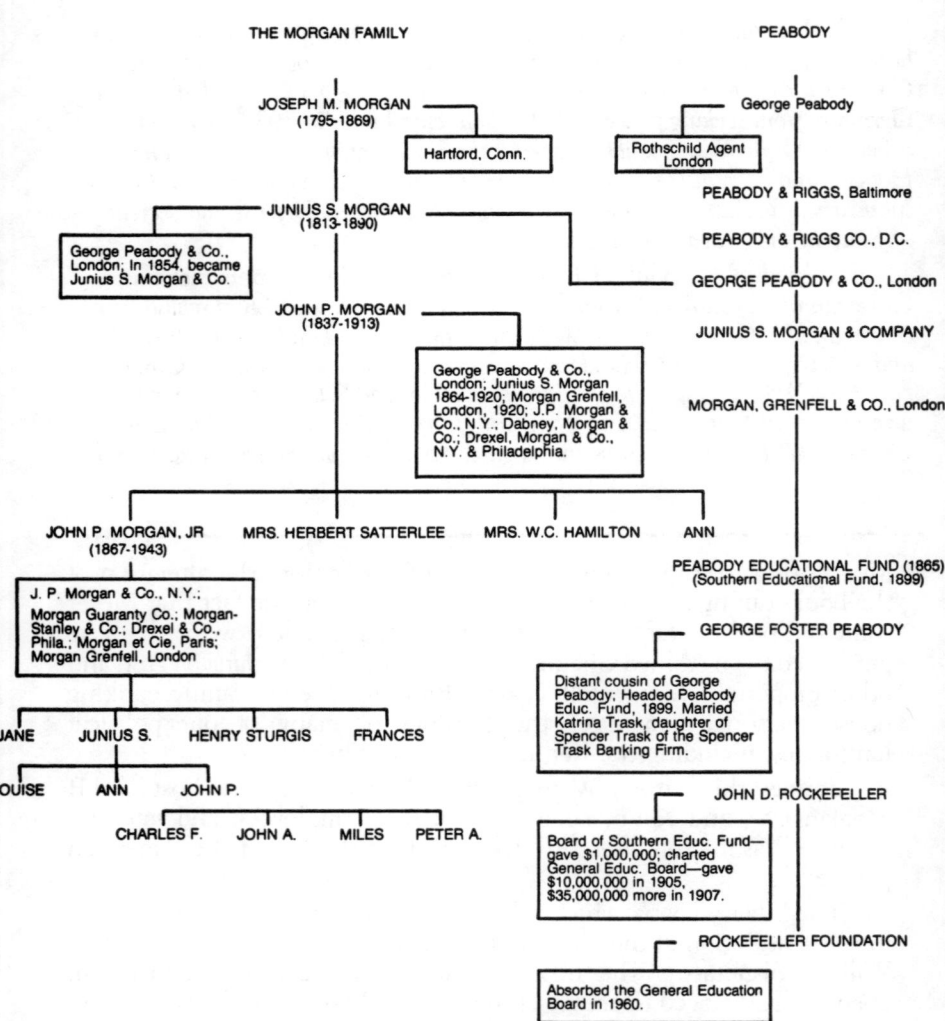

**CHART IV**

# CHART IV

The Peabody-Morgan chart shows the London Connection of these prominent banking firms, which have been headquartered in London since their inception. The Peabody fortune set up an Educational Fund in 1865, which was later absorbed by John D. Rockefeller into the General Educational Board in 1905, which, in turn, was absorbed by the Rockefeller Foundation in 1960.

---

to that firm when they had fulfilled their mission for Kuhn, Loeb Co. in the Treasury. Cravath and Henderson were the lawyers for Kuhn Loeb Co. Gilbert and Leffingwell subsequently received partnerships in J.P. Morgan Co.

Kuhn, Loeb Company, the nation's largest owners of railroad properties in this country and in Mexico, protected their interests during the First World War by having Woodrow Wilson set up a United States Railroad Administration. The Director-General was William McAdoo, and the Assistant Director-General was John Skelton Williams, Comptroller of the Currency. Warburg replaced this set up in 1918 with a tighter organization which he called the Federal Transportation Council. The purpose of both of these organizations was to prevent strikes against Kuhn, Loeb Company during the War, in case the railroad workers should try to get in wages some of the millions of dollars in wartime profits which Kuhn, Loeb received from the United States Government.

Among the important bankers present in Washington during the War was Herbert Lehman, of the rapidly rising firm of Lehman Brothers, Bankers, New York. Lehman was promptly put on the General Staff of the Army, and given the rank of Colonel.

The Lehmans had had prior experience in "taking the profits out of war", a double entendre and one of Baruch's favorite phrases. In *Men Who Rule America*, Arthur D. Howden Smith writes of the Lehmans during the Civil War, "They were often agents, fixers for both sides, intermediaries for confidential communications and handlers of the many illicit transactions in cotton and drugs for the Confederacy, purveyors of information for the North. The Lehmans, with Mayer in Montgomery, the first capital of the Confederacy, Henry in New Orleans, and Emanuel in New York were ideally situated to take advantage of every opportunity for profit which appeared. They seem to have missed few chances."[80]

---

[80]Arthur D. Howden Smith, *Men Who Rule America*, Bobbs Merrill, NY 1935, p. 112

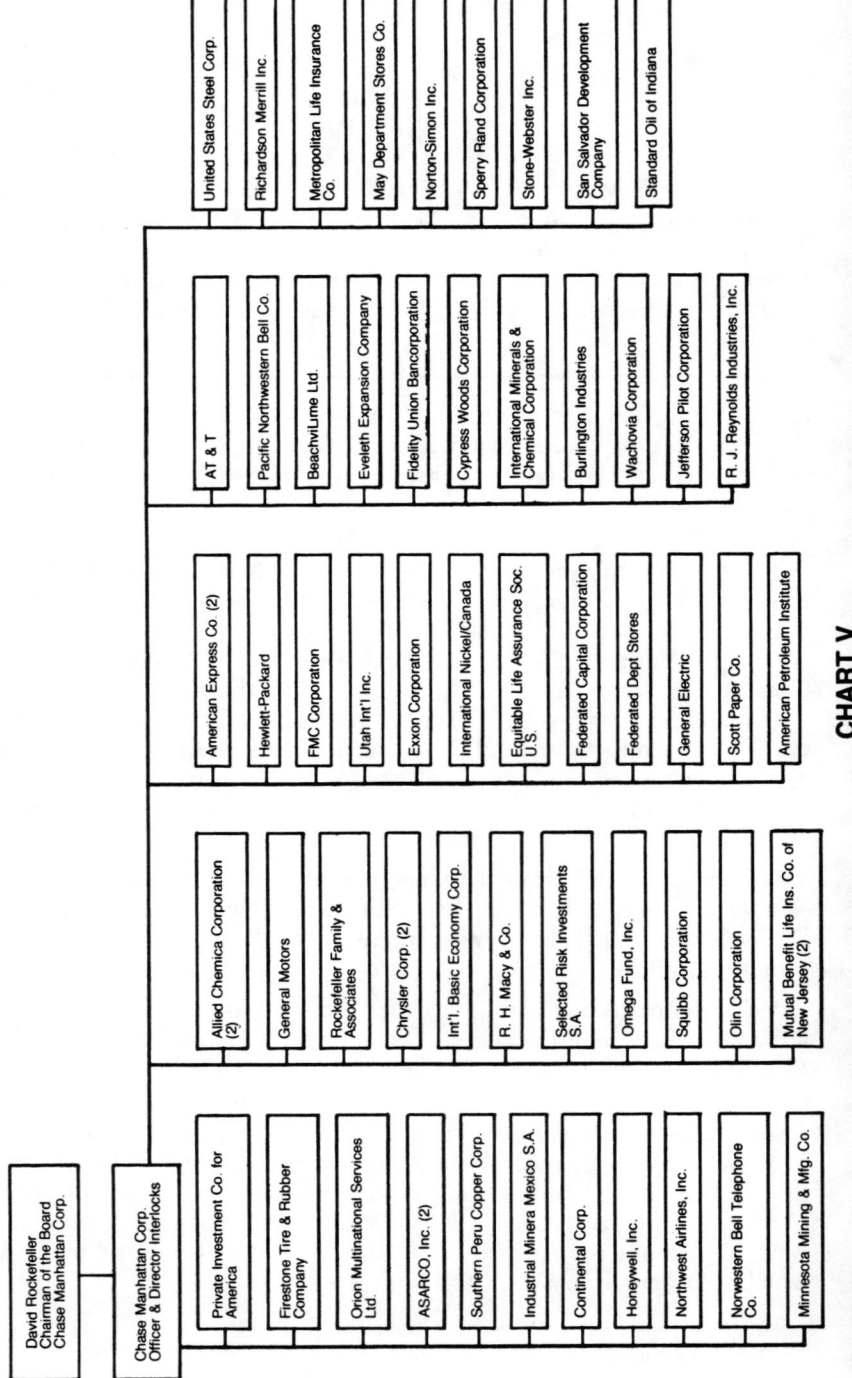

Federal Reserve Directors: A Study of Corporate and Banking Influence*

CHART V

# CHART V

*The David Rockefeller chart shows the link between the Federal Reserve Bank of New York, Standard Oil of Indiana, General Motors, and Allied Chemical Corporation (Eugene Meyer family) and Equitable Life (J.P. Morgan).*

---

Other appointments during the First World War were as follows:

J.W. McIntosh, director of the Armour meat-packing trust, who was made chief of Subsistence for the United States Army in 1918. He later became Comptroller of the Currency during Coolidge's Administration, and ex-officio member of the Federal Reserve Board. During the Harding Administration, he did his bit as Director of Finance for the United States Shipping Board when the Board sold ships to the Dollar Lines for a hundredth of their cost and then let the Dollar Line default on its payments. After leaving public service, J.W. McIntosh became a partner in J.W. Wollman Co., New York Stockbrokers.

W.P.G. Harding, Governor of the Federal Reserve Board, was also managing director of the War Finance Corporation under Eugene Meyer.

George R. James, member of the Federal Reserve Board in 1923-24, had been Chief of the Cotton Section of the War Industries Board.

Henry P. Davison, senior partner in J.P. Morgan Co., was appointed head of the American Red Cross in 1917 in order to get control of the three hundred and seventy million dollars cash which was collected from the American people in donations.

Ronald Ransom, banker from Atlanta, and Governor of the Federal Reserve Board under Roosevelt in 1938-39, had been the Director in Charge of Personnel for Foreign Service for the American Red Cross in 1918.

John Skelton Williams, Comptroller of the Currency, was appointed National Treasurer of the American Red Cross.

President Woodrow Wilson, the great liberal who signed the Federal Reserve Act and declared war against Germany, had an odd career for a man who is now enshrined as a defender of the common people. His chief supporter in both his campaigns for the Presidency was Cleveland H. Dodge, of Kuhn Loeb, who controlled National City Bank of New York. Dodge was also President of the Winchester Arms Company and Remington Arms Company. He was very close to President Wilson

Federal Reserve Directors: A Study of Corporate and Banking Influence*

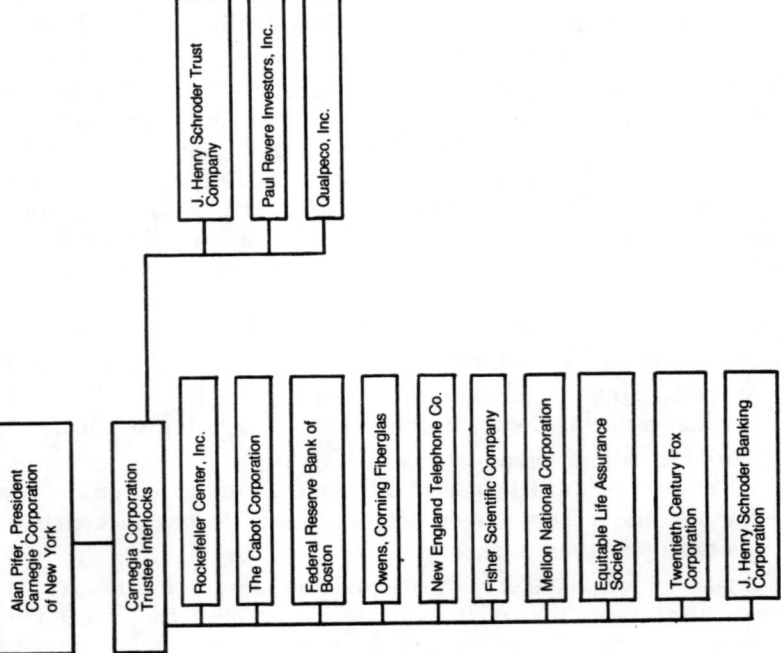

CHART VI

*Published 1976

## CHART VI

*This chart shows the interlocks between the Federal Reserve Bank of New York, J. Henry Schroder Banking Corp., J. Henry Schroder Trust Co., Rockefeller Center, Inc., Equitable Life Assurance Society (J.P. Morgan), and the Federal Reserve Bank of Boston.*

---

throughout the great democrat's political career. Wilson lifted the embargo on shipment of arms to Mexico on February 12, 1914, so that Dodge could ship a million dollars worth of arms and ammunition to Carranza and promote the Mexican Revolution. Kuhn, Loeb Co. which owned the Mexican National Railways System, had become dissatisfied with the administration of Huerta and had him kicked out.

When the British naval auxiliary Lusitania was sunk in 1915, it was loaded with ammunition from Dodge's factories. Dodge became Chairman of the "Survivors of Victims of the Lusitania Fund", which did so much to arouse the public against Germany. Dodge also was notorious for using professional gangsters against strikers in his plants, yet the liberal Wilson does not appear to have ever been disturbed by this.

Another clue to Wilson's peculiar brand of liberalism is to be found in Chaplin's book *Wobbly*, which relates how Wilson scrawled the word "REFUSED" across the appeal for clemency sent him by the aging and ailing Eugene Debs, who had been sent to Atlanta Prison for "speaking and writing against war". The charge on which Debs was convicted was "spoken and written denunciation of war". This was treason to the Wilson dictatorship, and Debs was imprisoned. As head of the Socialist Party, Debs ran for the Presidency from Atlanta Prison, the only man ever to do so, and polled more than a million votes. It was ironic that Debs' leadership of the Socialist Party, which at that time represented the desires of many Americans for an honest government, should fall into the sickly hands of Norman Thomas, a former student and admirer of Woodrow Wilson at Princeton University. Under Thomas' leadership, the Socialist Party no longer stood for anything, and suffered a steady decline in influence and prestige.

Wilson continued to be deeply involved in the Bolshevik Revolution, as were House and Wiseman. Vol. 3, p. 421 of House *Intimate Papers* records a cable from Sir William Wiseman to House from London, May 1, 1918, suggesting allied intervention at the invitation of the Bolsheviki

Federal Reserve Directors: A Study of Corporate and Banking Influence*

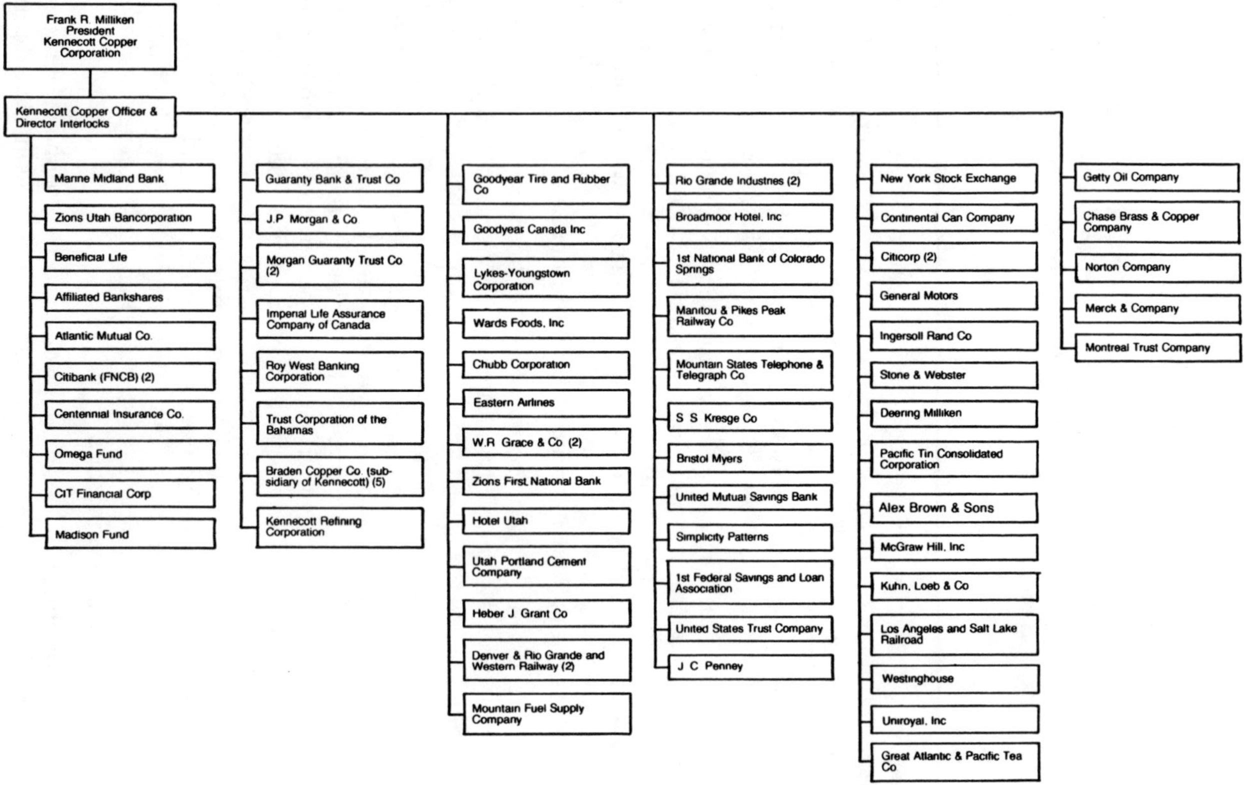

- Frank R. Milliken, President, Kennecott Copper Corporation
  - Kennecott Copper Officer & Director Interlocks
    - Marine Midland Bank
    - Zions Utah Bancorporation
    - Beneficial Life
    - Affiliated Bankshares
    - Atlantic Mutual Co.
    - Citibank (FNCB) (2)
    - Centennial Insurance Co.
    - Omega Fund
    - CIT Financial Corp
    - Madison Fund
    - Guaranty Bank & Trust Co
      - J.P. Morgan & Co
      - Morgan Guaranty Trust Co (2)
      - Imperial Life Assurance Company of Canada
      - Roy West Banking Corporation
      - Trust Corporation of the Bahamas
      - Braden Copper Co (subsidiary of Kennecott) (5)
      - Kennecott Refining Corporation
    - Goodyear Tire and Rubber Co
      - Goodyear Canada Inc
      - Lykes-Youngstown Corporation
      - Wards Foods, Inc
      - Chubb Corporation
      - Eastern Airlines
      - W.R. Grace & Co (2)
      - Zions First National Bank
      - Hotel Utah
      - Utah Portland Cement Company
      - Heber J Grant Co
      - Denver & Rio Grande and Western Railway (2)
      - Mountain Fuel Supply Company
    - Rio Grande Industries (2)
      - Broadmoor Hotel, Inc
      - 1st National Bank of Colorado Springs
      - Manitou & Pikes Peak Railway Co
      - Mountain States Telephone & Telegraph Co
      - S S Kresge Co
      - Bristol Myers
      - United Mutual Savings Bank
      - Simplicity Patterns
      - 1st Federal Savings and Loan Association
      - United States Trust Company
      - J C Penney
    - New York Stock Exchange
      - Continental Can Company
      - Citicorp (2)
      - General Motors
      - Ingersoll Rand Co
      - Stone & Webster
      - Deering Milliken
      - Pacific Tin Consolidated Corporation
      - Alex Brown & Sons
      - McGraw Hill, Inc
      - Kuhn, Loeb & Co
      - Los Angeles and Salt Lake Railroad
      - Westinghouse
      - Uniroyal, Inc
      - Great Atlantic & Pacific Tea Co
    - Getty Oil Company
      - Chase Brass & Copper Company
      - Norton Company
      - Merck & Company
      - Montreal Trust Company

**CHART VII**

*Published 1976

# CHART VII

*This chart shows the interlocks of the Federal Reserve Bank of New York with Citibank, Guaranty Bank and Trust Co. (J.P. Morgan), J.P. Morgan Co., Morgan Guaranty Trust Co., Alex Brown & Sons (Brown Brothers Harriman), Kuhn Loeb & Co., Los Angeles and Salt Lake RR (controlled by Kuhn Loeb Co.), and Westinghouse (controlled by Kuhn Loeb Co.).*

---

to help organize the Bolshevik forces. Lt. Col. Norman Thwaites, in his memoirs, *Velvet and Vinegar* says,

"Often during the years 1917-20 when delicate decisions had to be made, I consulted with Mr. (Otto) Kahn, whose calm judgment and almost uncanny foresight as to political and economic tendencies proved most helpful. Another remarkable man with whom I have been closely associated is Sir William Wiseman who was advisor on American affairs to the British delegation at the Peace Conference, and liaison officer between the American and British government during the war. He was rather more the Col. House of this country in his relations with Downing Street."[81]

In the summer of 1917, Woodrow Wilson named Col. House to head the American War Mission to the Interallied War Conference, the first American mission to a European council in history. House was criticized for naming his son-in-law, Gordon Auchincloss, as his assistant on this mission. Paul Cravath, the lawyer for Kuhn, Loeb Company, was third in charge of the American War Mission. Sir William Wiseman guided the American War Mission in its conferences. In *The Strangest Friendship in History*, Viereck writes,

"After America entered the War, Wiseman, according to Northcliffe, was the only man who had access at all times to the Colonel and to the White House. Wiseman rented an apartment in the house where the Colonel lived. David Lawrence referred to the Fifty-Third Street house (New York City) jestingly as the American No. 10 Downing St. . . . Col. House had a special code used only with Sir William Wiseman. Col. House was Bush, the Morgans were Haslam, and Trotsky was Keble."[82]

Thus these two "unofficial" advisors to the British and American governments had a code solely for each other, which no one else could understand. Even stranger was the fact that the international Communist

---

[81] Lt. Col. Norman Thwaites, *Velvet and Vinegar*, Grayson Co., London, 1932
[82] George Sylvester Viereck, *The Strangest Friendship in History, Woodrow Wilson and Col. House*, Liveright, N.Y. 1932, p. 172

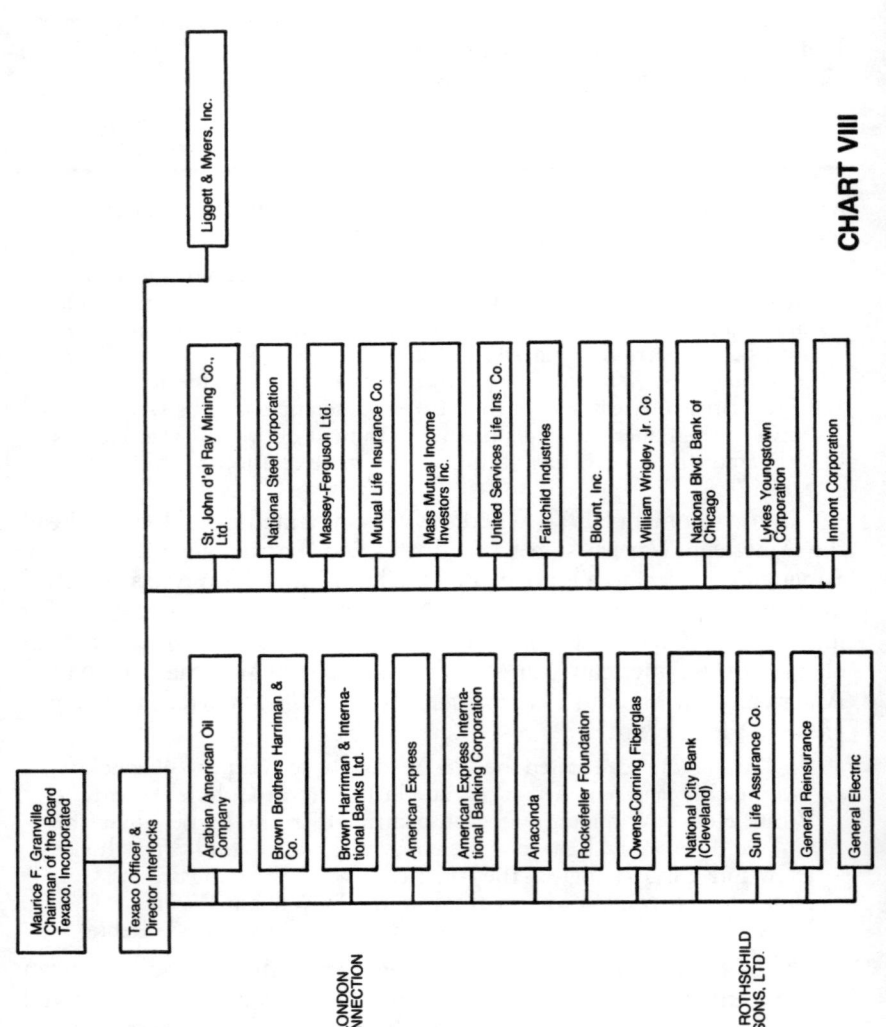

# CHART VIII

*This chart shows the link between the Federal Reserve Bank of New York, Brown Brothers Harriman, Sun Life Assurance Co. (N.M. Rothschild and Sons), and the Rockefeller Foundation.*

---

espionage apparatus for many years used Col. House's book, *Philip Dru, Administrator*, as their official code book. Francois Coty writes,

"Gorodin, Lenin's agent in China, was alleged to have with him a copy of the book published by Col. House, *Philip Dru, Administrator* and a code expert who lived in China told this writer that the purpose of having constant access to this book by Gorodin was to use it for coding and decoding messages."[83]

After the Armistice, Woodrow Wilson assembled the American Delegation to the Peace Conference, and embarked for Paris. It was, on the whole, a most congenial group, consisting of the bankers who had always guided Wilson's policies. He was accompanied by Bernard Baruch, Thomas W. Lamont of J.P. Morgan Co., Albert Strauss of J & W Seligman bankers, who had been chosen by Wilson to replace Paul Warburg on the Federal Reserve Board of Governors, J.P. Morgan, and Morgan lawyers Frank Polk and John W. Davis. Accompanying them were Walter Lippmann, Felix Frankfurter, Justice Brandeis, and other interested parties. Mason's biography of Brandeis states that "In Paris in June of 1919, Brandeis met with such friends as Paul Warburg, Col. House, Lord Balfour, Louis Marshall, and Baron Edmond de Rothschild."

Indeed, Baron Edmond de Rothschild served as the genial host to the leading members of the American Delegation, and even turned over his Paris mansion to them, although the lesser members had to rough it at the elegant Hotel Crillon with Col. House and his personal staff of 201 servants.

Baruch later testified before the Graham Committee of the Senate Foreign Relations Committee, "I was economic advisor with the peace mission. GRAHAM: Did you frequently advise with the President while there? BARUCH: Whenever he asked my advice I gave it. I had something to do with the reparations clauses. I was the American Commissioner in charge of what they called the Economic Section. I was a

---

[83]Francois Coty, *Tearing Away the Veil*, Paris, 1940

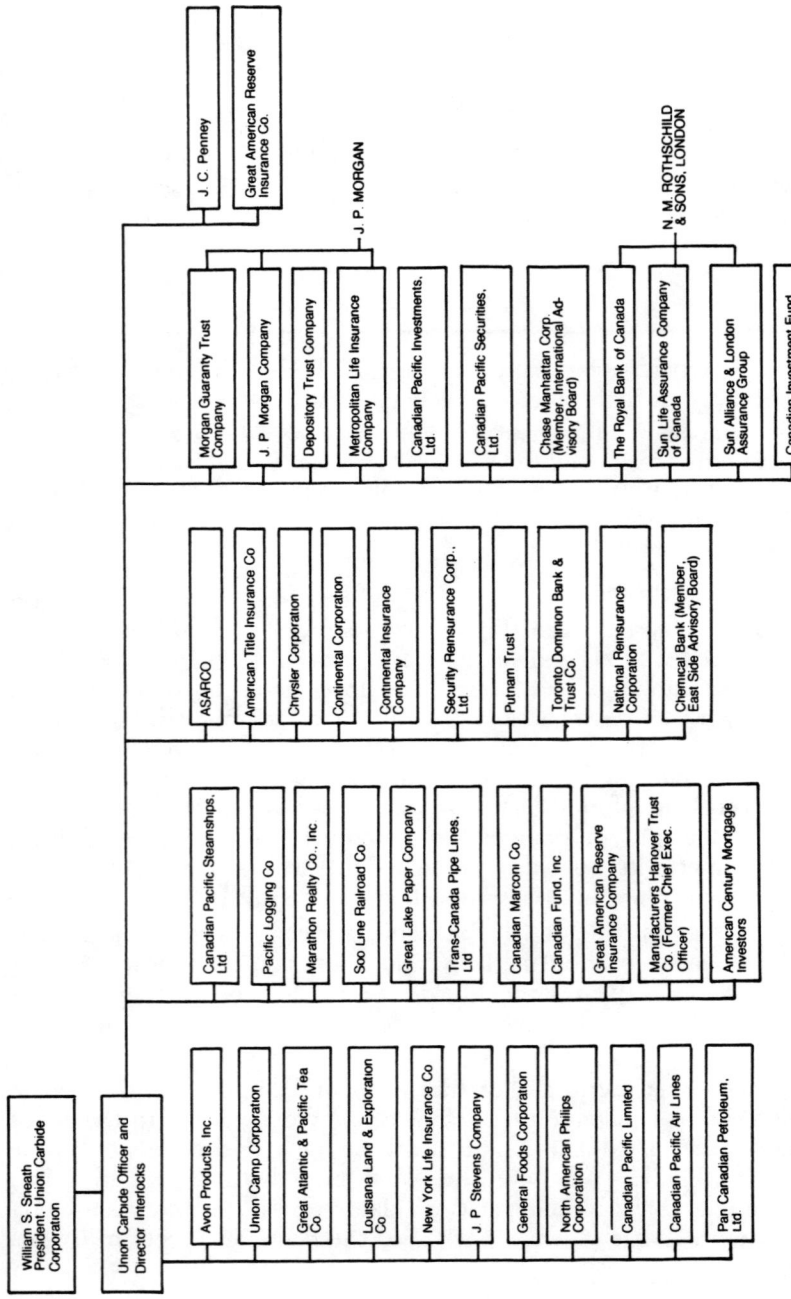

Federal Reserve Directors: A Study of Corporate and Banking Influence*

CHART IX

*Published 1976

# CHART IX

*This chart shows the interlocks between the Federal Reserve Bank of New York and J.P. Morgan Co., Morgan Guaranty Trust Co., and the Rothschild affiliates of Royal Bank of Canada, Sun Life Assurance Co. of Canada, Sun Alliance, and London Assurance Group.*

---

member of the Supreme Economic Council in charge of raw metals. GRAHAM: Did you sit in the council with the gentlemen who were negotiating the treaty? BARUCH: Yes, sir, some of the time. GRAHAM: All except the meetings that were participated in by the Five? (The Five being the leaders of the five allied nations). BARUCH: And frequently those also."

Paul Warburg accompanied Wilson on the American Commission to Negotiate Peace as his chief financial advisor. He was pleasantly surprised to find at the head of the German delegation his brother, Max Warburg, who brought along Carl Melchior, also of M.M. Warburg Company, William Georg von Strauss, Franz Urbig, and Mathias Erzberger.

Thomas W. Lamont states in his privately printed memoirs, *Across World Frontiers,* "The German delegation included two German bankers of the Warburg firm whom I happened to know slightly and with whom I was glad to talk informally, for they seemed to be striving earnestly to offer some reparations composition that might be acceptable to the Allies."[84] Lamont was also pleased to see Sir William Wiseman, chief advisor to the British delegation.

The bankers at the conference convinced Wilson that they needed an international government to facilitate their international monetary operations. Vol. IV, p. 52, *Intimate Papers of Col. House* quotes a message from Sir William Wiseman to Lord Reading, August 16, 1918, "The President has two main principles in view; there must be a League of Nations and it must be virile."

Wilson, who seems to have lived in a world of fantasy, was shocked when American citizens booed him during his campaign to have them sign over their hard won independence to what appeared to many to be an international dictatorship. He promptly went into a depression, and retired to his bedroom. His wife immediately shut the White House doors against Col. House, and from September 25, 1919 to April 13, 1920, she

---

[84] Thomas W. Lamont, *Across World Frontiers,* (Privately printed) 1950, p. 138

ruled the United States with the aid of an intimate friend, her "military aide", Col. Rixey Smith. As everyone was shut out of their deliberations, no one ever knew which of the pair functioned as the President, and which was the Vice President.

The admirers of Woodrow Wilson were led for decades by Bernard Baruch, who stated that Woodrow Wilson was the greatest man he ever knew. Wilson's appointments to the Federal Reserve Board, and that body's responsibility for financing the First World War, as well as Wilson's handing over the United States to the immigrant triumvirate during the War, made him appear to be the most important single effector of ruin in American history.

It is no wonder that after his abortive trip to Europe, where he was hissed and jeered in the streets by the French people, and snickered at in the halls of Versailles by Orlando and Clemenceau, Woodrow Wilson returned home to take to his bed. The sight of the destruction and death in Europe, for which he was directly responsible, was perhaps more of a shock than he could bear. The Italian Minister Pentaleoni expressed the feelings of the European peoples when he wrote that:

"Woodrow Wilson is a type of Pecksniff who was now disappeared amid universal execration."

It is America's misfortune that our subsidized press and educational system have been devoted to enshrining a man who colluded in causing so much death and sorrow throughout the world.

The financial cartel suffered only minor setbacks in those crucial years. On February 12, 1917, *The New York Times* reported that "The five members of the Federal Reserve Board were impeached on the floor of the House by Rep. Charles A. Lindbergh, Republican member of the House Banking and Currency Committee. According to Mr. Lindbergh, 'the conspiracy began in' 1906 when the late J.P. Morgan, Paul M. Warburg, a present member of the Federal Reserve Board, the National City Bank and other banking firms 'conspired' to obtain currency legislation in the interest of big business and the appointment of a special baord to administer such a law, in order to create industrial slaves of the masses, the aforesaid conspirators did conspire and are now conspiring to have the Federal Reserve Board administered so as to enable the conspirators to coordinate all kinds of big business and to keep themselves in control of big business in order to amalgamate all the trusts into one great trust in restraint and control of trade and commerce." The impeachment resolution was not acted on by the House.

*The New York Times* reported on August 10, 1918, "Mr. Warburg's term having expired, he voluntarily retired from the Federal Reserve Board." Thus the previous intimation that Mr. Warburg left he Federal Reserve Board because he had a brother in the Secret Service of a foreign country, namely, Germany, with whom we were at war, was not the cause of his retirement. In any case, he did not leave the Federal Reserve Administration, as he immediately took over J.P. Morgan's seat on the Federal Advisory Council, from which post he continued to administer the Federal Reserve System for the next ten years.

## CHAPTER NINE
# The Agricultural Depression

When Paul Warburg resigned from the Federal Reserve Board of Governors in 1918, his place was taken by Albert Strauss, partner in the international banking house of J & W Seligman. This banking house had large interests in Cuba and South America, and played a prominent part in financing the many revolutions in those countries. Its most notorious publicity came during the Senate Finance Committee's investigation in 1933, when it was brought out that J & W Seligman had given a $415,000 bribe to Juan Leguia, son of the President of Peru, in order to get that nation to accept a loan.

A partial list of Albert Strauss' directorships, according to "Who's Who", shows that he was: Chairman of the Board of the Cuba Cane Sugar Corporation; director, Brooklyn Manhattan Transit Co., Coney Island Brooklyn RR, New York Rapid Transit, Pierce-Arrow, Cuba Tobacco Corporation, and the Eastern Cuba Sugar Corporation.

Governor Delano resigned in August, 1918, to be commissioned a Colonel in the Army. The war ended on November 11, 1918.

William McAdoo was replaced in 1918 by Carter Glass as Secretary of the Treasury. Both Strauss and Glass were present during the secret meeting of the Federal Reserve Board on May 18, 1920, when the Agricultural Depression of 1920-21 was made possible.

One of the main lies about the Federal Reserve Act when it was being ballyhooed in 1913 was its promise to take care of the farmer. Actually, it has never taken care of anybody but a few big bankers. Prof. O.M.W. Sprague, Harvard economist, writing in the Quarterly Journal of Economics of February, 1914, said:

> "The primary purpose of the Federal Reserve Act is to make sure that there will always be an available supply of money and credit in this country to meet unusual *banking* requirements." There is nothing in that wording to help the farmer.

The First World War had introduced into this country a general prosperity, as revealed by the stocks of heavy industry on the New York Exchange in 1917-18, by the increase in the amount of money circulated, and by the enormous bank clearings during the whole of 1918. It was the assigned duty of the Federal Reserve System to get back the vast amount of money and credit which had escaped their control during this time of prosperity. This was done by the Agricultural Depression of 1920-21.

The operations of the Federal Reserve Open Market Committee in 1917-18, while Paul Warburg was still Chairman, show a tremendous increase in purchases of bankers' and trade acceptances. There was also a great increase in the purchase of United States Government securities, under the leadership of the able Eugene Meyer, Jr. A large part of the stock market speculation in 1919, at the end of the War when the market was very unsettled, was financed with funds borrowed from Federal Reserve Banks with Government securities as collateral. Thus the Federal Reserve System set up the Depression, first by causing inflation, and then raising the discount rate and making money dear.

In 1914, Federal Reserve Bank rates had dropped from six percent to four percent, had gone to a further low of three percent in 1916, and had stayed at that level until 1920. The reason for the low interest rate was the necessity for floating the billion dollar Liberty Loans. At the beginning of each Liberty Loan Drive, the Federal Reserve Board put a hundred million dollars into the New York money market through its open market operations, in order to provide a cash impetus for the drive. The most important role of the Liberty Bonds was to soak up the increase in circulation of the medium of exchange (integer of account) brought about by the large amount of currency and credit put out during the war. Laborers were paid high wages, and farmers received the highest prices for their produce they had ever known. These two groups accumulated millions of dollars in cash which they did not put into Liberty Bonds. That money was effectively out of the hands of the Wall Street group which controlled the money and credit of the United States. They wanted it back, and that is why we had the Agricultural Depression of 1920-21.

Much of the money was deposited in small country banks in the Middle West and West which had refused to have any part of the Federal Reserve System, the farmers and ranchers of those regions seeing no good reason why they should give a group of international financiers control of their money. The main job of the Federal Reserve System was to break these small country banks and get back the money which had been paid out to the farmers during the war, in effect, ruin them, and this it proceeded to do.

First of all, a Federal Farm Loan Board was set up which encouraged the farmers to invest their accrued money in land on long term loans, which the farmers were eager to do. Then inflation was allowed to take its course in this country and in Europe in 1919 and 1920. The purpose of the inflation in Europe was to cancel out a large portion of the war debts owned by the Allies to the American people, and its purpose in this country was to draw in the excess moneys which had been distributed to the working people in the form of higher wages and bonuses for production. As prices went higher and higher, the money which the workers had accumulated became worth less and less, inflicting upon them an unfair drain, while the propertied classes were enriched by the inflation because of the enormous increase in the value of land and manufactured goods. The workers were thus effectively impoverished, but the farmers, who were as a class more thrifty, and who were more self-sufficient, had to be handled more harshly.

G.W. Norris, in "Collier's Magazine" of March 20, 1920, said:

"Rumor has it that two members of the Federal Reserve Board had a plain talk with some New York bankers and financiers in December, 1919. Immediately afterwards, there was a notable decline in transactions on the stock market and a cessation of company promotions. It is understood that action in the same general direction has already been taken in other sections of the country, as evidence of the abuse of the Federal Reserve System to promote speculation in land and commodities appeared."

Senator Robert L. Owen, Chairman of the Senate Banking and Currency Committee, testified at the Senate Silver Hearings in 1939 that:

"In the early part of 1920, the farmers were exceedingly prosperous. They were paying off the mortgages and buying a lot of new land, at the instance of the Government—had borrowed money to do it—and then they were bankrupted by a sudden contraction of credit and currency which took place in 1920. What took place in 1920 was just the reverse of what should have been taking place. Instead of liquidating the excess of credits created by the war through a period of years, the Federal Reserve Board met in a meeting which was not disclosed to the public. They met on the 18th of May, 1920, and it was a secret meeting. They spent all day conferring; the minutes made sixty printed pages, and they appear in Senate Document 310 of February 19, 1923. The Class A Directors, the Federal Reserve Advisory Council, were present, but the Class B Directors, who represented business, commerce, and agriculture, were not present. The Class C Directors, representing the people of the United States, were not present and were not invited to be present. Only the big bankers were there, and their work of that day resulted in a contraction of credit which had the effect the next year of reducing the national income fifteen billion dollars, throwing millions of people out of employment, and reducing the value of lands and ranches by twenty billion dollars."

Carter Glass, member of the Board in 1920 as Secretary of the Treasury, wrote in his autobiography, *Adventure in Constructive Finance* published in 1928; "Reporters were not present, of course, as they should not have been and as they never are at any bank board meeting in the world."[85]

---

[85]Carter Glass, *Adventure in Constructive Finance*, Doubleday, N.Y. 1928

It was Carter Glass who had complained that, if a suggested amendment by Senator LaFollette were passed, on the Federal Reserve Act of 1913, to the effect that no member of the Federal Reserve Board should be an official or director or stockholder of any bank, trust company, or insurance company, we would end up by having mechanics and farm laborers on the Board. Certainly mechanics and farm laborers could have caused no more damage to the country than did Glass, Strauss, and Warburg at the secret meeting of the Federal Reserve Board.

Senator Brookhart of Iowa testified that at that secret meeting Paul Warburg, also President of the Federal Advisory Council, had a resolution passed to send a committee of five to the Interstate Commerce Commission and ask for an increase in railroad rates. As head of Kuhn, Loeb Co. which owned most of the railway mileage in the United States, he was already missing the huge profits which the United States Government had paid during the war, and he wanted to inflict new price raises on the American people.

Senator Brookhart also testified that:

"I went into Myron T. Herrick's office in Paris, and told him that I came there to study cooperative banking. He said to me, 'as you go over the countries of Europe, you will find that the United States is the only civilized country in the world that by law is prohibiting its people from organizing a cooperative system.' I went up to New York and talked to about two hundred people. After talking cooperation and standing around waiting for my train—I did not specifically mention cooperative banking, it was cooperation in general—a man called me off to one side and said, 'I think Paul Warburg is the greatest financier we have ever produced. He believes a lot more of your cooperative ideas than you think he does, and if you want to consult anybody about the business of cooperation, he is the man to consult, because he believes in you, and you can rely on him.' A few minutes later I was steered up against Mr. Warburg himself, and he said to me, 'You are absolutely right about this cooperative idea. I want to let you know that the big bankers are with you. I want to let you know that now, so that you will not start anything on cooperative banking and turn them against you.' I said, 'Mr. Warburg, I have already prepared and tomorrow I am going to offer an amendment to the Lant Bill authorizing the establishment of cooperative national banks.' That was the intermediate credit act which was then pending to authorize the establishment of cooperative national banks. That was the extent of my conversation with Mr. Warburg, and we have not had any since."

Mr. Wingo testified that in April, May, June and July of 1920, the manufacturers and merchants were allowed a very large increase in credits. This was to tide them through the contraction of credit which was intended to ruin the American farmers, who, during this period, were denied all credit.

At the Senate Hearings in 1923, Eugene Meyer, Jr. put his finger on a primary reason for the Federal Reserve Board's action in raising the interest rate to 7% on agricultural and livestock paper:

"I believe," he said, "that a great deal of trouble would have been avoided if a larger number of the eligible non-member banks had been members of the Federal Reserve System." Meyer was correct in pointing this out. The purpose of the Board's action was to break those state and joint land stock banks which had steadfastly refused to surrender their freedom to the banker's dictatorship set up by the System. Kemmerer in the *ABC of the Federal Reserve System* had written in 1919 that:

"The tendency will be toward unification and simplicity which will be brought about by the state institutions, in increasing numbers, becoming stockholders and depositors in the reserve banks." However, the state banks had not responded.

The Senate Hearings of 1923 investigating the causes of the Agricultural Depression of 1920-21 had been demanded by the American people. The complete record of the secret meeting of the Federal Reserve Board on May 18, 1920 had been printed in the "Manufacturers' Record" of Baltimore, Maryland, a magazine devoted to the interests of small Southern manufacturers.

Benjamin Strong, Governor of the Federal Reserve Bank of New York, and close friend of Montagu Norman, the Governor of the Bank of England, claimed at these Hearings:

"The Federal Reserve System has done more for the farmer than he has yet begun to realize."

Emmanuel Goldenweiser, Director of Research for the Board of Governors, claimed that the discount rate was raised purely as an anti-inflationary measure, but he failed to explain why it was a raise aimed solely at farmers and workers, while at the same time the System protected the manufacturers and merchants by assuring them increased credits.

The final statement on the Federal Reserve Board's causing the Agricultural Depression of 1920-21 was made by William Jennings Bryan. In "Hearst's Magazine" of November, 1923, he wrote:

"The Federal Reserve Bank that should have been the farmer's greatest protection has become his greatest foe. The deflation of the farmer was a crime deliberately committed."

## CHAPTER TEN
# The Money Creators

The editorial page of *The New York Times*, January 18, 1920, carried an interesting comment on the Federal Reserve System. The unidentified writer, perhaps Paul Warburg, stated, "The Federal Reserve is a fount of credit, not of capital." This is one of the most revealing statements ever made about the Federal Reserve System. It says that the Federal Reserve System will never add anything to our capital structure, or to the formation of capital, because it is organized to produce credit, to create money for credit money and speculations, instead of providing capital funds for the improvement of commerce and industry. Simply stated, capitalization would mean the providing of notes backed by a precious metal or other commodity. Reserve notes are unbacked paper loaned at interest.

On July 25, 1921, Senator Owen stated on the editorial page of *The New York Times*, "The Federal Reserve Board is the most gigantic financial power in all the world. Instead of using this great power as the Federal Reserve Act intended that it should, the board....delegated this power to the banks, threw the weight of its influence toward the support of the policy of German inflation." The senator whose name was on the Act saw that it was not performing as promised.

After the Agricultural Depression of 1920-21, the Federal Reserve Board of Governors settled down to eight years of providing rapid credit expansion of the New York bankers, a policy which culminated in the Great Depression of 1929-31 and helped paralyze the economic structure of the world. Paul Warburg had resigned in May, 1918, after the monetary system of the United States had been changed from a bond-secured currency to a currency based upon commercial paper and the shares of the Federal Reserve Banks. Warburg returned to his five hundred thousand dollar a year job with Kuhn, Loeb Company, but he continued to determine the policy of the Federal Reserve System, as President of the Federal Advisory Council and as Chairman of the Executive Committee of the American Acceptance Council.

From 1921 to 1929, Paul Warburg organized three of the greatest trusts in the United States, the International Acceptance Bank, largest acceptance bank in the world, Agfa Ansco Film Corporation, with headquarters in Belgium, and I.G. Farben Corporation whose American branch Warburg set up as I.G. Chemical Corporation. The Westinghouse Corporation is also one of his creations.

In the early 1920s, the Federal Reserve System played the decisive role in the re-entry of Russia into the international finance structure. Winthrop and Stimson continued to be the correspondents between Russian and American bankers, and Henry L. Stimson handled the negotiations concluding in our recognition of the Soviet after Roosevelt's election in 1932. This was an anti-climax, because we had long before resumed exchange relations with Russian financiers.

The Federal Reserve System began purchasing Russian gold in 1920, and Russian currency was accepted on the Exchanges. According to Colonel Ely Garrison, in his autobiography, and according to the United States Naval Secret Service Report on Paul Warburg, the Russian Revolution had been financed by the Rothschilds and Warburgs, with a member of the Warburg family carrying the actual funds used by Lenin and Trotsky in Stockholm in 1918.

An article in the English monthly "Fortnightly", July, 1922, says:

"During the past year, practically every single capitalistic institution has been restored. This is true of the State Bank, private banking, the Stock Exchange, the right to possess money to unlimited amount, the right of inheritance, the bill of exchange system, and other institutions and practices involved in the conduct of private industry and trade. A great part of the former nationalized industries are now found in semi-independent trusts."

The organization of powerful trusts in Russia under the guise of Communism made possible the receipt of large amounts of financial and technical help from the United States. The Russian aristocracy had been wiped out because it was too inefficient to manage a modern industrial state. The international financiers provided funds for Lenin and Trotsky to overthrow the Czarist regime and keep Russia in the First World War. Peter Drucker, spokesman for the oligarchy in America, declared in an article in the *Saturday Evening Post* in 1948, that:

"RUSSIA IS THE IDEAL OF THE MANAGED ECONOMY TOWARDS WHICH WE ARE MOVING."

In Russia, the issuance of sufficient currency to handle the needs of their economy occurred only after a government had been put in power which had absolute control of the people. During the 1920s, Russia issued large quantities of so-called "inflation money", a managed currency. The same "Fortnightly" article (of July, 1922) observed that:

"As economic pressure produced the 'astronomical dimensions system' of currency; it can never destroy it. Taken alone, the system is self-contained, logically perfected, even intelligent. And it can perish only through collapse or destruction of the political edifice which it decorates."

"Fortnightly" also remarked, in 1929, that:

"Since 1921, the daily life of the Soviet citizen is no different from that of the American citizen, and the Soviet system of government is more economical."

Admiral Kolchak, leader of the White Russian armies, was supported by the international bankers, who sent British and American troops to Siberia in order to have a pretext for printing Kolchak rubles. At one time in 1920, the bankers were manipulating on the London Exchange the old Czarist rubles, Kerensky rubles and Kolchak rubles, the values of all three fluctuating according to the movements of the Allied troops aiding Kolchak. Kolchak also was in possession of considerable amounts of gold which had been seized by his armies. After his defeat, a trainload of this gold disappeared in Siberia. At the Senate Hearings in 1921 on the Federal Reserve System, it was brought out that the System had been receiving this gold. Congressman Dunbar questioned Governor W.P.G. Harding of the Federal Reserve Board as follows:

DUNBAR: "In other words, Russia is sending a great deal of gold to the European countries, which in turn send it to us?"

HARDING: "This is done to pay for the stuff bought in this country and to create dollar exchange."

DUNBAR: "At the same time, that gold came from Russia through Europe?"

HARDING: "Some of it is thought to be Kolchak gold, coming through Siberia, but it is none of the Federal Reserve Banks' business. The Secretary of the Treasury has issued instructions to the assay office not to take any gold which does not bear the mint mark of a friendly nation."

Just what Governor Harding meant by "a friendly nation" is not clear. In 1921, we were not at war with any country, but Congress was already beginning to question the international gold dealings of the Federal Reserve System. Governor Harding could very well shrug his shoulders and say that it was none of the Federal Reserve Banks' business where the gold came from. Gold knows no nationality or race. The United States by law had ceased to be interested in where its gold came from in 1906, when Secretary of the Treasury Shaw made arrangements with several of the larger New York banks (ones in which he had interests) to purchase gold with advances of cash from the United States Treasury, which would then purchase the gold from these banks. The Treasury could claim that it did not know where its gold came from since their office only registers the bank from which it made the purchase. Since 1906, the Treasury has not known from which of the international gold merchants it was buying its gold.

The international gold dealings of the Federal Reserve System, and its active support in helping the League of Nations to force all the nations of Europe and South America back on the gold standard for the benefit of international gold merhants like Eugene Meyer, Jr. and Albert Strauss, is best demonstrated by a classic incident, the sterling credit of 1925.

J.E. Darling wrote, in the English periodical, "Spectator", on January 10, 1925 that:

> "Obviously, it is of the first importance to the United States to induce England to resume the gold standard as early as possible. An American controlled Gold Standard, which must inevitably result in the United States becoming the world's supreme financial power, makes England a tributary and satellite, and New York the world's financial centre."

Mr. Darling fails to point out that the American people have as little to do with this as the British people, and at resumption of the gold standard by Britain would benefit only that small group of international gold mercants who own the world's gold. No wonder that "Banker's Magazine" gleefully remarked in July, 1925 that:

> "The outstanding event of the past half year in the banking world was the restoration of the gold standard."

The First World War changed the status of the United States from that of a debtor nation to the position of the world's greatest creditor nation, a title formerly occupied by England. Since debt is money, according to the Governor Marriner Eccles of the Federal Reserve Board, this also made us the richest nation of the world. The war also caused the removal of the headquarters of the world's acceptance market from London to New York, and Paul Warburg became the most powerful trade acceptance banker in the world. The mainstay of the international financiers, however, remained the same. The gold standard was still the basis of foreign exchange, and the small group of internationals who owned the gold controlled the monetary systems of the Western nations.

Professor Gustav Cassel wrote in 1928:

> "The American dollar, not the gold standard, is the world's monetary standard. The American Federal Reserve Board has the power to determine the purchasing power of the dollar by making changes in the rate of discount, and thus controls the monetary standard of the world."

If this were true, the members of the Federal Reserve Board would be the most powerful financiers in the world. Occasionally their membership includes such influential men as Paul Warburg or Eugene Meyer, Jr., but usually they are a rubber-stamp committee for the Federal Advisory Council and the London bankers.

In May, 1925, the British Parliament passed the Gold Standard Act, putting Great Britain back on the gold standard. The Federal Reserve System's major role in this event came out on March 16, 1926, when George Seay, Governor of the Federal Reserve Bank of Richmond, testified before the House Banking and Currency Committee that:

"A verbal understanding, confirmed by correspondence, extended Great Britain a two hundred million dollar gold loan or credit. All negotiations were conducted between Benjamin Strong, Governor of the Federal Reserve Bank of New York and Mr. Montagu Norman, Governor of the Bank of England. The purpose of this loan was to help England get back on the gold standard, and the loan was to be met by investment of Federal Reserve funds in bills of exchange and foreign securities."

The Federal Reserve Bulletin of June, 1925, stated that:

"Under its arrangement with the Bank of England the Federal Reserve Bank of New York undertakes to sell gold on credit to the Bank of England from time to time during the next two years, but not to exceed $200,000,000 outstanding at any one time."

A two hundred million dollar gold credit had been arranged by a verbal understanding between the international bankers, Benjamin Strong and Montagu Norman. It was apparent by this time that the Federal Reserve System had other interests at heart than the financial needs of American business and industry. Great Britain's return to the gold standard was further facilitated by an additional gold loan of a hundred million dollars from J.P. Morgan Company. Winston Churchill, British Chancellor of the Exchequer, complained later that the cost to the British government of this loan was $1,125,000 the first year, this sum representing the profit to J.P. Morgan Company in that time.

The matter of changing the discount rate, for instance, has never been satisfactorily explained. Inquiry at the Federal Reserve Board in Washington elicited the reply that "the condition of the money market is the prime consideration behind changes in the rate." Since the money market is in New York, it takes no imagination to deduce that New York bankers may be interested in changes of the rate and often attempt to influence it.

Norman Lombard, in the periodical "World's Work" writes that:

"In their consideration and disposal of proposed changes of policy, the Federal Reserve Board should follow the procedure and ethics observed by our court of law. Suggestions that there should be a change of rate or that the Reserve Banks should buy or sell securities may come from anyone and with no formality or written argument. The suggestion may be made to a Governor or Director of the Federal Reserve System over the telephone or at his club over the luncheon table, or it may be made in the course of a casual call on a member of the Federal Reserve Board. The interests of the one proposing the change need not be revealed, and his name and any suggestions he makes are usually kept secret. If it concerns the matter of open market operations, the public has no inkling of the decision until the regular weekly statement appears, showing changes in the holdings of the Federal Reserve Banks. Meanwhile, there is no public discussion, there is no statement of the reasons for the decision, or of the names of those opposing or favoring it."

The chances of the average citizen meeting a Governor of the Federal Reserve System at his club are also slight.

The House Hearings on Stabilization of the Purchasing Power of the Dollar in 1928 proved conclusively that the Federal Reserve Board worked in close cooperation with the heads of European central banks, and that the Depression of 1929-31 was planned at a secret luncheon of the Federal Reserve Board and those heads of European central banks in 1927. The Board has never been made responsible to the public for its decisions or actions. The constitutional checks and balances seem not to operate in finance.

The true allegiance of the members of the Federal Reserve Board has always been to the central bankers. The three features of the central bank, its ownership by private stockholders who receive rent and profit for their use of the nation's credit, absolute control of the nation's financial resources, and mobilization of the nation's credit to finance foreigners, all were demonstrated by the Federal Reserve System during the first fifteen years of its operations.

Further demonstration of the international purposes of the Federal Reserve Act of 1913 is provided by the "Edge Amendment" of December 24, 1919, which authorizes the organization of corporations expressly for "engaging in international or foreign banking or other international or foreign financial operations, including the dealing in gold or bullion, and the holding of stock in foreign corporations." In commenting on this amendment, E.W. Kemmerer, economist from Princeton University, remarked that:

"The federal reserve system is proving to be a great influence in the internationalizing of American trade and American finance."

The fact that this internationalizing of American trade and American finance has been a direct cause for involving us in two world wars does not disturb Mr. Kemmerer. There is plenty of evidence to show how Paul Warburg used the Federal Reserve System as the instrument for getting trade acceptance adopted on a wide scale by American businessmen.

The use of trade acceptances, (which are the currency of international trade) by bankers and corporations in the United States prior to 1915 was practically unknown. The rise of the Federal Reserve System exactly parallels the increase in the use of acceptances in this country, nor is this a coincidence. The men who wanted the Federal Reserve System were the men who set up acceptance banks and profited by the use of acceptances.

As early as 1910, the National Monetary Commission began to issue pamphlets and other propanganda urging bankers and businessmen in this country to adopt trade acceptances in their transactions. For three years the Commission carried on this campaign, and the Aldrich Plan included a broad provision authorizing the introduction and use of bankers' acceptances into the American system of commercial paper.

The Federal Reserve Act of 1913 as passed by Congress did not specifically authorize the use of acceptances, but the Federal Reserve Board in 1915 and 1916 defined "trade acceptance", further defined by Regulation A Series of 1920, and further defined by Series 1924. One of the first official acts of the Board of Governors in 1914 was to grant acceptances a preferentially low rate of discount at Federal Reserve Banks. Since acceptances were not being used in this country at that time, no explanation of business exigency could be advanced for this action. It was apparent that someone in power on the Board of Governors wanted the adoptance of acceptances.

The National Bank Act of 1864, which was the determining financial authority of the United States until November, 1914, did not permit banks to lend their credit. Consequently, the power of banks to create money was greatly limited. We did not have a bank of issue, that is, a central bank, which could create money. To get a central bank, the bankers caused money panic after money panic on the business people of the United States, by shipping gold out of the country, creating a money shortage, and then importing it back. After we got our central bank, the Federal Reserve System, there was no longer any need for a money panic, because the banks could create money. However, the panic as an instrument of power over the business and financial community was used again on two important occasions, in 1920, causing the Agricultural Depression, because state banks and trust companies had refused to join the Federal Reserve System, and in 1929, causing the Great Depression, which centralized nearly all power in this country in the hands of a few great trusts.

A trade acceptance is a draft drawn by the seller of goods on the purchaser, and accepted by the purchaser, with a time of expiration stamped upon it. The use of trade acceptances in the wholesale market supplies short-term, assured credit to carry goods in process of production, storage, transit, and marketing. It facilitates domestic and foreign commerce. Seemingly, then, the bankers who wished to replace the open-book account system with the trade acceptance system were progressive men who wished to help American import-export trade. Much propaganda was issued to that effect, but this was not really the story.

The open-book system, heretofore used entirely by American business people, allowed a discount for cash. The acceptance system discourages the use of cash, by allowing a discount for credit. The open-book system also allowed much easier terms of payment, with liberal extensions on the debt. The acceptance does not allow this, since it is a short-term credit with the time-date stamped upon it. It is out of the seller's hands, and in the hands of a bank, usually an acceptance bank, which does not allow any extension of time. Thus, the adoption of acceptances by American businessmen during the 1920's greatly facilitated the domination and swallowing up of small business into huge trusts, which accelerated the crash of 1929.

Trade acceptances had been used to some extent in the United States before the Civil War. During that war, exigencies of trade had destroyed the acceptance as a credit medium, and it had not come back into favor in this country, our people preferring the simplicity and generosity of the open- book system. Open-book accounts are single-name commercial paper, bearing only the name of the debtor. Acceptances are two-name paper, bearing the name of the debtor and the creditor. Thus they became commodities to be bought and sold by banks. To the creditor, under the open-book system, the debt is a liability. To the acceptance bank holding an acceptance, the debt is an asset. The men who set up acceptance banks in this country, under the leadership of Paul Warburg, secured control of the billions of dollars of credit existing as open accounts on the books of American businessmen.

Governor Marriner Eccles of the Federal Reserve Board stated before the House Banking and Currency Committee that: "Debt is the basis for the creation of money."

Large holders of trade acceptances got the use of billions of dollars worth of credit-money, besides the rate of interest charged upon the acceptance itself. It is obvious why Paul Warburg should have devoted so much time, money, and energy to getting acceptances adopted by this country's banking machinery.

On September 4, 1914, the National City Bank accepted the first time-draft drawn on a national bank under provisions of the Federal Reserve Act of 1913. This was the beginning of the end of the open-book account system as an important factor in wholesale trade. Beverly Harris, vice-president of the National City Bank of New York, issued a pamphlet in 1915 stating that:

"Merchants using the open account system are usurping the functions of bankers."

In *The New York Times* on June 14, 1920, Paul Warburg, Chairman of the American Acceptance Council, said:

"Unless the Federal Reserve Board puts itself heart and soul behind the untrammeled development of acceptances as a prime investment for banks of the Federal Reserve Banks the future safe and sound development of the system will be jeopardized."

This was a statement of the purpose of Warburg and his bunch who wanted "monetary reform" in this country. They were out to get control of all credit in the United States, and they got it, by means of the Federal Reserve System, the acceptance system, and the lack of concern by the citizens.

The First World War was a boon to the introduction of trade acceptances, and the volume jumped to four hundred million dollars in 1917, growing through the 1920s to more than a billion dollars a year, which culminated in a high peak just before the Great Depression of 1929-31. The Federal Reserve Bank of New York's charts show that its use of acceptances reached a peak in November, 1929, the month of the stock market crash, and declined sharply thereafter. The acceptance people by then had gotten what they wanted, which was control of American business and industry. "Fortune Magazine" in February of 1950 pointed out that:

"Volume of acceptances declined from $1,732 million in 1929 to $209 million in 1940, because of the concentration of acceptance banking in a few hands, and the Treasury's low-interest policy, which made direct loans cheaper than acceptance. There has been a slight upturn since the war, but it is often cheaper for large companies to finance imports from their own coffers."

In other words, the "large companies" more accurately, the great trusts, now have control of credit and have not needed acceptances. Besides the barrage of propaganda issued by the Federal Reserve System itself, the National Association of Credit Men, the American Bankers' Association, and other fraternal organizations of the New York bankers devoted much time and money to distributing acceptance propaganda. Even their flood of lectures and pamphlets proved insufficient, and in 1919 Paul Warburg organized the American Acceptance Council, which was devoted entirely to acceptance propaganda.

The first convention held by this association at Detroit, Michigan, on June 9, 1919, coincided with the annual convention of the National Association of Credit Men, held there on that date, so that "interested observers might with facility participate in the lectures and meetings of both groups," according to a pamphlet issued by the American Acceptance Council.

Paul Warburg was elected President of this organization, and later became chairman of the Executive Committee of the American Acceptance Council, a position which he held until his death in 1932. The Council published lists of corporations using trade acceptances, all of them businesses in which Kuhn, Loeb Co. or its affiliates held control. Lectures given before the Council or by members of the Council were attractively bound and distributed free by the National City Bank of New York to the country's businessmen.

Louis T. McFadden, Chairman of the House Banking and Currency Committee, charged in 1922 that the American Acceptance Council was exercising undue influence on the Federal Reserve Board and called for a Congressional investigation, but Congress was not interested.

At the second annual convention of the American Acceptance Council, held in New York on December 2, 1920, President Paul Warburg stated:

> "It is a great satisfaction to report that during the year under review it was possible for the American Acceptance Council to further develop and strengthen its relations with the Federal Reserve Board."

During the 1920s Paul Warburg, who had resigned from the Federal Reserve Board after holding a position as Governor for a year in wartime, continued to exercise direct personal influence on the Federal Reserve Board by meeting with the Board as President of the Federal Advisory Council and as President of the American Acceptance Council. He was, from its organization in 1920 until his death in 1932, Chairman of the Board of the International Acceptance Bank of New York, the largest acceptance bank in the world. His brother, Felix M. Warburg, also a partner in Kuhn, Loeb Co., was director of the International Acceptance Bank and Paul's son, James Paul Warburg, was Vice-President. Paul Warburg was also a director on other important acceptance banks in this country, such as the Westinghouse Acceptance Bank, which were organized in the United States immediately after the World War, when the headquarters of the international acceptance market was moved from London to New York, and Paul Warburg became the most powerful acceptance banker in the world.

Paul Warburg became an even more legendary figure by his memorialization as "Daddy Warbucks" in the comic strip, "Little Orphan Annie". The strip celebrated a homeless waif and her dog who are adopted by "the richest man in the world", Daddy Warbucks, a takeoff on "Warburg", who has almost magical powers and can accomplish anything by the power of his limitless wealth. Those in the know snickered when "Annie", the musical comedy version of this story, had a highly successful run of several years on Broadway, because the vast majority of the audience had no idea that this was merely another Warburg operation.

It was the transference of the acceptance market from England to this country which gave rise to Thomas Lamont's ecstatic speech before the Academy of Political Science in 1917 that:

> "The dollar, not the pound, is now the basis for international exchange."

Americans were proud to hear that, but they did not realize at what a price.

Visible proof of the undue influence of the American Acceptance Council on the Federal Reserve Board, about which Congressman McFadden complained, is the chart showing the rate-pattern of the

Federal Reserve Bank of New York during the 1920s. The Bank's official discount rate follows exactly for nine years the ninety-day bankers' acceptance rate, and the Federal Reserve Bank of New York sets the discount rate for the rest of the Reserve Banks.

Throughout the 1920s the Board of Governors retained two of its first members, C.S. Hamlin and Adolph C. Miller. These men found themselves careers as arbiters of the nation's monetary policy. Hamlin was on the Board from 1914 until 1936, when he was appointed Special Counsel to the Board, while Miller served from 1914 until 1931. These two men were allowed to stay on the Board so many years because they were both eminently respectable men who gave the Board a certain prestige in the eyes of the public. During these years one important banker after another came on the Board, served for awhile, and went on to better things. Neither Miller nor Hamlin ever objected to anything that the New York bankers wanted. They changed the discount rate and they performed open market operation with Government securities whenever Wall Street wanted them to. Behind them was the figure of Paul Warburg, who exercised a continuous and dominant influence as President of the Federal Advisory Council, on which he had such men of common interests with himself as Winthrop Aldrich and J.P. Morgan. Warburg was never too occupied with his duties of organizing the big international trusts to supervise the nation's financial structures. His influence from 1902, when he arrived in this country as an immigrant from Germany, until 1932, the year of his death, was dependent on his European alliance with the banking cartel. Warburg's son, James Paul Warburg, continued to exercise such influence, being appointed Franklin D. Roosevelt's Director of the Budget when that great man assumed office in 1933, and setting up the Office of War Information, our official propaganda agency during the Second World War.

In *The Fight for Financial Supremacy*, Paul Einzig, editorial writer for the London Economist, wrote that:

"Almost immediately after World War I a close cooperation was established between the Bank of England and the Federal Reserve authorities, and more especially with the Federal Reserve Bank of New York.* This cooperation was largely due to the cordial relations existing between Mr. Montagu Norman of the Bank of England and Mr. Benjamin Strong, Governor of the Federal Reserve Bank of New York until 1928. On several occasions the discount rate policy of the Federal Reserve Bank of New York was guided by a desire to help the Bank of England.

---

*William Boyce Thompson (Wall Street operator) commented to Clarence Barron, Nov. 27, 1920, "Why should the Federal Reserve Bank have private wires all over the country and talk daily by cable with the Bank of England?" p. 327 *"They Told Barron".*

There has been close cooperation in the fixing of discount rates between London and New York."[86]

---

[86]Paul Einzig, *The Fight For Financial Supremacy*, Macmillan, 1931

# CHAPTER ELEVEN
# Lord Montagu Norman

The collaboration between Benjamin Strong and Lord Montagu Norman is one of the greatest secrets of the twentieth century. Benjamin Strong married the daughter of the president of Bankers Trust in New York, and subsequently succeeded to its presidency. Carroll Quigley, in *Tragedy and Hope* says: "Strong became Governor of the Federal Reserve Bank of New York as the joint nominee of Morgan and of Kuhn, Loeb Company in 1914."[87]

Lord Montagu Norman is the only man in history who had both his maternal grandfather and his paternal grandfather serve as Govenrors of the Bank of England. His father was with Brown, Shipley Company, the London Branch of Brown Brothers (now Brown Brothers Harriman). Montagu Norman (1871-1950) came to New York to work for Brown Brothers in 1894, where he was befriended by the Delano family, and by James Markoe, of Brown Brothers. He returned to England, and in 1907 was named to the Court of the Bank of England. In 1912, he had a nervous breakdown, and went to Switzerland to be treated by Jung, as was fashionable among the powerful group which he represented.*

Lord Montagu Norman was Governor of the Bank of England from 1916 to 1944. During this period, he participated in the central bank conferences which set up the Crash of 1929 and a worldwide depression. In *The Politics of Money* by Brian Johnson, he writes, "Strong and Norman, intimate friends, spent their holidays together at Bar Harbour and in the South of France." Johnson says, "Norman therefore became Strong's alter ego. . . . "Strong's easy money policies on the New York money market from 1925-28 were the fulfillment of his agreement with Norman to keep New York interest rates below those of London. For the sake of international cooperation, Strong withheld the steadying hand of high interest rates from New York until it was too late. Easy money in New

---

[87]Carroll Quigley, *Tragedy and Hope*, Macmillan, New York, p. 326
*When people of this class are stricken by guilt feelings while plotting world wars and economic depressions which will bring misery, suffering and death to millions of the world's inhabitants, they sometimes have qualms. These qualms are jeered at by their peers as "a failure of nerve". After a bout with their psychiatrists, they return to their work with renewed gusto, with no further digressions of pity for "the little people" who are to be their victims.

York had encouraged the surging American boom of the late 1920s, with its fantastic heights of speculation."[88]

Benjamin Strong died suddenly in 1928. *The New York Times* obituary, Oct. 17, 1928, describes the conference between the directors of the three great central banks in Europe in July, 1927, "Mr. Norman, Bank of England, Strong of the New York Federal Reserve Bank, and Dr. Hjalmar Schacht of the Reichsbank, their meeting referred to at that time as a meeting of 'the world's most exclusive club'. No public reports were ever made of the foreign conferences, which were wholly informal, but which covered many important questions of gold movements, the stability of world trade, and world economy."

The meetings at which the future of the world's economy are decided are always reported as being "wholly informal", off the record, no reports made to the public, and on the rare occasions when outraged Congressmen summon these mystery figures to testify about their activities they merely trace the outline of steps taken, and develop no information about what was really said or decided.

At the Senate Hearings on the Federal Reserve System in 1931, H. Parker Willis, one of the authors and First Secretary of the Federal Reserve Board from 1914 until 1920, pointedly asked Governor George Harrison, Strong's successor as Governor of the Federal Reserve Bank of New York:

"What is the relationship between the Federal Reserve Bank of New York and the money committee of the Stock Exchange?"

"There is no relationship." Governor Harrison replied.

"There is no assistance or cooperation in fixing the rate in any way?" asked Willis.

"No," said Governor Harrison. "although on various occasions they advise us of the state of the money situation, and what they think the rate ought to be." This was an absolute contradiction of his statement that "There is no relationship". The Federal Reserve Bank of New York which set the discount rate for the other Reserve Banks, actually maintained a close liason with the money committee of the Stock Exchange.

The House Stabilization Hearings of 1928 proved conclusively that the Governors of the Federal Reserve System had been holding conferences with heads of the big European central banks. Even had the Congressmen known the details of the plot which was to culminate in the Great Depression of 1929-31, there would have been nothing they could have done to stop it. The international bankers who controlled gold movements could inflict their will on any country, and the United States was as helpless as any other.

Notes from these House Hearings follow:

---

[88]Brian Johnson, *The Politics of Money*, McGraw Hill, New York, 1970, p. 63.

MR. BEEDY: "I notice on your chart that the lines which produce the most violent fluctuations are found under 'Money Rates in New York.' As the rates of money rise and fall in the big cities the loans that are made on investments seem to take advantage of them, at present, a quite violent change, while industry in general does not seem to avail itself of these violent changes, and that line is fairly even, there being no great rises or declines.

GOVERNOR ADOLPH MILLER: This was all more or less in the interests of the international situation. They sold gold credits in New York for sterling balances in London.

REPRESENTATIVE STRONG: (No relation to Benjamin): Has the Federal Reserve Board the power to attract gold to this country?

E.A. GOLDENWEISER, research director for the Board: The Federal Reserve Board could attract gold to this country by making money rates higher.

GOVERNOR ADOLPH MILLER: I think we are very close to the point where any further solicitude on our part for the monetary concerns of Europe can be altered. The Federal Reserve Board last summer, 1927, set out by a policy of open market purchases, followed in course by reduction on the discount rate at the Reserve Banks, to ease the credit situation and to cheapen the cost of money. The official reasons for that departure in credit policy were that it would help to stabilize international exchange and stimulate the exportation of gold.

CHAIRMAN MCFADDEN: Will you tell us briefly how that matter was brought to the Federal Reserve Board and what were the influences that went into the final determination?

GOVERNOR ADOLPH MILLER: You are asking a question impossible for me to answer.

CHAIRMAN MCFADDEN: Perhaps I can clarify it—where did the suggestions come from that caused this decision of the change of rates last summer?

GOVERNOR ADOLPH MILLER: The three largest central banks in Europe had sent representatives to this country. There were the Governor of the Bank of England, Mr. Montagu Norman, the President of the German Reichsbank, Mr. Hjalmar Schacht, and Professor Rist, Deputy Governor of the Bank of France. These gentlemen were in conference with officials of the Federal Reserve Bank of New York. After a week or two, they appeared in Washington for the better part of a day. They came down the evening of one day and were the guests of the Governors of the Federal Reserve Board the following day, and left that afternoon for New York.

CHAIRMAN MCFADDEN: Were the members of the Board present at this luncheon?

GOVERNOR ADOLPH MILLER: Oh, yes, it was given by the Governors of the Board for the purpose of bringing all of us together.

CHAIRMAN MCFADDEN: Was it a social affair, or were matters of importance discussed?

GOVERNOR MILLER: I would say it was mainly a social affair. Personally, I had a long conversation with Dr. Schacht alone before the luncheon, and also one of considerable length with Professor Rist. After the luncheon I began a conversation with Mr. Norman, which was joined in by Governor Strong of New York.

CHAIRMAN MCFADDEN: Was that a formal meeting of the Board?

GOVERNOR ADOLPH MILLER: No.

CHAIRMAN MCFADDEN: It was just an informal discussion of the matters they had been discussing in New York?

GOVERNOR MILLER: I assume so. It was mainly a social occasion. What I said was mainly in the nature of generalities. The heads of these central banks also spoke in generalities.

MR. KING: What did they want?

GOVERNOR MILLER: They were very candid in answers to questions. I wanted to have a talk with Mr. Norman, and we both stayed behind after luncheon, and were joined by the other foreign representatives and the officials of the New York Reserve Bank. *These gentlemen were all pretty concerned with the way the gold standard was working.* They were therefore desirous of seeing an easy money market in New York and lower rates, which would deter gold from moving from Europe to this country. That would be very much in the interest of the international money situation which then existed.

MR. BEEDY: Was there some understanding arrived at between the representatives of these foreign banks and the Federal Reserve Board or the New York Federal Reserve Bank?

GOVERNOR MILLER: Yes.

MR. BEEDY: It was not reported formally?

GOVERNOR MILLER: No. Later, there came a meeting of the Open-Market Policy Committee, the investment policy committee of the Federal Reserve System, by which and to which certain recommendations were made. My recollection is that about eighty million dollars worth of securities were purchased in August consistent with this plan.

CHAIRMAN MCFADDEN: Was there any conference between the members of the Open Market Committee and those bankers from abroad?

GOVERNOR MILLER: They may have met them as individuals, but not as a committee.

MR. KING: How does the Open-Market Committee get its ideas?

GOVERNOR MILLER: They sit around and talk about it. I do not know whose idea this was. It was distinctly a time in which there was a cooperative spirit at work.

CHAIRMAN MCFADDEN: You have outlined here negotiations of very great importance.

GOVERNOR MILLER: I should rather say conversations.

CHAIRMAN MCFADDEN: Something of a very definite character took place?

GOVERNOR MILLER: Yes.

CHAIRMAN MCFADDEN: A change of policy on the part of our whole financial system which has resulted in one of the most unusual situations that has ever confronted this country financially (the stock market speculation boom of 1927-1929). It seems to me that a matter of that importance should have been made a matter of record in Washington.

GOVERNOR MILLER: I agree with you.

REPRESENTATIVE STRONG: Would it not have been a good thing if there had been a direction that those powers given to the Federal Reserve System should be used for the continued stabilization of the purchasing power of the American dollar rather than be influenced by the interests of Europe?

GOVERNOR MILLER: I take exception to that term "influence". Besides, there is no such thing as stabilizing the American dollar without stabilizing every other gold currency. They are tied together by the gold standard. Other eminent men who come here are very adroit in knowing how to approach the folk who make up the personnel of the Federal Reserve Board.

MR. STEAGALL: The visit of these foreign bankers resulted in money being cheaper in New York?

GOVERNOR MILLER: Yes, exactly.

CHAIRMAN MCFADDEN: I would like to put in the record all who attended that luncheon in Washington.

GOVERNOR MILLER: In addition to the names I have given you, there was also present one of the younger men from the Bank of France. I think all members of the Federal Reserve Board were there. Under Secretary of the Treasury Ogden Mills was there, and the Assistant Secretary of the Treasury, Mr. Schuneman, also, two or three men from the State Department and Mr. Warren of the Foreign Department of the Federal Reserve Bank of New York. Oh yes, Governor Strong was present.

CHAIRMAN MCFADDEN: This conference, of course, with all of these foreign bankers did not just happen. The prominent bankers from Germany, France, and England came here at whose suggestion?

GOVERNOR MILLER: A situation had been created that was distinctly embarrassing to London by reason of the impending withdrawal of a certain amount of gold which had been recovered by France and that had originally been shipped and deposited in the Bank of England by the French Government as a war credit. There was getting to be some tension of mind in Europe because France was beginning to put her house in order for a *return to the gold standard*. The situation was one which called for some moderating influence.

MR. KING: Who was the moving spirit who got those people together?

GOVERNOR MILLER: That is a detail with which I am not familiar.

REPRESENTATIVE STRONG: Would it not be fair to say that the fellows who wanted the gold were the ones who instigated the meeting?

GOVERNOR MILLER: They came over here.

REPRESENTATIVE STRONG: The fact is that they came over here, they had a meeting, they banqueted, they talked, they got the Federal Reserve Board to lower the discount rate, and to make the purchases in the open market, and they got the gold.

MR. STEAGALL: Is it true that action stabilized the European currencies and upset ours?

GOVERNOR MILLER: *Yes, that was what it was intended to do.*

CHAIRMAN MCFADDEN: Let me call your attention to the recent conference in Paris at which Mr. Goldenweiser, director of research for the Federal Reserve Board, and Dr. Burgess, assistant Federal Reserve Agent of the Federal Reserve Bank of New York, were in consultation with the representatives of the other central banks. Who called the conference?

GOVERNOR MILLER: My recollection is that it was called by the Bank of France.

GOVERNOR YOUNG: No, it was the *League of Nations* who called them together."

The secret meeting between the Governors of the Federal Reserve Board and the heads of the European central banks was not called to stabilize anything. It was held to discuss the best way of getting the gold held in the United States by the System back to Europe to force the nations of that continent back on the gold standard. The League of Nations had not yet succeeded in doing that, the objective for which that body was set up in the first place, because the Senate of the United States had refused to let Woodrow Wilson betray us to an international monetary authority. It took the Second World War and Franklin D. Roosevelt to do that. Meanwhile, Europe had to have our gold and the Federal Reserve System gave it to them, five hundred million dollars worth. The movement of that gold out of the United States caused the deflation of the stock boom, the end of the business prosperity of the 1920s and the Great Depression of 1929-31, the worst calamity which has ever befallen this nation. It is entirely logical to say that the American people suffered that depression as a punishment for not joining the League of Nations. The bankers knew what would happen when that five hundred million dollars worth of gold was sent to Europe. They wanted the Depression because it put the business and finance of the United States in their hands.

The Hearings continue:

Mr. Beedy: "Mr. Ebersole of the Treasury Department concluded his remarks at the dinner we attended last night by saying that the Federal Reserve System did not want stabilization and the American businessman did not want it. They want these fluctuations in prices, not only in securities but in commodities, in trade generally, because those who are now in control are making their profits out of that very instability. If control of these people does not come in a legitimate way, there may be an attempt to produce it by general upheavals such as have characterized society in days gone by. Revolutions have been promoted by dissatisfaction with existing conditions, the control being in the hands of the few, and the many paying the bills.

CHAIRMAN MCFADDEN: I have here a letter from a member of the Federal Reserve Board who was summoned to appear here. I would like to have it put in the record. It is from Governor Cunningham:

Dear Mr. Chairman:

For the past several weeks I have been confined to my home on account of illness and am now preparing to spend a few weeks away from Washington for the purpose of hastening convalescence.

Edward H. Cunningham

This is in answer to an invitation extended him to appear before our Committee. I also have a letter from George Harrison, Deputy Governor of the Federal Reserve Bank of New York.

My dear Mr. Congressman:

Governor Strong sailed for Europe last week. He has not been at all well since the first of the year, and, while he did appear before your Committee last March, it was only shortly after that that he suffered a very severe attack of shingles, which has sorely racked his nerves.

George L. Harrison, May 19, 1928

I also desire to place in the record a statement in the New York Journal of Commerce, dated May 22, 1928, from Washington:

'It is stated in well-informed circles here that the chief topic being taken up by Governor Strong of the Federal Reserve Bank of New York on his present visit to Paris is the arrangement of stabilization credits for France, Rumania, and Yugoslavia. A second vital question Mr. Strong will take up is the amount of gold France is to draw from this country.' "

Further questioning by Chairman McFadden about the strange illness of Benjamin Strong brought forth the following testimony from Governor Charles S. Hamlin of the Federal Reserve Board on May 23rd, 1928:

"All I know is that Governor Strong has been very ill, and he has gone over to Europe primarily, I understand, as a matter of health. Of course, he knows well the various offices of the European central banks and undoubtedly will call on them."

Governor Benjamin Strong died a few weeks after his return from Europe, without appearing before the Committee.

The purpose of these hearings before the House Committee on Banking and Currency in 1928 was to investigate the neccessity for passing the Strong bill, presented by Representative Strong (no relation to Benjamin, the international banker), which would have provided that the Federal Reserve System be empowered to act to stabilize the purchasing power of the dollar. This had been one of the promises made by Carter Glass and Woodrow Wilson when they presented the Federal Reserve Act before Congress in 1912, and such a provision had actually been put in the Act by Senator Robert L. Owen, but Carter Glass' House Committee on Banking and Currency had struck it out. The traders and speculators did not want the dollar to become stable, because they would no longer be able to make a profit. The citizens of this country had been led to gamble on the stock market in the 1920s because the traders had created a nationwide condition of instability.

The Strong Bill of 1928 was defeated in Congress.

The financial situation in the United States during the 1920s was characterized by an inflation of speculative values only. It was a tradermade situation. Prices of commodities remained low, despite the overpricing of securities on the exchange.

The purchasers did not expect their securities to pay dividends. The idea was to hold them awhile and sell them at a profit. It had to stop somewhere, as Paul Warburg remarked in March, 1929. Wall Street did not let it stop until the people had put their savings into these over-priced securities. We had the spectacle of the President of the United States, Calvin Coolidge, acting as a shill for the stock market operators when he recommended to the American people that they continue buying on the market, in 1927. There had been uneasiness about the inflated condition of the market, and the bankers showed their power by getting the President of the United States, the Secretary of the Treasury, and the Chairman of the Board of Governors of the Federal Reserve System to issue statements that brokers' loans were not too high, and that the condition of the stock market was sound.

Irving Fisher warned us in 1927 that the burden of stabilizing prices all over the world would soon fall on the United States. One of the results of the Second World War was the establishment of an International Monetary Fund to do just that. Professor Gustav Cassel remarked in the same year that:

> "The downward movement of prices has not been a spontaneous result of forces beyond our control. It is the result of a policy deliberately framed to bring down prices and give a higher value to the monetary unit."

The Democratic Party, after passing the Federal Reserve Act and leading us into the First World War, assumed the role of an opposition party during the 1920s. They were on the outside of the political fence, and were supported during those lean years by liberal handouts from Bernard Baruch, according to his biography. How far outside of it they were, and how little chance they had in 1928, is shown by a plank in the official Democratic Party platform adopted at Houston on June 28, 1928:

> "The administration of the Federal Reserve System for the advantage of the stock-market speculators should cease. It must be administered for the benefit of farmers, wage-earners, merchants, manufacturers, and others engaged in constructive business."

This idealism insured defeat for its protagonist, Al Smith, who was nominated by Franklin D. Roosevelt. The campaign against Al Smith also was marked by appeals to religious intolerance, because he was a Catholic. The bankers stirred up anti-Catholic sentiment all over the country to achieve the election of their World War I protege, Herbert Hoover.

Instead of being used to promote the financial stability of the country, as had been promised by Woodrow Wilson when the Act was passed, financial instability has been steadily promoted by the Federal Reserve Board. An official memorandum issued by the Board on March 13, 1939, stated that:

> "The Board of Governors of the Federal Reserve System opposes any bill which proposes a stable price level."

Politically, the Federal Reserve Board was used to advance the election of the bankers' candidates during the 1920s. The "Literary Digest" on August 4, 1928, said, on the occasion of the Federal Reserve Board raising the rate to five percent in a Presidential year:

"This reverses the politically desirable cheap money policy of 1927, and gives smooth conditions on the stock market. It was attacked by the Peoples' Lobby of Washington, D.C. which said that 'This increase at a time when farmers needed cheap money to finance the harvesting of their crops was a direct blow at the farmers, who had begun to get back on their feet after the Agricultural Depression of 1920-21.'"

"The New York World" said on that occasion:

"Criticism of Federal Reserve Board policy by many investors is not based on its attempt to deflate the stock market, but on the charge that the Board itself, by last year's policy, is completely responsible for such stock market inflation as exists."

A damning survey of the Federal Reserve System's first fifteen years appears in the "North American Review" of May, 1919, by H. Parker Willis, professional economist who was one of the authors of the Act and First Secretary of the Board from 1914 until 1920. He expresses complete disillusionment.

"My first talk with President-elect Wilson was in 1912. Our conversation related entirely to banking reform. I asked whether he felt confident we could secure the administration of a suitable law and how we should get it applied and enforced. He answered: 'We must rely on American business idealism.' He sought for something which could be trusted to afford opportunity to American Idealism. It did serve to finance the World War and to revise American banking practices. The element of idealism that the President prescribed and believed we could get on the principle of noblesse oblige from American bankers and businessmen was not there. Since the inauguration of the Federal Reserve Act we have suffered one of the most serious financial depressions and revolutions ever known in our history, that of 1920-21. We have seen our agriculture pass through a long period of suffering and even of revolution, during which one million farmers left their farms, due to difficulties with the price of land and the odd status of credit conditions. We have suffered the most extensive era of bank failures ever known in this country. Forty-five hundred banks have closed their doors since the Reserve System began functioning. In some Western towns there have been times when all banks in that community failed, and given banks have failed over and over again. There has been little difference in liability to failure between members and non-member banks of the Federal Reserve System.

"Wilson's choice of the first members of the Federal Reserve Board was not especially happy. They represented a composite group chosen for the express purpose of placating this, that, or the other big interest. It was not strange that appointees used their places to pay debts. When the Board was considering a resolution to the effect that future members of the reserve system should be appointed solely on merit, because of the demonstrated incompetence of some of their number. Comptroller John Skelton Williams moved to strike out the word 'solely' and in this he was sustained by the Board. The inclusion of *certain elements* (Warburg,

Strauss, etc) in the Board gave an opportunity for catering to special interests that was to prove disastrous later on.

"President Wilson erred, as he often erred, in supposing that the holding of an important office would transform an incumbent and revivify his patriotism. The Reserve Board reached the low ebb of the Wilson period with the appointment of a member who was chosen for his ability to get delegates for a Democratic candidate for the Presidency. However, this level was not the dregs reached under President Harding. He appointed an old crony, D.R. Crissinger, as Governor of the Board, and named several other super-serviceable politicians to other places. Before his death he had done his utmost to debauch the whole undertaking. The System has gone steadily downhill ever since.

"Reserve Banks had hardly assumed their first form when it became apparent that local bankers had sought to use them as a means of taking care of 'favorite sons', that is, persons who had by common consent become a kind of general charge upon the banking community, or inefficients of various kinds. When reserve directors were to be chosen, the country bankers often refused to vote, or, when they voted, cast their ballots as directed by city correspondents. In these circumstances popular or democratic control of reserve banks was out of the question. Reasonable efficiency might have been secured if honest men, recognizing their public duty, had assumed power. If such men existed, they did not get on the Federal Reserve Board. In one reserve bank today the chief management is in the hands of a man who never did a day's actual banking in his life, while in another reserve institution both Governor and Chairman are the former heads of now defunct banks. They naturally have a high failure record in their district. In a majority of districts the standard of performance as judged by good banking standards is disgracefully low among reserve executive officials. The policy of the Federal Reserve Bank of Philadelphia is known in the System as the 'Friends and Relatives Banks'.

"It was while making war profits in considerable amounts that someone conceived the idea of using the profits to provide themselves with phenomenally costly buildings. Today the Reserve Banks must keep a full billion dollars of their money constantly at work merely to pay their own expenses in normal times.

"The best illustration of what the System has done and not done is offered by the experience which the country was having with speculation, in May, 1929. Three years prior to that, the present bull market was just getting under way. In the autumn of 1926 a group of bankers, among them one of world famous name, were sitting at a table in a Washington hotel. One of them raised the question whether the low discount rates of the System were not likely to encourage speculation.

" 'Yes', replied the famous banker, 'they will, but that cannot be helped. It is the price we must pay for helping Europe.'

"It may well be questioned whether the encouragement of speculation by the Board has been the price paid for helping Europe or whether it is the price paid to induce a certain class of financiers to help Europe, but in either case European conditions should not have had anything to do with the Board's discount policy. The fact of the matter is that the Federal Reserve Banks do not come into contact with the community.

"The 'small man' from Maine to Texas has gradually been led to invest his savings in the stock market, with the result that the rising tide of speculation, transacted at a higher and higher rate of speed, has swept over the legitimate business of the country.

"In March, 1928, Roy A. Young, Governor of the Board, was called before a Senate committee. 'Do you think the brokers' loans are too high?; he was asked.

" 'I am not prepared to say whether brokers' loans are too high or too low,' he replied. 'but I am sure they are safely and conservatively made.'

"Secretary of the Treasury Mellon in a formal statement assured the country that they were not too high, and Coolidge, using material supplied him by the Federal Reserve Board, made a plain statement to the country that they were not too high. The Federal Reserve Board, charged with the duty of protecting the interests of the average man, thus did its utmost to assure the average man that he should feel no alarm about his savings. Yet the Federal Reserve Board issued on February 2, 1929, a letter addressed to the Reserve Bank Directors cautioning them against the grave danger of further speculation.

"What could be expected from a group of men such as composed the Board, a set of men who were solely interested in standing from under when there was any danger of friction, displaying a bovine and canine appetite for credit and praise, while eager only to 'stand in' with the 'big men' whom they know as the masters of American finance and banking?"

H. Parker Willis omitted any reference to Lord Montague Norman and the machinations of the Bank of England which were about to result in the Crash of 1929 and the Great Depression.

# CHAPTER TWELVE
# The Great Depression

R.G. Hawtrey, the English economist, said, in the March, 1926 American Economic Review:

"When external investment outstrips the supply of general savings the investment market must carry the excess with money borrowed from the banks. A remedy is control of credit by a rise in bank rate."

The Federal Reserve Board applied this control of credit, but not in 1926, nor as a remedial measure. It was not applied until 1929, and then the rate was raised as a punitive measure, to freeze out everybody but the big trusts.

Professor Cassel, in the *Quarterly Journal of Economics*, August 1928, wrote that:

"The fact that a central bank fails to raise its bank rate in accordance with the actual situation of the capital market very much increases the strength of the cyclical movement of trade, with all its pernicious effects on social economy. A rational regulation of the bank rate lies in our hands, and may be accomplished only if we perceive its importance and decide to go in for such a policy. With a bank rate regulated on these lines the conditions for the development of trade cycles would be radically altered, and indeed, our familiar trade cycles would be a thing of the past."

This is the most authoritative premise yet made relating that our business depressions are artificially precipitated. The occurrence of the Panic of 1907, the Agricultural Depression of 1920, and the Great Depression of 1929, all three in good crop years and in periods of national prosperity, suggests that premise is not guesswork. Lord Maynard Keynes pointed out that most theories of the business cycle failed to relate their analysis adequately to the money mechanism. Any survey or study of a depression which failed to list such factors as gold movements and pressures on foreign exchange would be worthless, yet American economists have always dodged this issue.

The League of Nations had achieved its goal of getting the nations of Europe back on the gold standard by 1928, but three-fourths of the world's gold was in France and the United States. The problem was how to get that gold to countries which needed it as a basis for money and credit. The answer was action by the Federal Reserve System.

Following the secret meeting of the Federal Reserve Board and the heads of the foreign central banks in 1927, the Federal Reserve Banks in a few months doubled their holdings of Government securities and acceptances, which resulted in the exportation of five hundred million dollars in gold in that year. The System's market activities forced the rates of call money down on the Stock Exchange, and forced gold out of the country. Foreigners also took this opportunity to purchase heavily in Government securities because of the low call money rate.

"The agreement between the Bank of England and the Washington Federal Reserve authorities many months ago was that we would force the export of 725 million of gold by reducing the bank rates here, thus helping the stabilization of France and Europe and putting France on a gold basis."[89] (April 20, 1928)

On February 6, 1929, Mr. Montagu Norman, Governor of the Bank of England, came to Washington and had a conference with Andrew Mellon, Secretary of the Treasury. Immediately after that mysterious visit, the Federal Reserve Board abruptly changed its policy and pursued a high discount rate policy, abandoning the cheap money policy which it had inaugurated in 1927 after Mr. Norman's other visit. The stock market crash and the deflation of the American people's financial structure was scheduled to take place in March. To get the ball rolling, Paul Warburg gave the official warning to the traders to get out of the market. In his annual report to the stockholders of his International Acceptance Bank, in March, 1929, Mr. Warburg said:

"If the orgies of unrestrained speculation are permitted to spread, the ultimate collapse is certain not only to affect the speculators themselves, but to bring about a general depression involving the entire country."

During three years of "unrestrained speculation", Mr. Warburg had not seen fit to make any remarks about the condition of the Stock Exchange. A friendly organ, *The New York Times*, not only gave the report two columns on its editorial page, but editorially commented on the wisdom and profundity of Mr. Warburg's observations. Mr. Warburg's concern was genuine, for the stock market bubble had gone much farther than it had been intended to go, and the bankers feared the consequences if the people realized what was going on. When this report in *The New York Times* started a sudden wave of selling on the Exchange, the bankers grew panicky, and it was decided to ease the market somewhat. Accordingly, Warburg's National City Bank rushed twenty-five million dollars in cash to the call money market, and postponed the day of the crash.

The revelation of the Federal Reserve Board's final decision to trigger the Crash of 1929 appears, amazingly enough, in *The New York Times*. On April 20, 1929, the *Times* headlined, "Federal Advisory Council Mystery

---

[89]Clarence W. Barron, *They Told Barron*, Harpers, New York, 1930, p. 353

Meeting in Washington. Resolutions were adopted by the council and transmitted to the board, but their purpose was closely guarded. An atmosphere of deep mystery was thrown about the proceedings both by the board and the council. Every effort was made to guard the proceedings of this extraordinary session. Evasive replies were given to newspaper correspondents."

Only the innermost council of "The London Connection" knew that it had been decided at this "mystery meeting" to ring down the curtain on the greatest speculative boom in American history. Those in the know began to sell off all speculative stocks and put their money in government bonds. Those who were not privy to this secret information, and they included some of the wealthiest men in America, continued to hold their speculative stocks and lost everything they had.

In *FDR, My Exploited Father-in-Law*, Col. Curtis B. Dall, who was a broker on Wall Street at that time, writes of the Crash, "Actually it was the calculated 'shearing' of the public by the World Money-Powers, triggered by the planned sudden shortage of the supply of call money in the New York money market."[90] Overnight, the Federal Reserve System had raised the call rate to twenty percent. Unable to meet this rate, the speculators' only alternative was to jump out of windows.

The New York Federal Reserve Bank rate, which dictated the national interest rate, went to six percent on November 1, 1929. After the investors had been bankrupted, it dropped to one and one-half percent on May 8, 1931. Congressman Wright Patman in "A Primer On Money", says that the money supply decreased by eight billion dollars from 1929 to 1933, causing 11,630 banks of the total of 26, 401 in the United States to go bankrupt and close their doors.

The Federal Reserve Board had already warned the stockholders of the Federal Reserve Banks to get out of the Market, on February 6, 1929, but it had not bothered to say anything to the rest of the people. Nobody knew what was going on except the Wall Street bankers who were running the show. Gold movements were completely unreliable. The *Quarterly Journal of Economics* noted that:

> "The question has been raised, not only in this country, but in several European countries, as to whether customs statistics record with accuracy the movements of the precious metals, and, when investigation has been made, confidence in such figures has been weakened rather than strengthened. Any movement between France and England, for instance, should be recorded in each country, but such comparison shows an average yearly discrepancy of fifty million francs for France and eighty-five million francs for England. These enormous discrepancies are not accounted for."

The Right Honorable Reginald McKenna stated that:

---

[90]Col. Curtis B. Dall, *F.D.R., My Exploited Father-in-Law*, Liberty Lobby, Wash., D.C. 1970

"Study of the relations between changes in gold stock and movement in price levels shows what should be very obvious, but is by no means recognized, that the gold standard is in no sense automatic in operation. The gold standard can be, and is, usefully managed and controlled for the benefit of a small group of international traders."

"In August 1929, the Federal Reserve Board raised the rate to six percent. The Bank of England in the next month raised its rate from five and one-half percent to six and one-half percent. Dr. Friday in the September, 1929, issue of *Review of Reviews*, could find no reason for the Board's action:

"The Federal Reserve statement for August 7, 1929, shows that signs of inadequacy for autumn requirements do not exist. Gold resources are considerably more than the previous year, and gold continues to move in, to the financial embarrassment of Germany and England. The reasons for the Board's action must be sought elsewhere. The public has been given only the hint that 'This problem has presented difficulties because of certain peculiar conditions'. Every reason which Governor Young advanced for lowering the bank rate last year exists now. Increasing the rate means that not only is there danger of drawing gold from abroad, but imports of the yellow metal have been in progress for the last four months. To do anything to accentuate this is to take the responsibility for bringing on a world-wide credit deflation."

Thus we find that not only was the Federal Reserve System responsible for the First World War, which it made possible by enabling the United States to finance the Allies, but its policies brought on the world-wide depression of 1929-31. Governor Adolph C. Miller stated at the Senate Investigation of the Federal Reserve Board in 1931 that:

"If we had had no Federal Reserve System, I do not think we would have had as bad a speculative situation as we had, to begin with."

Carter Glass replied, "You have made it clear that the Federal Reserve Board provided a terrific credit expansion by these open market transactions."

Emmanuel Goldenweiser said, "In 1928-29 the Federal Board was engaged in an attempt to restrain the rapid increase in security loans and in stock market speculation. The continuity of this policy of restraint, however, was interrupted by reductions in bill rates in the autumn of 1928 and the summer of 1929."

Both J. P. Morgan and Kuhn, Loeb Co. had "preferred lists" of men to whom they sent advance announcements of profitable stocks. The men on these preferred lists were allowed to purchase these stocks at cost, that is, anywhere from 2 to 15 points a share less than they were sold to the public. The men on these lists were fellow bankers, prominent industrialists, powerful city politicians, national Committeemen of the Republican and Democratic Parties, and rulers of foreign countries. The men on these lists were notified of the coming crash, and sold all but so-called gilt-edged stocks, General Motors, Dupont, etc. The prices on these stocks also sank to record lows, but they came up soon afterwards. How the big bankers operated in

1929 is revealed by a *Newsweek* story on May 30, 1936, when a Roosevelt appointee, Ralph W. Morrison, resigned from the Federal Reserve Board:

"The consensus of opinion is that the Federal Reserve Board has lost an able man. He sold his Texas utilities stock to Insull for ten million dollars, and in 1929 called a meeting and ordered his banks to close out all security loans by September 1. As a result, they rode through the depression with flying colors."

Predictably enough, all of the big bankers rode through the depression "with flying colors." The people who suffered were the workers and farmers who had invested their money in get-rich stocks, after the President of the United States, Calvin Coolidge, and the Secretary of the Treasury, Andrew Mellon, had persuaded them to do it.

There had been some warnings of the approaching crash in England, which American newspapers never saw. *The London Statist* on May 25, 1929 said:

"The banking authorities in the United States apparently want a business panic to curb speculation."

*The London Economist* on May 11, 1929, said:

"The events of the past year have seen the beginnings of a new technique, which, if maintained and developed, may succeed in 'rationing the speculator without injuring the trader.'"

Governor Charles S. Hamlin quoted this statement at the Senate hearings in 1931 and said, in corroboration of it:

"That was the feeling of certain members of the Board, to remove Federal Reserve credit from the speculator without injuring the trader."

Governor Hamlin did not bother to point out that the "speculators" he was out to break were the school-teachers and small town merchants who had put their savings into the stock market, or that the "traders" he was trying to protect were the big Wall Street operators, Bernard Baruch and Paul Warburg.

When the Federal Reserve Bank of New York raised its rate to six percent on August 9, 1929, market conditions began which culminated in tremendous selling orders from October 24 into November, which wiped out a hundred and sixty billion dollars worth of security values. That was a hundred and sixty billions which the American citizens had one month and did not have the next. Some idea of the calamity may be had if we remember that our enormous outlay of money and goods in the Second World War amounted to not much more than two hundred billions of dollars, and a great deal of that remained as negotiable securities in the national debt. The stock market crash is the greatest misfortune which the United States has ever suffered.

The Academy of Political Science of Columbia University in its annual meeting in January, 1930, held a post-mortem on the Crash of 1929. Vice-

President Paul Warburg was to have presided, and Director Ogden Mills was to have played an important part in the discussion. However, these two gentlemen did not show up. Professor Oliver M.W. Sprague of Harvard University remarked of the crash:

> "We have here a beautiful laboratory case of the stock market's dropping apparently from its own weight."

It was pointed out that there was no exhaustion of credit, as in 1893, nor any currency famine, as in the Panic of 1907, when clearing-house certificates were resorted to, nor a collapse of commodity prices, as in 1920. What then, had caused the crash? The people had purchased stocks at high prices and expected the prices to continue to rise. The prices had to come down, and they did. It was obvious to the economists and bankers gathered over their brandy and cigars at the Hotel Astor that the people were at fault. Certainly the people had made a mistake in buying over-priced securities, but they had been talked into it by every leading citizen from the President of the United States on down. Every magazine of national circulation, every big newspaper, and every prominent banker, economist, and politician, had joined in the big confidence game of urging people to buy those over-priced securities. When the Federal Reserve Bank of New York raised its rate to six percent, in August 1929, people began to get out of the market, and it turned into a panic which drove the prices of securities down far below their natural levels. As in previous panics, this enabled both Wall Street and foreign operators in the know to pick up "blue-chip" and gilt-edged" securities for a fraction of their real value.

The Crash of 1929 also saw the formation of giant holding companies which picked up these cheap bonds and securities, such as the Marine Midland Corporation, the Lehman Corporation, and the Equity Corporation. In 1929 J.P. Morgan Company organized the giant food trust, Standard Brands. There was an unequalled opportunity for trust operators to enlarge and consolidate their holdings.

Emmanuel Goldenweiser, director of research for the Federal Reserve System, said, in 1947:

> "It is clear in retrospect that the Board should have ignored the speculative expansion and allowed it to collapse of its own weight."

This admission of error eighteen years after the event was small comfort to the people who lost their savings in the Crash.

The Wall Street Crash of 1929 was the beginning of a world-wide credit deflation which lasted through 1932, and from which the Western democracies did not recover until they began to rearm for the Second World War. During this depression, the trust operators achieved further control by their backing of three international swindlers, The Van Sweringen brothers, Samuel Insull, and Ivar Kreuger. These men pyramided billions of dollars worth of securities to fantastic heights. The bankers who promoted them and floated their stock issue could have stopped them at any time, by calling loans of less than a million dollars, but they let these men go on until they had incorporated many industrial and financial properties into holding companies, which the banks then took over for nothing. Insull piled up public utility holdings throughout the Middle West, which the banks got for a fraction of their worth. Ivar Kreuger was backed by Lee Higginson Company, supposedly one of the nation's most reputable banking houses. *The Saturday Evening Post* called him "more than a financial titan", and the English review *Fortnightly* said, in an article written December 1931, under the title, "A Chapter in Constructive Finance": "It is as a financial irrigator that Kreuger has become of such vital importance to Europe."*

"Financial irrigator" we may remember, was the title bestowed upon Jacob Schiff by *Newsweek Magazine*, when it described how Schiff had bought up American railroads with Rothschild's money.

*The New Republic* remarked on January 25th, 1933, when it commented on the fact that Lee Higginson Company had handled Kreuger and Toll Securities on the American market:

"Three-quarters of a billion dollars was made away with. Who was able to dictate to the French police to keep secret the news of this extremely important *suicide* for some hours, during which somebody sold Kreuger securities in large amounts, thus getting out of the market before the debacle?"

The Federal Reserve Board could have checked the enormous credit expansion of Insull and Kreuger by investigating the security on which their loans were being made, but the Governors never made any examination of the activities of these men.

The modern bank with the credit facilities it affords, gives an opportunity which had not previously existed for such operators as Kreuger to make an appearance of abundant capital by the aid of borrowed capital. This enables the speculator to buy securities with securities. The only limit to the amount he can corner is the amount to which the banks will back him, and, if a speculator is being promoted by a reputable banking house, as Kreuger was promoted by Lee Higginson Company, the only way he could be stopped would be by an investigation of his actual financial resources, which in Kreuger's case would have proved to be nil.

The leader of the American people during the Crash of 1929 and the subsequent depression was Herbert Hoover. After the first break of the

---

*NOTE: Ivar Kreuger, we may recall, was occasionally the personal guest of his old friend, President Herbert Hoover, at the White House. Hoover seems to have maintained a cordial relationship with many of the most prominent swindlers of the twentieth century, including his partner, Emile Francqui. The receivership of the billion dollar Kreuger Fraud was handled by Samuel Untermeyer, former counsel for Pujo Committee hearings.

market (the five billion dollars in security values which disappeared on October 24, 1929) President Hoover said:

"The fundamental business of the country, that is, production and distribution of commodities, is on a sound and prosperous basis."

His Secretary of the Treasury, Andrew Mellon, stated on December 25, 1929, that:

"The Government's business is in sound condition."

His own business, the Aluminum Company of America, apparently was not doing so well, for he had reduced the wages of all employees by ten percent.

*The New York Times* reported on April 7, 1931, "Montagu Norman, Governor of the Bank of England, conferred with the Federal Reserve Board here today. Mellon, Meyer, and George L. Harrison, Governor of the Federal Reserve Bank of New York, were present."

The London Connection had sent Norman over this time to ensure that the Great Depression was proceeding according to schedule. Congressman Louis McFadden had complained, as reported in *The New York Times*, July 4, 1930, "Commodity prices are being reduced to 1913 levels. Wages are being reduced by the labor surplus of four million unemployed. The Morgan control of the Federal Reserve System is exercised through control of the Federal Reserve Bank of New York, the mediocre representation and acquiescense of the Federal Reserve Board in Washington." As the depression deepened, the trust's lock on the American economy strengthened, but no finger was pointed at the parties who were controlling the system.

# CHAPTER THIRTEEN
# The 1930's

In 1930 Herbert Hoover appointed to the Federal Reserve Board an old friend from World War I days, Eugene Meyer, Jr., who had a long record of public service dating from 1915, when he went into partnership with Bernard Baruch in the Alaska-Juneau Gold Mining Company. Meyer had been a Special Advisor to the War Industries Board on Non-Ferrous Metals (gold, silver, etc.); Special Assistant to the Secretary of War on aircraft production; in 1917 he was appointed to the National Committee on War Savings, and was made Chairman of the War Finance Corporation from 1918-1926. He then was appointed chairman of the Federal Farm Loan Board from 1927-29. Hoover put him on the Federal Reserve Board in 1930, and Franklin D. Roosevelt created the Reconstruction Finance Corporation for him in 1932, and he headed the International Bank for Reconstruction and Development in 1946. Meyer must have been a man of exceptional ability to hold so many important posts. However, there were some Senators who did not believe he should hold any Government office, because of his family background as an international gold dealer and his mysterious operations in billions of dollars of Government securities in the First World War. Consequently, the Senate held Hearings to determine whether Meyer ought to be on the Federal Reserve Board.

At these Hearings, Representative Louis T. McFadden, Chairman of the House Banking and Currency Committee, said:

"Eugene Meyer, Jr. has had his own crowd with him in the government since he started in 1917. His War Finance Corporation personnel took over the Federal Farm Loan System, and almost immediately afterwards, the Kansas City Joint Stock Land Bank and the Ohio Joint Stock Land Bank failed."

REPRESENTATIVE RAINEY: Mr. Meyer, when he nominally resigned as head of the Federal Farm Loan Board, did not really cease his activities there. He left behind him an able body of wreckers. They are continuing his policies and consulting with him. Before his appointment, he was frequently in consultation with Assistant Secretary of the Treasury Dewey. Just before his appointment, the Chicago Joint Land Stock Bank, the Dallas Joint Stock Land Bank, the Kansas City Joint Land Stock Bank, and the Des Moines Land Bank were all functioning. Their bonds were selling at par. The then farm loan commissioner had an understanding with Secretary Dewey that nothing would be done without the consent and approval of the Federal Farm Loan Board. A few days afterwards, United States Marshals, with pistols strapped at their sides, and sometimes with drawn pistols, entered these five banks and demanded that the banks be turned over to them. Word went out all over the United States, through the newspapers, as to what had happened, and these banks were ruined. This led to the breach with the old Federal Farm Loan Board, and to the resignation of three of its members, and the appointment of Mr. Meyer to be head of that Board.

SENATOR CAREY: Who authorized the marshals to take over the banks?

REP. RAINEY: Assistant Secretary of the Treasury Dewey. That started the ruin of all these rural banks, and the Gianninis bought them up in great numbers."

*World's Work* of February 1931, said:

"When the World War began for us in 1917, Mr. Eugene Meyer, Jr. was among the first to be called to Washington. In April, 1918, President Wilson named him Director of the War Finance Corporation. This corporation loaned out 700 million dollars to banking and financial institutions."

The Senate Hearings on Eugene Meyer, Jr. continued:

REPRESENTATIVE MCFADDEN: "Lazard Freres, the international banking house of New York and Paris, was a Meyer family banking house. It frequently figures in imports and exports of gold, and one of the important functions of the Federal Reserve System has to do with gold movements in the maintenance of its own operations. In looking over the minutes of the hearing we had last Thursday, Senator Fletcher had asked Mr. Meyer, 'Have you any connections with international banking?' Mr. Meyer had answered, 'Me? Not personally.' This last question and answer do not appear in the stenographic transcript. Senator Fletcher remembers asking the question and the answer. It is an odd omission.

SENATOR BROOKHART: I understand that Mr. Meyer looked it over for corrections.

REPRESENTATIVE MCFADDEN: Mr. Meyer is a brother-in-law of George Blumenthal, a member of the firm of J.P. Morgan Company, which represents the Rothschild interests. He also is a liason officer between the French Government and J.P. Morgan. Edmund Platt, who had eight years to go on a term of ten years as Governor of the Federal Reserve Board, resigned to make room for Mr. Meyer. Platt was given a Vice-Presidency of Marine Midland Corporation by Meyer's brother-in-law Alfred A. Cook. Eugene Meyer, Jr. as head of the War Finance Corporation, engaged in the placing of two billion dollars in Government securities, placed many of those orders first with the banking house now located at 14 Wall Street in the name of Eugene Meyer, Jr. Mr. Meyer is now a large stockholder in the Allied Chemical Corporation. I call your attention to House Report No. 1635, 68th Congress, 2nd Session, which reveals that *at least twenty-four million dollars in bonds were duplicated. Ten billion dollars worth of bonds were surreptitiously destroyed.* Our committee on Banking and Currency found the records of the War Finance Corporation under Eugene Meyer, Jr. extremely faulty. While the books were being brought before our committee by the people who were custodians of them and taken back to the Treasury at night, the committee discovered that alterations were being made in the permanent records."

The record of public service did not prevent Eugene Meyer, Jr. from continuing to serve the American people on the Federal Reserve Board, as Chairman of the Reconstruction Finance Corporation, and as head of the International Bank.

President Rand, of the Marine Midland Corporation, questioned about his sudden desire for the services of Edmund Platt, said:

"We pay Mr. Platt $22,000 a year, and we took his secretary over, of course." This meant another five thousand a year.

Senator Brookhart showed that Eugene Meyer, Jr. administered the Federal Farm Loan Board against the interests of the American farmer, saying:

"Mr. Meyer never loaned more than 180 million dollars of the capital stock of 500 million dollars of the farm loan board, so that in aiding the farmers he was not even able to use half of the capital."

MR. MEYER: Senator Kenyon wrote me a letter which showed that I cooperated with great advantage to the people of Iowa.

SENATOR BROOKHART: "You went out and took the opposite side from the Wall Street crowd. They always send somebody out to do that. I have not yet discovered in your statements much interest in making loans to the farmers at large, or any real effort to help their condition. In your two years as head of the Federal farm loan board you made very few loans compared to your capital. You loaned only one-eighth of the demand, according to your own statement."

Despite the damning evidence uncovered at these Senate Hearings, Eugene Meyer, Jr. remained on the Federal Reserve Board.

During this tragic period, chairman Louis McFadden of the House Banking and Currency Committee continued his lone crusade against the "London Connection" which had wrecked the nation. On June 10, 1932, McFadden addressed the House of Representatives:

"Some people think the Federal Reserve banks are United States Government institutions. They are not government institutions. They are private credit monopolies which prey upon the people of the United

States for the benefit of themselves and their foreign customers. The Federal Reserve banks are the agents of the foreign central banks. Henry Ford has said, 'The one aim of these financiers is world control by the creation of inextinguishable debts.' The truth is the Federal Reserve Board has usurped the Government of the United States by the arrogant credit monopoly which operates the Federal Reserve Board and the Federal Reserve Banks."

On January 13, 1932, McFadden had introduced a resolution indicting the Federal Reserve Board of Governors for "Criminal Conspiracy":

"Whereas I charge them, jointly and severally, with the crime of having treasonably conspired and acted against the peace and security of the United States and having treasonably conspired to destroy constitutional government in the United States. Resolved, that the Committee on the Judiciary is authorized and directed as a whole or by subcommittee to investigate the official conduct of the Federal Reserve Board and agents to determine whether, in the opinion of the said committee, they have been guilty of any high crime or misdemeanour which in the contemplation of the Constitution requires the interposition of the Constitutional powers of the House."

No action was taken on this Resolution. McFadden came back on December 13, 1932 with a motion to impeach President Herbert Hoover. Only five Congressmen stood with him on this, and the resolution failed. The Republican majority leader of the House remarked, "Louis T. McFadden is now politically dead."

On May 23, 1933, McFadden introduced House Resolution No. 158, Articles of Impeachment against the Secretary of the Treasury, two Assistant Secretaries of the Treasury, the Federal Reserve Board of Governors, and officers and directors of the Federal Reserve Banks for their guilt and collusion in causing the Great Depression. "I charge them with having unlawfully taken over 80 billion dollars from the United States Government in the year 1928, the said unlawful taking consisting of the unlawful recreation of claims against the United States Treasury to the extent of over 80 billion dollars in the year 1928, and in each year subsequent, and by having robbed the United States Government and the people of the United States by their theft and sale of the gold reserve of the United States."

The Resolution never reached the floor. A whispering campaign that McFadden was insane swept Washington, and in the next Congressional elections, he was overwhelmingly defeated by thousands of dollars poured into his home district of Canton, Pennsylvania.

In 1932, the American people elected Franklin D. Roosevelt President of the United States. This was hailed as the freeing of the American people from the evil influence which had brought on the Great Depression, the ending of Wall Street domination, and the disappearance of the banker from Washington.

Roosevelt owed his political career to a fortuitous circumstance. As Assistant Secretary of the Navy during World War I, because of old school ties, he had intervened to prevent prosecution of a large ring of homosexuals in the Navy which included several Groton and Harvard chums. This brought him to the favorable attention of a wealthy international homosexual set which travelled back and forth between New York and Paris, and which was presided over by Bessie Marbury, of a very old and prominent New York family. Bessie's "wife", who lived with her for a number of years, was Elsie de Wolfe, later Lady Mendl in a "mariage de convenance", the arbiter of the international set. They recruited J.P. Morgan's youngest daughter, Anne Morgan, into their circle, and used her fortune to restore the Villa Trianon in Paris, which became their headquarters. During World War I, it was used as a hospital. Bessie Marbury expected to be awarded the Legion of Honor by the French Government as a reward, but J.P. Morgan, Jr., who despised her for corrupting his youngest sister, requested the French Government to withhold the award, which they did. Smarting from this rebuff, Bessie Marbury threw herself into politics, and became a power in the Democratic National Party. She had also recruited Eleanor Roosevelt into her circle, and, during a visit to Hyde Park, Eleanor confided that she was desperate to find something for "poor Franklin" to do, as he was confined to a wheelchair, and was very depressed.

"I know what we'll do," exclaimed Bessie. "We'll run him for Governor of New York!" Because of her power, she succeeded in this goal, and Roosevelt later became President.

One of the men Roosevelt brought down from New York with him as a Special Advisor to the Treasury was Earl Bailie of J & W Seligman Company, who had become notorious as the man who handed the $415,000 bribe to Juan Leguia, son of the President of Peru, in order to get the President to accept a loan from J & W Seligman Company. There was a great deal of criticism of this appointment, and Mr. Roosevelt, in keeping with his new role as defender of the people, sent Earl Bailie back to bribing in New York.

Franklin D. Roosevelt himself was an international banker of ill repute, having floated large issues of foreign bonds in this country in the 1920s. These bonds defaulted, and our citizens lost millions of dollars, but they still wanted Mr. Roosevelt as President. The New York Directory of Directors lists Mr. Roosevelt as President and Director of United European Investors, Ltd., in 1923 and 1924, which floated many millions of German marks in this country, all of which defaulted. Poor's Directory of Directors lists him as a director of The International Germanic Trust Company in 1928. Franklin D. Roosevelt was also an advisor to the

Federal International Banking Corporation, an Anglo-American outfit dealing in foreign securities in the United States.

Roosevelt's law firm of Roosevelt and O'Connor during the 1920s represented many international corporations. His law partner, Basil O'Connor, was a director in the following corporations:

Cuban-American Manganese Corporation, Venezuela-Mexican Oil Corporation, Honduras Timber Corporation, Federal International Corporation, West Indies Sugar Corporation, American Reserve Insurance Corporation, Warm Springs Foundation. He was director in other corporations, and later head of the American Red Cross.

When Franklin D. Roosevelt took office as President of the United States, he appointed as Director of the Budget James Paul Warburg, son of Paul Warburg, and Vice President of the International Acceptance Bank and other corporations. Roosevelt appointed as Secretary of the Treasury W.H. Woodin, one of the biggest industrialists in the country, Director of the American Car and Foundry Company and numerous other locomotive works, Remington Arms, The Cuba Company, Consolidated Cuba Railroads, and other big corporations. Woodin was later replaced by Henry Morgenthau, Jr., son of the Harlem real estate operator who had helped put Woodrow Wilson in the White House. With such a crew as this, Roosevelt's promises of radical social changes showed little likelihood of fulfillment. One of the first things he did was to declare a bankers' moratorium, to help the bankers get their records in order.

*World's Work* says:

"Congress has left Charles G. Dawes and Eugene Meyer, Jr. free to appraise, *by their own methods*, the security which prospective borrowers of the two billion dollar capital may offer."

Roosevelt also set up the Securities Exchange Commission, to see to it that no new faces got into the Wall Street gang, which caused the following colloquy in Congress:

REPRESENTATIVE WOLCOTT: At hearings before this committee in 1933, the economists showed us charts which proved beyond all doubt that the dollar value of commodities followed the price level of gold. It did not, did it?

LEON HENDERSON: No.

REPRESENTATIVE GIFFORD: Wasn't Joe Kennedy put in [as Chairman of the Securities Exchange Committee] by President Roosevelt because he was sympathetic with big business?

LEON HENDERSON: I think so.

Paul Einzig pointed out in 1935 that:

"President Roosevelt was the first to declare himself openly in favor of a monetary policy aiming at a deliberately engineered rise in prices. In a negative sense his policy was successful. Between 1933 and 1935 he succeeded in reducing private indebtedness, but this was done at the cost of increasing public indebtedness." In other words, he eased the burden of debts off of the rich onto the poor, since the rich are few and the poor many.

Senator Robert L. Owen, testifying before the House Committee on Banking and Currency in 1938, said:

"I wrote into the bill which was introduced by me in the Senate on June 26, 1913, a provision that the powers of the System should be employed to promote a stable price level, which meant a dollar of stable purchasing, debt-paying power. It was stricken out. The powerful money interests got control of the Federal Reserve Board through Mr. Paul Warburg, Mr. Albert Strauss, and Mr. Adolph C. Miller and they were able to have that secret meeting of May 18, 1920, and bring about a contraction of credit so violent it threw five million people out of employment. In 1920 that Reserve Board deliberately caused the Panic of 1921. The same people, unrestrained in the stock market, expanding credit to a great excess between 1926 and 1929, raised the price of stocks to a fantastic point where they could not possibly earn dividends, and when the people realized this, they tried to get out, resulting in the Crash of October 24, 1929."

Senator Owen did not go into the question of whether the Federal Reserve Board could be held repsonsible to the public. Actually, they cannot. They are public officials who are appointed by the President, but their salaries are paid by the private stockholders of the Federal Reserve Banks.

Governor W.P.G. Harding of the Federal Reserve Board testified in 1921 that:

"The Federal Reserve Bank is an institution owned by the stockholding member banks. The Government has not a dollar's worth of stock in it."

However, the Government does give the Federal Reserve System the use of its billions of dollars of credit, and this gives the Federal Reserve its characteristic of a central bank, the power to issue currency on the Government's credit. We do not have Federal Government notes or gold certificates as currency. We have Federal Reserve Bank notes, issued by the Federal Reserve Banks, and every dollar they print is a dollar in their pocket.

W. Randolph Burgess, of the Federal Reserve Bank of New York, stated before the Academy of Political Science in 1930 that:

"In its major principles of operation the Federal Reserve System is no different from other banks of issue, such as the Bank of England, the Bank of France, or the Reichsbank."

All of these central banks have the power of issuing currency in their respective countries. Thus, the people do not own their own money in Europe, nor do they own it here. It is privately printed for private profit. The people have no sovereignty over their money, and it has developed that they have no sovereignty over other major political issues such as foreign policy.

As a central bank of issue, the Federal Reserve System had behind it all the enormous wealth of the American people. When it began operations in 1913, it created a serious threat to the central banks of the impoverished countries of Europe. Becuase it represented this great wealth, it attracted far more gold than was desirable in the 1920s, and it was apparent that soon all of the world's gold would be piled up in this country. This would make the gold standard a joke in Europe, because they would have no gold over there to back their issue of money and credit. It was the Federal Reserve's avowed aim in 1927, after the secret meeting with the heads of the foreign central banks, to get large quantities of that gold sent back to Europe, and its methods of doing so, the low interest rate and heavy purchases of Government securities, which created vast sums of new money, intensified the stock market speculation and made the stock market crash and resultant depression a national disaster.

Since the Federal Reserve System was guilty of causing this disaster, we might suppose that they would have tried to alleviate it. However, through the dark years of 1931 and 1932, the Governors of the Fedral Reserve Board saw the plight of the American people steadily worsening and did nothing to help them. This was more criminal than the original plotting of the Depression. Anyone who lived through those years in this country remembers the widespread unemployment, the misery, and the hunger of our people. At any time during those years the Federal Reserve Board could have acted to relieve this situation.

The problem was to get some money back into circulation. So much of the money normally used to pay rent and food bills had been sucked into Wall Street that there was no money to carry on the business of living. In many areas, people printed their own money on wood and paper for use in their communities, and this money was good, since it represented obligations to each other which people fulfilled.

The Federal Reserve System was a central bank of issue. It had the power to, and did, when it suited its owners, issue millions of dollars of money. Why did it not do so in 1931 and 1932? The Wall Street bankers were through with Mr. Herbert Hoover, and they wanted Franklin D. Roosevelt to come in on a wave of glory as the saviour of the nation. Therefore, the American people had to starve and suffer until March of 1933, when the White Knight came riding in with his crew of Wall Street bribers and put some money into circulation. That was all there was to it. As soon as Mr. Roosevelt took office, the Federal Reserve began to buy Government securities at the rate of ten million dollars a week for ten weeks, and created a hundred million dollars in new money, which alleviated the critical famine of money and credit, and the factories started hiring people again.

During the Roosevelt Administration, The Federal Reserve Board, insofar as the public was concerned, was Marriner Eccles, an emulator and admirer of "the Chief". Eccles was a Utah banker, President of the First Securities Corporation, a family investment trust consisting of a number of banks which Eccles had picked up cheap during the Agricultural Depression of 1920-21. Eccles also was a director of such corporations as Pet Milk Company, Mountain States Implement Company, and Amalgamated Sugar. As a big banker, Eccles fitted in well with the group of powerful men who were operating Roosevelt.

There was some discussion in Congress as to whether Eccles ought to be on the Federal Reserve Board at the same time he had all of these banks in Utah, but he testified that he had very little to do with the First Securities Corporation besides being President of it, and so he was confirmed as Chairman of the Board.

Eugene Meyer, Jr. now resigned from the Board to spend more of his time lending the two billion dollar capital of the Reconstruction Finance Corporation, and determining the value of collateral by his own methods.

The Banking Act of 1935, which greatly increased Roosevelt's power over the nation's finances, was an integral part of the legislation by which he proposed to extend his reign in the United States. It was not opposed by the people as was the National Recovery Act, because it was not so naked an infringement of their liberties. It was, however, an important measure. First of all, it extended the terms of office of the Federal Reserve Board of Governors to fourteen years, or, three and a half times the length of a Presidential term. This meant that a President assuming office who might be hostile to the Board could not appoint a majority to it who would be favorable to him. Thus, a monetary policy inaugurated before a President came into the White House would go on regardless of his wishes.

The Banking Act of 1935 also repealed the clause of the Glass-Steagall Banking Act of 1933, which had provided that a banking house could not be on the Stock Exchange and also be involved in investment banking. This clause was a good one, since it prevented a banking house from lending money to a corporation which it owned. Still it is to be remembered that this clause covered up some other provisions in that Act, such as the creation of the Federal Deposit Insurance Corporation, providing insurance money to the amount of 150 million dollars, to guarantee fifteen billion dollars worth of deposits. This increased the power of the big bankers over small banks and gave them another excuse to investigate them. The Banking Act of 1933 also legislated that all earnings of the Federal Reserve Banks must by law go to the banks themselves. At last the provision in the Act that the Government share in the profits was gotten rid of. It had never been observed, and the increase in the assets of the Federal Reserve Banks from 143 million dollars in 1913 to 45 billion dollars in 1949 went entirely to the private stockholders of the banks. Thus, the one constructive provision of the Banking Act of 1933 was repealed in 1935, and also the Federal Reserve Banks were now permitted to loan directly to industry, competing with the member banks, who could not hope to match their capacity in arranging large loans.

When the provision that banks could not be involved in investment banking and operate on the Stock Exchange was repealed in 1935, Carter Glass, originator of that provision, was asked by reporters:

"Does that mean that J.P. Morgan can go back into investment banking?"

"Well, why not?" replied Senator Glass. "There has been an outcry all over the country that the banks will not make loans. Now the Morgans can go back to underwriting."

Because that provision was unfavorable to them, the bankers had simply clamped down on making loans until it was repealed.

*Newsweek* of March 14, 1936, noted that:

> "The Federal Reserve Board fired nine chairmen of Reserve Banks, explaining that 'it intended to make the chairmanships of the Reserve Banks largely a part-time job on an honorary basis.'"

This was another instance of the centralization of control in the Federal Reserve System. The regional district system had never been an important factor in the administration of monetary policy, and the Board was not cutting down on its officials outside of Washington. The Chairman of the Senate Committee on Banking and Currency had asked, during the Gold Reserve Hearings of 1934:

> "Is it not true, Governor Young, that the Secretary of the Treasury for the past twelve years has dominated the policy of the Federal Reserve Banks and the Federal Reserve Board with respect to the purchase of United States bonds?"

Governor Young had denied this, but it had already been brought out that on both of his hurried trips to this country in 1927 and 1929 to dictate Federal Reserve policy, Governor Montagu Norman of the Bank of England had gone directly to Andrew Mellon, Secretary of the Treasury, to get him to purchase Government securities on the open market and start the movement of gold out of this country back to Europe.

The Gold Reserve Hearings had also brought in other people who had more than a passing interest in the operations of the Federal Reserve System. James Paul Warburg, just back from the London Economic Conference with Professor O.M.W. Sprague and Henry L. Stimson, came in to declare that he thought we ought to modernize the gold standard. Frank Vanderlip suggested that we do away with the Federal Reserve Board and set up a Federal Monetary Authority. This would have made no difference to the New York bankers, who would have selected the personnel anyway. And Senator Robert L. Owen, longtime critic of the system, made the following statement:

"The people did not know the Federal Reserve Banks were organized for profit-making. They were intended to stabilize the credit and currency supply of the country. That end has not been accomplished. Indeed, there has been the most *remarkable variation* in the purchasing power of money since the System went into effect. The Federal Reserve men are chosen by the big banks, through discreet little campaigns, and they naturally follow the ideals which are portrayed to them as the soundest from a financial point of view."

Benjamin Anderson, economist for the Chase National Bank of New York, said:

"At the moment, 1934, we have 900 million dollars excess reserves. In 1924, with increased reserves of 300 million, you got some three or four billion in bank expansion of credit very quickly. That extra money was put out by the Federal Reserve Banks in 1924 through buying government securities and was the cause of the rapid expansion of bank credit. The banks continued to get excess reserves because more gold came in, and because, whenever there was a slackening, the Federal Reserve people would put out some more. They held back a bit in 1926. Things firmed up a bit that year. And then in 1927 they put out less than 300 million additional reserves, set the wild stock market going, and that led us right into the smash of 1929."

Dr. Anderson also stated that:

"The money of the Federal Reserve Banks is money they created. When they buy Government securities they create reserves. They pay for the Government securities by giving checks on themselves, and those checks come to the commercial banks and are by them deposited in the Federal Reserve Banks, and then money exists which did not exist before."

SENATOR BULKLEY: It does not increase the circulating medium at all?

ANDERSON: No.

This is an explanation of the manner in which the Federal Reserve Banks increased their assets from 143 million dollars to 45 billion dollars in thirty-five years. They did not produce anything, they were nonproductive enterprises, and yet they had this enormous profit, merely by creating money, 95 percent of it in the form of credit, which did not add to the circulating medium. It was not distributed among the people in the form of wages, nor did it increase the buying power of the farmers and workers. It was credit-money created by bankers for the use and profit of bankers, who increased their wealth by more than forty billion dollars in a few years because they had obtained control of the Government's credit in 1913 by passing the Federal Reserve Act.

Marriner Eccles also had much to say about the creation of money. He considered himself an economist, and had been brought into the Government service by Stuart Chase and Rexford Guy Tugwell, two of Roosevelt's early brain-trusters. Eccles was the only one of the Roosevelt crowd who stayed in office throughout his administration.

Before the House Banking and Currency Committee on June 24, 1941, Governor Eccles said:

"Money is created out of the *right* to issue credit-money."

Turning over the Government's credit to private bankers in 1913 gave them unlimited opportunities to create money. The Federal Reserve System could also destroy money in large quantities through open market operations. Eccles said, at the Silver Hearings of 1939:

"When you sell bonds on the open market, you extinguish reserves."

Extinguishing reserves means wiping out a basis for money and credit issue, or, tightening up on money and credit, a condition which is usually even more favorable to bankers than the creation of money. Calling in or destroying money gives the banker immediate and unlimited control of the financial situation, since he is the only one with money and the only one with the power to issue money in a time of money shortage. The money panics of 1873, 1893, 1920-21, and 1929-31, were characterized by a drawing in of the circulating medium. In economical terms, this does not sound like such a terrible thing, but when it means that people do not have money to pay their rent or buy food, and when it means that an employer has to lay off three-fourths of his help because he cannot borrow the money to pay them, the enormous guilt of the bankers and the long record of suffering and misery for which they are responsible would suggest that no punishment might be too severe for their crimes against their fellowmen.

On September 30, 1940, Governor Eccles said:

"If there were no debts in our money system, there would be no money."

This is an accurate statement about our money system. Instead of money being created by the production of the people, the annual increase in goods and services, it is created by the bankers out of the debts of the people. Because it is inadequate, it is subject to great fluctuations and is basically unstable. These fluctuations are also a source of great profit. For that reason, the Federal Reserve Board has consistently opposed any legislation which attempts to stabilize the monetary system. Its position has been set forth definitively in Chairman Eccles' letter to Senator Wagner on March 9, 1939, and the Memorandum issued by the Board on March 13, 1939.

Chairman Eccles wrote that:

". . . you are advised that the Board of Governors of the Federal Reserve System does not favor the enactment of Senate Bill No. 31, a bill to amend the Federal Reserve Act, or any other legislation of this general character."

The Memorandum of the Board stated, in its "Memorandum on Proposals to maintain prices at fixed levels":

"The Board of Governors oposes any bill which proposes a stable price level, on the grounds that prices do not depend primarily on the price or cost of money; that the Board's control over money cannot be made complete; and that steady average prices, even if obtainable by official action, would not insure lasting prosperity."

Yet William McChesney Martin, the Chairman of the Board of Governors in 1952, said before the Subcommittee on Debt Control, the Patman Committee, on March 10, 1952 that "One of the fundamental purposes of the Federal Reserve Act is to protect the value of the dollar."

Senator Flanders questioned him: "Is that specifically stated in the original legislation setting up the Federal Reserve System?"

"No," replied Mr. Martin, "but it is inherent in the entire legislative history and in the surrounding circumstances."

Senator Robert L. Owen has told use how it was taken out of the original legislation against his will, and that the Board of Governors has opposed such legislation. Apparently Mr. Martin does not know this.

Steady average prices, indeed, are impossible so long as we have the speculators on the stock exchange driving prices up and down in order to reap profits for themselves. Despite Governor Eccles' insistence that steady average prices would not *insure* lasting prosperity, they could do much to bring about this condition. A man on a yearly wage of $2,500 is not more prosperous if the price of bread increases five cents a loaf during the year.

In 1935, Eccles said before the House Committee on Banking and Currency:

"The Government controls the gold reserve, that is, the power to issue money and credit, thus largely regulating the price structure."

This is an almost direct contradiction of Eccles' statement in 1939 that prices do not depend, primarily, on the price or cost of money.

In 1935, Governor Eccles stated before the House Committee:

"The Federal Reserve Board has the power of open market operations. Open-market operations are the most important single instrument of control over the volume and cost of credit in this country. When I say "credit" in this connection, I mean money, because by far the largest part of money in use by the people of this country is in the form of bank credit or bank deposits. When the Federal Reserve Banks buy bills or securities in the open market, they increase the volume of the people's money and lower its cost; and when they sell in the open market they decrease the volume of money and increase its cost. Authority over these operations, which affect the welfare of the whole people, must be invested in a body representing the national interest."

Governor Eccles testimony exposes the heart of the money machine which Paul Warburg revealed to his incredulous fellow bankers at Jekyll Island in 1910. Most Americans comment that they cannot understand how the Federal Reserve System operates. It remains beyond understanding, not because it is complex, but because it is so simple. If a confidence man comes up to you and offers to demonstrate his marvelous money machine, you watch while he puts in a blank piece of paper, and cranks out a $100 bill. That is the Federal Reserve System. You then offer to buy this marvelous money machine, but you cannot. It is owned by the private stockholders of the Federal Reserve Banks, whose identities can be traced partially, but not completely, to "the London Connection."

At the House Banking and Currency Committee Hearings on June 6, 1960, Congressman Wright Patman, Chairman, questioned Carl E. Allen, President of the Federal Reserve Bank of Chicago. (p. 4). PATMAN: "Now Mr. Allen, when the Federal Reserve Open Market Committee buys a million dollar bond you create the money on the credit of the Nation to pay for that bond, don't you? ALLEN: That is correct. PATMAN: And the credit of the Nation is represented by Federal Reserve Notes in that case, isn't it? If the banks want the actual money, you give Federal Reserve notes in payment, don't you? ALLEN: That could be done, but nobody wants the Federal Reserve notes. PATMAN: Nobody wants them, because the banks would rather have the credit as reserves."

This is the most incredible part of the Federal Reserve operation and one which is difficult for anyone to understand. How can any American citizen grasp the concept that there are people in this country who have the power to make an entry in a ledger that the government of the United States now owes them one billion dollars, and to collect the principal and interest on this "loan"?

Congressman Wright Patman tells us in "The Primer of Money", p. 38 of going into a Federal Reserve Bank and asking to see their bonds on which the American people are paying interest. After being shown the bonds, he asked to see their cash, but they only had some ledgers and blank checks. Patman says,

> "The cash, in truth, does not exist and has never existed. What we call 'cash reserves' are simply bookkeeping credits entered upon ledgers

of the Federal Reserve Banks. The credits are created by the Federal Reserve Banks and then passed along through the banking system."

Peter L. Bernstein, in *A Primer On Money, Banking and Gold* says:

"The trick in the Federal Reserve notes is that the Federal reserve banks lose no cash when they pay out this currency to the member banks. Federal Reserve notes are not redeemable in anything except what the Government calls 'legal tender'—that is, money that a creditor must be willing to accept from a debtor in payment of sums owned him. But since all Federal Reserve notes are themselves declared by law to be legal money, they are really redeemable only in themselves ... they are an irredeemable obligation issued by the Federal Reserve Banks."[91]

As Congressman Patman puts it,

"The dollar represents a one dollar debt to the Federal Reserve System. The Federal Reserve Banks create money out of thin air to buy Government bonds from the United States Treasury, lending money into circulation at interest, by bookkeeping entries of checkbook credit to the United States Treasury. The Treasury writes up an interest bearing bond for one billion dollars. The Federal Reserve gives the Treasury a one billion dollar credit for the bond, and has created out of nothing a one billion dollar debt which the American people are obligated to pay with interest." (Money Facts, House Banking and Currency Committee, 1964, p. 9)

Patman continues,

"Where does the Federal Reserve system get the money with which to create Bank Reserves? Answer. It doesn't get the money, it creates it. When the Federal Reserve writes a check, it is creating money. The Federal Reserve is a total moneymaking machine. It can issue money or checks."

In 1951, the Federal Reserve Bank of New York published a pamphlet, "A Day's Work at the Federal Reserve Bank of New York." On page 22, we find that:

"There is still another and more important element of public interest in the operation of banks beside the safekeeping of money; banks can 'create' money. One of the most important factors to remember in this connection is that the supply of money affects the general level of prices—the cost of living. The Cost of Living Index and money supply are parallel."

The decisions of the Federal Reserve Board, or rather, the decisions which they are told to make by "parties unknown", affect the daily lives of every American by the effect of these decisions on prices. Raising the interest rate, or causing money to become "dearer" acts to limit the amount of money available in the market, as does the raising of reserve

---

[91] Peter L. Bernstein, *A Primer On Money, Banking and Gold*, Vintage Books, New York, 1965, p. 104

requirements by the Federal Reserve System. Selling bonds by the Open Market Committee also extinguishes reserves and lowers the money supply. Buying government securities on the open market "creates" more money, as does lowering the interest rate and making money "cheaper". It is axiomatic that an increase in the money supply brings prosperity, and that a decrease in the money supply brings on a depression. Dramatic increases in the money supply which outstrip the supply of goods brings on inflation, "too much money chasing too few goods". A more esoteric aspect of the monetary system is "velocity of circulation", which sounds much more technical than it is. This is the speed at which money changes hands; if it is gold buried in the peasant's garden, that is a slow velocity of circulation, caused by a lack of confidence in the economy or the nation. Very rapid velocity of circulation, such as the stock market boom of the late 1920s, means quick turnover, spending and investment of money, and it stems from confidence, or overconfidence, in the economy. With a high velocity of circulation, a smaller money supply circulates among as many people and goods as a larger money supply would circulate with a slower velocity of circulation. We mention this because the velocity of circulation, or confidence in the economy, also is greatly affected by the Federal Reserve actions. Milton Friedman comments in *Newsweek*, May 2, 1983, "The Federal Reserve's major function is to determine the money supply. It has the power to increase or decrease the money supply at any rate it chooses."

This is an enormous power, because increasing the money supply can cause the re-election of an administration, while decreasing it can cause an administration to be defeated. Friedman goes on to criticize the Federal Reserve, "How is it that an institution which has so poor a record of performance nevertheless has so high a public reputation and even commands a considerable measure of credibility for its forecasts?"

All open market transactions, which affect the money supply, are conducted for a single System account by the Federal Reserve Bank of New York on behalf of all the Federal Reserve Banks, and supervised by an officer of the Federal Reserve Bank of New York. The conferences at which decisions are made to buy or sell securities by the Open Market Committee remain closed to the public, and the deliberations also remain a mystery. On May 8, 1928, *The New York Times* reported that Adolph C. Miller, Governor of the Federal Reserve Board, testifying before the House Banking and Currency Committee, stated that open market purchases and rediscount rates were established through "conversations". At that time, the purchases on the open market amounted to seventy or eighty million dollars a day, and would be ten times that today. These are vast sums to be manipulated on the basis of mere "conversations", but that is as much information as we can obtain.

Because of these mysterious transactions which affect the life, liberty and happiness of every American citizen, there have been numerous proposals such as Senate Document No. 23, presented by Mr. Logan on January 24, 1939, that "The Government should create, issue and circulate all the currency and credit needed to satisfy the spending power of the Government and the buying power of consumers. The privilege of creating and issuing money is not only the supreme prerogative of Government, but it is the Government's greatest creative opportunity."

On March 21, 1960, Congressman Wright Patman used a simple illustration in the Congressional Record of how banks "create money".

"If I deposit $100 with my bank and the reserve requirements imposed by the Federal Reserve Bank are 20% then the bank can make a loan to John Doe of up to $80. Where does the $80 come from? It does not come out of my deposit of $100; on the contrary, the bank simply credits John Doe's account with $80. The bank can acquire Government obligations by the same procedure, by simply creating deposits to the credit of the government. Money creating is a power of the commercial banks ... Since 1917 the Federal Reserve has given the private banks forty-six billion dollars of reserves."

How this is done is best revealed by Governor Eccles at Hearings before the House Committee on Banking and Currency on June 24, 1941:

ECCLES: "The banking system as a whole creates and extinguishes the deposits as they make loans and investments, whether they buy Government Bonds or whether they buy utility bonds or whether they make Farmers' loans.

MR. PATMAN: I am thoroughly in accord with what you say, Governor, but the fact remains that they created the money, did they not?

ECCLES: Well, the banks create money when they make loans and investments."

On September 30, 1941, before the same Committee, Governor Eccles was asked by Representative Patman:

"How did you get the money to buy those two billion dollars worth of Government securities in 1933?

ECCLES: We created it.

MR. PATMAN: Out of what?

ECCLES: Out of the right to issue credit money.

MR. PATMAN: And there is nothing behind it, is there, except our Government's credit?

ECCLES: That is what our money system is. If there were no debts in our money system, there wouldn't be any money."

On June 17, 1942, Governor Eccles was interrogated by Mr. Dewey.

ECCLES: "I mean the Federal Reserve, when it carries out an open market operation, that is, if it purchases Government securities in the open market, it puts new money into the hands of the banks which creates idle deposits.

DEWEY: There are no excess reserves to use for this purpose?

DEWEY: Whenever the Federal Reserve System buys Government securities in the open market, or buys them direct from the Treasury, either one, that is what it does.

DEWEY: What are you going to use to buy them with? You are going to create credit?

ECCLES: That is all we have ever done. That is the way the Federal Reserve System operates. The Federal Reserve System creates money. It is a bank of issue."

At the House Hearings of 1947, Mr. Kolburn asked Mr. Eccles:

"What do you mean by monetization of the public debt?

ECCLES: I mean the bank creating money by the purchase of Government securities. All money is created by debt—either private or public debt.

FLETCHER: Chairman Eccles, when do you think there is a possibility of returning to a free and open market, instead of this pegged and artificially controlled financial market we now have?

ECCLES: Never. Not in your lifetime or mine."

Congressman Jerry Voorhis is quoted in *U.S. News*, August 31, 1959, as questioning Secretary of Treasury Anderson, "Do you mean that Banks, in buying Government securities, do not lend out their customers' deposits? That they create the money they use to buy the securities? ANDERSON; That is correct. Banks are different from other lending institutions. When a savings association, an insurance company, or a credit union makes a loan, it lends the very dollar that its customers have previously paid in. But when a bank makes a loan, it simply adds to the borrower's deposit account in the bank by the amount of the loan. The money is not taken from anyone. It is new money, recreated by the bank, for the use of the borrower."

Strangely enough, there has never been a court trial on the legality or Constitutionality of the Federal Reserve Act. Although it is on much the same shaky grounds as the National Recovery Act, or NRA, which was challenged in Schechter Poultry v. United States of America, 29 U.S. 495, 55 US 837.842 (1935), the NRA was ruled unconstitutional by the Supreme Court on the grounds that "Congress may not abdicate or transfer to others its legitimate functions. Congress cannot Constitutionally delegate its legislative authority to trade or industrial associations or groups so as to empower them to make laws."

Article 1, Sec. 8 of the Constitution provides that "The Congress shall have Power to borrow money on the credit of the United States . . . and to coin Money, regulate the value thereof, and of foreign Coin, and fix the Standard of Weights and Measures." According to the NRA decision, Congress cannot delegate this power to the Federal Reserve System, nor can it delegate its legislative authority to the Federal Reserve System to allow the System to fix the rate of bank reserves, the rediscount rate, or the volume of money. All of these are "legislated" by the Federal Reserve Board, meeting in legislative sessions to determine these matters and to issue "laws" or regulations fixing them.

The Second World War gave the big bankers who owned the Federal Reserve System a chance to unload on the country billions of dollars printed early in 1930, in the biggest counterfeiting operation in history, all legalized by Roosevelt's government, of course. Henry Hazlitt writes in the January 4, 1943 issue of *Newsweek Magazine:*

"The money that began to appear in circulation a week ago, December 21, 1942, was really printing press money in the fullest sense of the term, that is, money which has *no collateral of any kind behind it.* The Federal Reserve statement that 'The Board of Governors, after consulation with the Treasury Department, has authorized Federal Reserve Banks to utilize at this time the existing stocks of currency printed in the early thirties, known as 'Federal Reserve Banknotes'. We repeat, these notes have absolutely no collateral of any kind behind them."

Governor Eccles also testified to some other interesting matters of the Federal Reserve and war finance at the Senate Hearings on the Office of Price Administration in 1944:

"The currency in circulation was increased from seven billion dollars in four years to twenty-one and a half billion. We are losing some considerable amounts of gold during the war period. As our exports have gone out, largely on a lend-lease basis, we have taken imports on which we have given dollar balances. These countries are now drawing off these dollar balances in the form of gold.

MR. SMITH: Governor Eccles, what is the objective that the foreign governments are after in this projected program whereby we would contribute gold to an international fund?

GOVERNOR ECCLES: I would like to discuss OPA, and leave the stabilization fund for a time when I am prepared to go into it.

MR. SMITH: Just a minute. I feel that this fund is very pertinent to what we are talking about today.

MR. FORD: I believe that the stabilization fund is entirely off the OPA and consequently we ought to stick to the business at hand."

The Congressmen never did get to discuss the Stabilization Fund, another setup whereby we would give the impoverished countries of Europe back the gold which had been sent over here. In 1945, Henry Hazlitt, commenting in *Newsweek* of January 22, on Roosevelt's annual budget message to Congress, quoted Roosevelt as saying:

"I shall later recommend legislation reducing the present high gold reserve requirements of the Federal Reserve Banks."

Hazlitt pointed out that the reserve requirement was not high, it was just what it had been for the past thirty years. Roosevelt's purpose was to free more gold from the Federal Reserve System and make it available for the Stabilization Fund, later called the International Monetary Fund, part of the World Bank for Reconstruction and Development, the equivalent of the League Finance Committee which would have swallowed the financial sovereignty of the United States if the Senate had let us join it. Consequently, the American people suffered the Great Depression as a result of not joining the League of Nations.

## CHAPTER FOURTEEN
# Congressional Exposé

"Mr. Volcker's politics is something of an enigma."—*New York Times*

Since 1933 when Eugene Meyer resigned from the Federal Reserve Board of Governors, no member of the international banking families has personally served on the Board of Governors. They have chosen to work from behind the scenes through carefully selected presidents of the Federal Reserve Bank of New York and other employees.

The present chairman of the Federal Reserve Board of Governors is Paul Volcker. His appointment was greeted by one well-known economist with the following prediction, "Volcker's selection has been by far the worst. Carter has put Dracula in charge of the blood bank. To us, it means a crash and depression in the 80s is more certain than ever."

Col. E.C. Harwood's *Research Report*, August 6, 1979, gave much the same view. "Paul Volcker is from the same mold as the unsound money men who have misguided the monetary actions of this nation for the past five decades. The outcome probably will be equally as disastrous for the dollar and the U.S. economy."

Despite these gloomy views, the report from *The New York Times* on the selection of Volcker was positively esctatic. On July 26, 1979, *The Times* commented that Volcker learned "the business" from Robert Roosa, now partner of Brown Brothers Harriman, and that Volcker had been part of the Roosa Brain Trust at the Federal Reserve Bank of New York, and, later, at the Treasury in the Kennedy administration. "David Rockefeller, the chairman of Chase, and Mr. Roosa were strong influences in the Mr. Carter decision to name Mr. Volcker for the Reserve Board chairmanship."

*The New York Times* did not point out that David Rockefeller and Robert Roosa had previously chosen Mr. Carter, a member of the Trilateral Commission, as the presidential candidate of the Democratic Party, or that Mr. Carter would hardly refuse to appoint their choice of Paul Volcker as the new Chairman of the Federal Reserve Board. Nor is it straining the point to be reminded that this manner of selection of the Chairman of the Board of Governors is directly in the line of royal prerogative going back to George Peabody's initial agreement with N.M. Rothschild, to the Jekyll Island meeting, and to the enactment of the Federal Reserve Act.

*The Times* noted that "Volcker's choice was approved by European banks in Bonn, Frankfurt and Zurich." William Simon, former Secretary of Treasury, was quoted as saying "a marvelous choice." *The Times* further noted that the Dow market rose on Volcker's nomination, registering the best gains in three weeks for a rise of 9.73 points, and that the dollar rose sharply on foreign exchange at home and abroad.

Who was Volcker, that his appointment could have such an effect on the stock market and the value of the dollar in foreign exchange? He represented the most powerful houses of "the London Connection," Brown Brothers Harriman, and the London houses which directed the Rockefeller empire. On July 29, 1979, *The Times* had said of Volcker, "New Man Will Chart His Own Course".

Volcker's background shows that this was nonsense. His course has always been charted for him by his masters in London. He attended Princeton, obtained an M.A. at Harvard, and went to the London School of Economics 1951-52, the banker's graduate school. He then came to the Federal Reserve Bank of New York as an economist from 1952-57, economist at Chase Manhattan Bank, 1957-61, with Treasury Department 1961-65, as deputy under secretary for monetary affairs, 1963-65, and under secretary for monetary affairs, 1969-74. He then became President of the Federal Reserve Bank of New York from 1975-79, when Carter, at the behest of Robert Roosa and David Rockefeller, appointed him Chairman of the Federal Reserve Board of Governors. He was succeeded as President of Federal Reserve Bank of New York by Anthony Solomon, a Harvard Ph.D. who was with the OPA 1941-42 and with the government financial mission to Iran 1942-46. He operated a canned food company in Mexico from 1951-61, was president of International Investment Corp. for Yugoslavia 1969-72 (a communist country), under secretary for monetary affairs at Treasury 1977-80. In short, Solomon's background was much the same as Paul Volcker's.

*The New York Times* stated on December 2, 1981, "For years the Federal Reserve was the second or third most secret institution in town. The Sunshine Act of 1976 penetrated the curtain a trifle. The board now holds a public meeting once a week on Wednesday at 10 a.m., but not to discuss Monetary policy, which is still regarded as top secret and not to be discussed in public." *The Times* mentioned that when Open Market Committee meetings are held, Solomon and Volcker sit together at the head of the table and relay the instructions which they have received from abroad.

Behind Volcker and Solomon stands Robert Roosa, Secretary of the Treasury in Carter's shadow cabinet, and representing Brown Brothers Harriman, the Trilateral Commission, the Council on Foreign Relations, the Bilderbergers, and the Royal Economic Institute. He is a trustee of the

Rockefeller Foundation*, and a director of Texaco and American Express companies. Dr. Martin Larson points out that "The international consortium of financiers known as the Bilderbergers, who meet annually in profound secrecy to determine the destiny of the western world, is a creature of the Rockefeller-Rothschild alliance, and that it held its third meeting on St. Simons Island, only a short distance from Jekyll Island." Larson also states that "The Rockefeller interests work in close alliance with the Rothschilds and other central banks."**

On June 18, 1983, President Ronald Reagan ended months of speculation by announcing that he was reappointing Paul Volcker as Chairman of the Federal Reserve Board of Governors for another four year term, although Volcker's term was not up until August 6, 1983. Reagan's reappointment of a Carter appointee puzzled some political observers, but apparently he had succumbed to considerable pressure, as indicated by a lead editorial in *The Washington Post*, June 10, 1983, "There is no one who matches Mr. Volcker in both political standing and grasp of the intricate networks that make up the world's financial system." The anonymous writer gave no documentation for his elevation of Volcker to the standing of the world's greatest financier, and as for his political standing, *The New York Times* commented on June 19, 1983, "Mr. Volcker's politics is something of an enigma." His "non-political" stance conforms with the Washington tradition of "the political independence of the Fed" which has been maintained for many years. However, the problem of its dependence on "the London connection" has never been discussed in Washington.

In reality, Volcker is more of a politician than an economist. After attending the London School of Economics, and finding out who issues the orders of the international financial community, Volcker has ever since played the game. Not once has he failed to carry out the orders of the "London Connection".

Can it really be possible that "The London Connection" exists, and that men like Volcker and Solomon receive their instructions, in however devious or indirect a manner, from foreign bankers? Let us look at the evidence, circumstantial, to be sure, but circumstantial evidence of the quality which has often sent men to the penitentiary or to the electric chair. John Moody pointed out in 1911 that seven men of the Morgan group, allied with the Standard Oil-Kuhn, Loeb group, ruled the United States. Where do these groups stand in the financial picture today?

*U.S. News* published on April 11, 1983, a list of the largest bank holding companies in the United States by assets as of December 31, 1982. Number 1 is Citicorp, New York, with assets of $130 billion. This is Baker and

---
*See Chart V
**See Chart I

Morgan's First National Bank of New York, merged with National City Bank in 1955, two of the largest purchasers of Federal Reserve Bank of New York stock in 1914. Number 3, is Chase Manhattan, New York, with assets of $80.9 billion. This is Chase and Bank of Manhattan merged, the Rockefeller and Kuhn Loeb group, also purchasers of Federal Reserve Bank of New York stock in 1914. Number 4 is Manufacturers Hanover of New York $64 billion, also purchaser of Federal Reserve Bank of New York stock in 1914. Number 5 is J.P. Morgan Company of New York, $58.6 billion in assets and holder of considerable Federal Reserve Bank stock. Number 6 is Chemical Bank of New York, $48.3 billion also purchaser of Federal Reserve stock in 1914. And Number 11, First Chicago Corporation, the First National Bank of Chicago which was principal correspondent of the Morgan-Baker bank in New York, and which furnished the first two presidents of the Federal Advisory Council.

The direct line which leads from the participants in the Jekyll Island Conference of 1910 to the present day is illustrated by a passage from "A Primer on Money", Committee on Banking and Currency, U.S. House of Representatives, 88th congress, 2d session, August 5, 1964, p. 75:

"The practical effect of requiring all purchases to be made through the open market is to take money from the taxpayer and give it to the dealers. It forces the Government to pay a toll for borrowing money. There are six 'bank' dealers: First National City Bank of New York; Chemical Corp. Exchange Bank, New York, Morgan Guaranty Trust Co., New York, Bankers Trust of New York, First National Bank of Chicago, and Continental Illinois Bank of Chicago."

Thus the banks which receive a "toll" on all money borrowed by the Government of the United States are the same banks which planned the Federal Reserve Act of 1913. There is ample evidence demonstrating the present preeminence of the same banks which set up the Federal Reserve System in 1914. For instance, Warren Brookes writes on the editorial page of *The Washington Post*, June 6, 1983:

"Citicorp (National City Bank and First National Bank of New York, merged in 1955) just recorded an 18.6% return on equity, J.P. Morgan, 17%, Chemical Bank and Bankers Trust, nearly 16%, an exceptional rate of return."

These are the banks which bought the first issue of Federal Reserve Bank stock in 1914, and which owned the controlling interest in the Federal Reserve Bank of New York, which sets the interest rate and is the bank for all open market operations.

These banks also profit steadily from the otherwise inexplicable fluctuations in monetary growth and interest rates. Brookes further comments on "actual monetary growth rates alternately gyrating from 0 to 17% in successive six month periods for three recession-wracked years. The two measures of money growth most admired by Milton Friedman M2 and M3, have actually shown little change on a year to year basis in the 1972-82 period."

Thus we have money growth rates gyrating from 0 to 17% but no actual year to year changes, which raises the question of why we cannot have stability of monetary growth throughout the year. The answer is that the big profits are made by these gyrations, and the next question is, who sets in motion these gyrations? The answer is "the London Connection".

To draw attention from the continued control of the bankers and their heirs, who obtained the government monopoly of the nation's money and credit in 1913, the paid propagandists of the controlled media monopoly and academia are constantly trotting forth new and more exotic theories of economics. Thus James Burnham, one of the National Review propagandists, won fame with a ridiculous theory of "the managers". He postulated that the old arbiters of wealth, the J.P. Morgans, the Warburgs and the Rothschilds had, by 1950, disappeared from the scene, being replaced by a new class of "managers". This theory, which had no foundation in fact, served to obscure the fact that the same people still controlled the monetary system of the world. The "managers" were just that, executives like Volcker who were front men, paid employees who would continue to receive their paychecks only as long as they carried out their employers' instructions. Burnham remains a well-paid propagandist at the *National Review*, which many prominent leaders, including President Reagan, believe to be a "conservative" publication.

From 1914 to 1982, a period in which many thousands of American banks went bankrupt, the original purchasers of Federal Reserve Bank stock have not only survived but they have consolidated their power. And what of "the London Connection"? Does it still exist, and is it still dictating the economic destiny of the United States? *The Washington Post*, May 19, 1983, carried a story datelined Nairobi, Kenya, noting the meeting of the African Development Bank. "The British merchant bank, Morgan Grenfell and a syndicate of the United States, Kuhn Loeb, Lehman Brothers International, the French Lazard Freres and Britain's Warburg are discreetly acting as financial advisors to about ten debt-plagued African states."

There are the same names we encountered in 1914, still managing the finances of the world, with profits for themselves but with disastrous results for everyone else. Perhaps we can look for relief to the present Administration of President Reagan. Unfortunately, before reaching him we have to run the gamut of the long list of his principal staff, composed a men from J. Henry Schroder, Brown Brothers Harriman, and other leading components of "The London Connection ".

Lopez Portillo, President of Mexico, in addressing the Mexican National Congress of Mexico in September, 1982, called the world credit boom of the past decade a financial pestilence akin to the Black Death which swept

Europe in the fourteenth century. "As in mediaeval times, it flattens country after country. It is transmitted by rats and it yields unemployment and misery, industrial bankruptcy and enrichment by speculation. The remedy prescribed by faith healers is forced inactivity and depriving the patient of food."

*Forbes Magazine* stated October 11, 1982, "The world gasps for liquidity, not because the supply of money has contracted but because too much of it now goes to pay off old debts rather than fund new productive investments."

The policy of high interest rates and tight money has been disastrous for the United States. In early 1983, a slight easing of money and credit promises some relief, but as long as the Federal Reserve system and its unseen manipulators continue their control of the money supply, we can expect more problems. *The Nation* on December 11, 1982, in commenting on economic problems, stated, "The blame for all this lies at the door of the Federal Reserve System working as usual on behalf of the international banking system."

The evidence of how the Federal Reserve System works on behalf of the international banking system is graphically illustrated by a series of charts drawn up by the staff of the Committee on Banking, Currency and Housing of the House of Representatives, 94th Congress, 2d session, August, 1976, "FEDERAL RESERVE DIRECTORS: A STUDY OF CORPORATE AND BANKING INFLUENCE".* We present as our Chart V page 49 of this study, showing the interlocking directorates of David Rockefeller. As our Chart VI we reproduce page 55 of this study, showing the interlocking directorates of Frank R. Milliken, one of the Class C Directors** of the Federal Reserve Bank of New York. In this chart are all the main personages in our story of the Jekyll Island conference: Citibank, J.P. Morgan and Company, Kuhn Loeb and Company, and many related firms. As Chart VII we reproduce page 53 of this study, showing the interlocking directorates of another Class C Directors of the Federal Reserve Bank of New York, Alan Pifer. As President of the Carnegie Corporation of New York, he interlocks with J. Henry Schroder Trust Company, J. Henry Schroder Banking Corporation, Rockefeller Center, Inc., Federal Reserve Bank of Boston, Equitable Life Assurance Society (J.P. Morgan), and others. Thus an August, 1976 study from the House Committee on Banking, Currency and Housing, brings before us all of our main cast of personages, functioning today just as they did in 1914.

---

*Due to space limitations, only five of the seventy-five charts in the study, all of which show the connections between prominent, powerful individuals with control in the Federal Reserve System have been selected to illustrate the connections between officers and directors of the twelve Federal Reserve Banks in 1976 and the firms listed in this book.
**"The three Class C Directors are appointed by the Board of Governors as representatives of the public interest as a whole." p. 34, Congressional Study, 1976.

This 120 page Congressional study details public policy functions of the Federal Reserve District Banks, how directors are selected, who is selected, the public relations lobbying factor, bank domination and bank examination, and corporate interlocks with Reserve banks. Charts were used to illustrate Class A, Class B, and Class C directorships of each district bank. For each branch bank a chart was designed giving information regarding bank appointed directors and those appointed by the Board of Governors of the Federal Reserve System.

In his Foreword to the study, Chairman Henry S. Reuss, (D-Wis) wrote:

"This Committee has observed for many years the influence of private interests over the essentially public responsibilities of the Federal Reserve System.

As the study makes clear, it is difficult to imagine a more narrowly-based board of directors for a public agency than has been gathered together for the twelve banks of the Federal Reserve System.

Only two segments of American society—banking and big business—have any substantial representation on the boards, and often even these become merged through interlocking directorates . . . . Small farmers are absent. Small business is barely visible. No women appear on the district boards and only six among the branches. Systemwide—including district and branch boards—only thirteen members from minority groups appear.

The study raises a substantial question about the Federal Reserve's oft-repeated claim of "independence". One might ask, independent from what? Surely not banking or big business, if we are to judge from the massive interlocks revealed by this analysis of the district boards.

The big business and banking dominance of the Federal Reserve System cited in this report can be traced, in part, to the original Federal Reserve Act, which gave member commercial banks the right to select two-thirds of the directors of each district bank. But the Board of Governors in Washington must share the responsibility for this imbalance. They appoint the so-called "public" members of the boards of each district bank, appointments which have largely reflected the same narrow interests of the bank-elected members . . . . Until we have basic reforms, the Federal Reserve System will be handicapped in carrying out its public responsibilities as an economic stabilization and bank regulatory agency. The System's mandate is too essential to the nation's welfare to leave so much of the machinery under the control of narrow private interests. Concentration of economic and financial power in the United States has gone too far."

In a section of the text entitled "The Club System", the Committee noted:

"This "club" approach leads the Federal Reserve to consistently dip into the same pools—the same companies, the same universities, the same bank holding companies—to fill directorships."

This Congressional study concludes as follows:

"Many of the companies on these tables, as mentioned earlier, have multiple interlocks to the Federal Reserve System. First Bank Systems; Southeast Banking Corporation; Federated Department Stores; Westinghouse Electric Corporation; Proctor and Gamble; Alcoa; Honeywell, Inc.; Kennecott Copper; Owens-Corning Fiberglas; all have two or more director ties to district or branch banks.

In Summary, the Federal Reserve directors are apparently representatives of a small elite group which dominates much of the economic life of this nation." END OF CONGRESSIONAL REPORT.

# ADDENDUM

As of 11:05 Tuesday, July 26, 1983, the list of member banks holding Federal Reserve Bank of New York stock includes twenty-seven New York City banks. Listed below are the number of shares held by ten of these banks, amounting to 66% of the total outstanding number of shares, namely 7,005,700:

|  | Shares | Percent |
|---|---|---|
| Bankers Trust Company | 438,831 | ( 6%) |
| Bank of New York | 141,482 | ( 2%) |
| Chase Manhattan Bank | 1,011,862 | (14%) |
| Chemical Bank | 544,962 | ( 8%) |
| Citibank | 1,090,813 | (15%) |
| European American Bank & Trust | 127,800 | ( 2%) |
| J. Henry Schroder Bank & Trust | 37,493 | ( .5%) |
| Manufacturers Hanover | 509,852 | ( 7%) |
| Morgan Guaranty Trust | 655,443 | ( 9%) |
| National Bank of North America | 105,600 | ( 2%) |

The tremendous number of shares held today as against the original purchases in 1914 is brought about by Section 5 of the original Federal Reserve Act which called for a member bank to buy and hold stock in the district Federal Reserve Bank equal to 6% of its capital and surplus.

Currently, shares held by five of the above named banks comprise 53% of the total Federal Reserve Bank of New York stock. An examination of the major stockholders of the New York City banks shows clearly that a few families, related by blood, marriage, or business interests, still control the New York City banks which, in turn, hold the controlling stock of the Federal Reserve Bank of New York.

It is notable that three of the banks holding Federal Reserve Bank of New York stock, in the amount of 270,893 shares, are subsidiaries of foreign banks. J. Henry Schroder Bank and Trust is listed by *Standard and Poors* as a subsidiary of Schroders Ltd. of London. The National Bank of North America is a subsidiary of the National Westminster Bank, one of London's "Big Five". European American Bank is a subsidiary of the European American Bank, Bahamas, LTD. It is interesting to note that the directors of the European American Bank & Trust include Milton F. Rosenthal, president and Chief Operating Officer of the international gold company,

Engelhard Minerals and Chemical; Hamilton F. Potter, a partner in Sullivan and Cromwell (J. Henry Schroder Bank & Trust attorneys); Edward H. Tuck, partner of Shearman and Sterling (Citibank's attorneys); F.H. Ulrich and Hans Liebkutsch, managing directors of the Deutsche Bank (Germany); E.J.W. Helmuth and Jack Lendley, directors of the giant Midland Bank of London, one of the "Big Five"; and Roger Alloo, Paul-Emmanuel Janssen, and Maurice Laure of the Societe Generale de Banque (Brussels, Belgium). [See Chart III]

This information, derived from the latest issue of the tabulation available from the Board of Governors, Federal Reserve System, is cited as current evidence which indicates that the controlling stock in the Federal Reserve Bank of New York, which sets the rate and scale of operations for the entire Federal Reserve System is heavily influenced by banks directly controlled by "The London Connection", that is, the Rothschild-controlled Bank of England. [See Chart I]

# APPENDIX I

E.C. Knuth, in *The Empire of the City*, priv. printed, 1946, p. 27, refers to "the Bank of England, the full partner of the American Administration in the conduct of the financial affairs of all the world" and cites the *Encyclopaedia Americana*, 1943 edition.

Barron cites Lord Swaythling, (April 8, 1923), "Lord Swaythling said, 'Exchange can only be run from London. This is the center in Exchange.' " (*They Told Barron*, by Clarence W. Barron, founder of Barron's Weekly, Harpers, New York, 1930, p. 27.)

Exchange, in the international financial world, means the transactions in money or securities, or simply, the "exchange" of the values of these securities. It is necessary that this "exchange" take place where the values can be established, and this place is the "City" in London.

London was established as the primary center of exchange because of the "Consols" of the Bank of England, bonds which could never be redeemed, but which paid a stable rate of return. Henry Clews writes, in *The Wall Street View*, Silver Burdett Co. 1900, p. 255, "The Consolidated Act of 1757 consolidated the debts of the nation of England at 3%, which were kept in an account at the Bank of England and is the great bulwark of its deposits." By osentatiously "dumping" "Consols" on the London Exchange after the Battle of Waterloo, in a pretended panic, Nathan Meyer Rothschild then secretly bought up the Consols sold in the panic by other holders at a low rate, and became the largest holder of Consols, and thus won control of the Bank of England in 1815.

## 12% Dividends

Although a Labor government nationalized the Bank of England in 1946, *The Great Soviet Encyclopaedia* points out (vol. I, p. 490c) that the Bank of England continues to pay 12% dividends per annum, just as it had done prior to the nationalization. The "Governor" is appointed by the government, in a situation similar to that in the United States, where the Governors of the Federal Reserve System are appointed by the President. However, as is pointed out in the *Encylcopaedia Americana* v. 13, p. 272, "In practice, the governors of the Bank of England have not hesitated to criticize and bring pressure on the government in public."

## Bank Rate

The interest rate set by the Bank of England is known as "the Bank rate", and it is a controlling factor in interest rates throughout the world, although rates in other countries may be higher or lower than this "Bank rate". The Bank of England manages the government debt, and is called upon to arbitrate in political affairs. It served as the intermediary with the Iran revolutionaries in negotiating for the return of the American hostages—a recent example.

We should not be surprised that the present Governor of the Bank of England, Sir Gordon Richardson is a prominent international financial figure, who appears elsewhere in these pages because of his connection with the J. Henry Schroder Banking Corporation of New York. He was Chairman of J. Henry Schroder Wagg in London from 1962 to 1972, when he became Governor of the Bank of England. He was also director of J. Henry Schroder Co., New York, and Schroder Banking Corp., New York. He also serves as director of Rolls Royce and Lloyd's Bank. Although he resides in London, he maintains a home in New York, and is listed in the current Manhattan directory simple as "G. Richardson, 45 Sutton Place S.", although a prior listing showed him at 4 Sutton Place. Sutton Place was developed as a fashionable address for the international set by Bessie Marbury, whom we earlier cited for her connection with the Morgan family and the Roosevelts.

The present directors of the Bank of England (1982) include Leopold de Rothschild of N.M. Rothschild & Sons, Sir Robert Clark, chairman of Hill Samuel Bank, the most influential bank after Rothschilds, John Clay, of Hambros Bank, and David Scholey, of Warburg Bank, and joint chairman of S.C. Warburg Co.

Anthony Sampson writes, in "The Changing Anatomy of Britain", Random House, New York, 1982, p. 279, "The more cosmopolitan banks with foreign experts and directors, such as Warburgs, Montagus, Rothschilds and Kleinworts, had also discovered a huge new source of profits in the market for Eurodollars which began in the late fifties and multiplied through the 60s . . . . British bankers themselves controlled relatively small funds, but they knew how to make money out of other people's money."

The Eurodollar market, a new development in "created money" is monopolized by the above firms.

### Eurodollar Empire

"Today, together with allies on the island of Manhattan (Britain's most important piece of real estate), the British Empire controls the entire $1.5 trillion Eurodollar financial market, another $300-$500 billion in the Cayman Islands, Bahamas, and $50-$100 billion in the Hong-Kong Singapore "Asia-dollar market". . . .Consider the $1.5 trillion Eurodollar market an "outlaw" market in the U.S. dollars over which this nation has no control. Here control and profits are overwhelmingly in the hands of London banks, who set the terms of lending and the interest rate on this mass of American dollars in relation to the London Interbank Borrowing

Rate (LIBOR)...U.S. banks like Citibank (New York City), on whose board of directors sits the powerful British financier, Lord Aldington, collaborate openly in this market. At the same time, British banks including the known central bank for the world's drug trade, the Hongkong and Shanghai Bank, pour into America to devour U.S. banks. In 1978 the Hongshang (Ed.—Hongkong and Shanghai Bank) took over New York's Marine Midland Bank, the state's 11th largest commercial bank... The British also control the creation of American dollars. While Federal Reserve Board Chairman Paul Volcker tightens credit against the domestic economy, British-controlled banks in the Cayman Islands (such as the European American Bank—Ed.) a British possession 20 miles off Florida, and in the Bermudas and a dozen other "free banking"computer terminals create hundreds of billions of American dollars. How is this done? There are no reserve ratios or other restrictions on the creation of dollar-denominated credits in the Empire's "free enterprise" banking. A $1 million bona fide credit coming from the United States can be turned into $20 to $100 million in dollar-denominated credits as it passes through the British system without reserve ratios."*

Not only the financial power, but also the legal power, has remained seated in Britain. *The Washington Post* commented on June 18, 1983 that after the American Revolution, all the old laws remained in effect in the new United States: Some of these laws of "English common law" dated back to 1278, long before America was discovered.

This enormous financial power of "the City" is revealed in many areas. Dean Acheson states, in "Present at the Creation", 1969, W.W. Norton, New York, p. 779, "We stayed at the embassy residence, the old J.P. Morgan mansion, 14 Prince's Gate, facing Hyde Park." How many Americans are aware that the U.S. Embassy residence in London is the J.P. Morgan home, or that Dean Acheson, a former Morgan employee, described himself as Secretary of State on p. 505, "My own attitude had long been, and was known to have been, pro-British." No one commented on an American Secretary of State's open bias in favor of England.

The Federal Reserve "created" money is not used only for financial matters; this money is also used to maintain the bankers' control of every aspect of political, economic and social life. It is used to bankroll the enormous expenditures of political candidates, the swollen budgets of universities, the huge outlays required to start newspapers or magazines, and a vast array of foundations, "think-tanks" and other instruments of mind control.

## Psychological Warfare

Few Americans know that almost every development in psychology in the United States in the past sixty-five years has been directed by the Bureau of Psychological Warfare of the British Army. A short time ago,

---
*\*Harpers Magazine*, Feb. 1980

the present writer learned a new name, The Tavistock Institute of London, also known as the Tavistock Institute of Human Relations. "Human relations" covers every aspect of human behavior, and it is the modest goal of the Tavistock Institute to obtain and exercise control over every aspect of human behaviour of American citizens.

Because of the intensive artillery barrages of World War I, many soldiers were permanently impaired by shell shock. In 1921, the Marguess of Tavistock, 11th Duke of Bedford, gave a building to a group which planned to conduct rehabilitation programs for shell shocked British soldiers. The group took the name of "Tavistock Institute" after its benefactor. The General Staff of the British Army decided it was crucial that they determine the breaking point of the soldier under combat conditions. The Tavistock Institute was taken over by Sir John Rawlings Reese, head of the British Army Psychological Warfare Bureau. A cadre of highly trained specialists in psychological warfare was built up in total secrecy. In fifty years, the name "Tavistock Institute" appears only twice in the Index of the *New York Times*, yet this group, according to LaRouche and other authorities, organized and trained the entire staffs of the Office of Strategic Services (OSS), the Strategic Bombing Survey, Supreme Headquarters of the Allied Expeditionary Forces, and other key American military groups during World War II. During World War II, the Tavistock Institute combined with the medical sciences division of the Rockefeller Foundation for esoteric experiments with mind-altering drugs. The present drug culture of the United States is traced in its entirety to this Institute, which supervised the Central Intelligence Agency's training programs. The "LSD counter culture" originated when Sandoz A.G., a Swiss pharmaceutical house owned by S.G. Warburg & Co., developed a new drug from lycergic acid, called LSD. James Paul Warburg (son of Paul Warburg who had written the Federal Reserve Act in 1910), financed a subsidiary of the Tavistock Institute in the United States called the Institute for Policy Studies, whose director, Marcus Raskin, was appointed to the National Security Council James Paul Warburg set up a CIA program to experiment with LSD on CIA agents, some of whom later committed suicide. This program, MK-Ultra, supervised by Dr. Gottlieb, resulted in huge lawsuits against the United States Government by the families of the victims.

The Institute for Policy Studies set up a campus subsidiary, Students for Democratic Society (SDS), devoted to drugs and revolution. Rather than finance SDS himself, Warburg used CIA funds, some twenty million dollars, to promote the campus riots of the 1960s.

The English Tavistock Institute has not restricted its activities to left-wing groups, but has also directed the programs of such supposedly "conservative" American think tanks as the Herbert Hoover Institute at Stanford University, Heritage Foundation, Wharton, Hudson, Massachusetts Institute of Technology, and Rand. The "sensitivity training" and "sexual encounter" programs of the most radical California groups such as Esalen Institute and its many imitators were all developed and implemented by Tavistock Institute psychologists.

One of the rare items concerning the Tavistock Institute appears in *Business Week*, Oct. 26, 1963, with a photograph of its building in the most expensive medical offices area of London. The story mentions "the Freudian bias" of the Institute, and comments that it is amply financed by British blue-chip corporations, including Unilever, British Petroleum, and Baldwin Steel. According to *Business Week*, the psychological testing programs and group relations training programs of the Institute were implemented in the United States by the University of Michigan and the University of California, which are hotbeds of radicalism and the drug network.

It was the Marquess of Tavistock, 12th Duke of Bedford, whom Rudolf Hess flew to England to contact about ending World War II. Tavistock was said to be worth $40 million in 1942. In 1945, his wife committed suicide by taking an overdose of pills.

# BIOGRAPHIES

### NELSON ALDRICH (1841-1915)
Senator from Rhode Island; head of National Monetary Commission; his daughter Abby Aldrich married John D. Rockefeller, Jr.; he became the grandfather of his namesake. Nelson Aldrich Rockefeller, as well as the present David Rockefeller and Laurence Rockefeller.

### WILLIAM JENNINGS BRYAN (1860-1925)
Woodrow Wilson's Secretary of State, three times losing presidential candidate of the Democratic Party, in 1896, 1900, and 1908, and head of the Democratic Party.

### ALFRED OWEN CROZIER (1863-1939)
A prominent attorney in Grand Rapids, Cincinnati, and New York, Crozier wrote eight books on legal and monetary problems, focussing on his opposition to the supplanting of Constitutional money by the corporation currency printed by private firms for their profit.

### CLARENCE DILLON (1882-1979)
Born in San Antonio, Texas, son of Samuel and Bertha Lapowitz. Harvard, 1905. Married Anne Douglass of Milwaukee. His son, C. Douglas Dillon (later Secretary of the Treasury, 1961-65) was born in Geneva, Switzerland in 1909 while they were abroad. Dillon met William A. Read, founder of the Wall Street bond broker William A. Read and Company, through introduction by Harvard classmate William A. Phillips in 1912 and Dillon joined Read's Chicago office in that year. He moved to New York in 1914. Read died in 1916, and Dillon bought a majority interest in the firm. During World War I, Bernard Baruch, chairman of the War Industries Board, (known as the Czar of American industry) asked Dillon to be assistant chairman of the War Industries Board. In 1920, William A. Read & Company name was changed to Dillon, Read & Company. Dillon was director of American Foreign Securities Corporation, which he had set up in 1915 to finance the French Government's purchases of munitions in the United States. His righthand man at Dillon Read, James Forrestal, became Secretary of the Navy, later Secretary of Defense, and died under mysterious circumstances at a Federal hospital. In 1957, Fortune Magazine listed Dillon as one of the richest men in the United States, with a fortune then estimated to be from $150 to $200 million.

## COLONEL EDWARD MANDEL HOUSE (1858-1938)
Son of a Rothschild agent in Texas. Succeeded in electing five consecutive governors of Texas; became Woodrow Wilson's advisor in 1912. Cooperated with Paul Warburg to get the Federal Reserve Act passed by Congress in 1913.

## ROBERT MARION LAFOLLETTE:
Served in Senate from Wisconsin 1905-25. Led agrarian reformers in opposing Eastern bankers and their plans for the Federal Reserve Act. Ran for President in 1924 on Progressive-Socialist ticket.

## CHARLES AUGUSTUS LINDBERGH, SR. (Sweden 1860-1924)
Congressman from Minnesota (1907-1917) who led the fight against enactment of the Federal Reserve Act in 1913. He served until 1917 when he resigned to run for governor of Minnesota. He ran a good campaign despite adverse newspaper attacks led by *The New York Times*. His campaign was adversely affected when Federal agents burned his books, including *Why Is Your Country At War?* and the papers and contents of his home office in Little Falls, Minnesota.

## LOUIS T. McFADDEN (1876-1936)
Congressman and Chairman of the House Banking and Currency Committee, 1927-33; courageously opposed the manipulators of the Federal Reserve System in the 1920's and the 1930's. Introduced bills to impeach Federal Reserve Board of Governors and allied officials. After three attempts on his life, he died mysteriously.

## JOHN PIERPONT MORGAN (1837-1913)
Considered the dominant American financier at the turn of the century. *Who's Who* in 1912 stated he "controls over 50,000 miles of railroads in the United States." Organized United States Steel Corporation. Became representative of House of Rothschild through his father, Junius S. Morgan, who had become London partner of George Peabody & Company, later Junius S. Morgan Company, a Rothschild agent. John Pierpont Morgan, Jr. succeeded his father as head of the Morgan empire.

## WRIGHT PATMAN (1893-1976)
Congressman and Chairman of the House Banking and Currency Committee 1963-74. Led the fight in Congress to stop the manipulators of the Federal Reserve System from 1937 to his death in 1976.

## CONGRESSMAN ARSENE PUJO
Served in Congress 1903-1913. Democrat from Louisiana. Chairman of House Banking and Currency Committee. Chairman of "Pujo Hearings" Subcommittee, 1912.

### SIR GORDON RICHARDSON (1915-    )
Head of the Bank of England since 1973. Chairman J. Henry Schroder Wagg, London, 1962-72; director of J. Henry Schroder Banking Corporation, New York; Schroder Banking Corporation, New York; Lloyd's Bank, London; Rolls Royce.

### JACOB SCHIFF (1847-1920)
Born in Rothschild house in Frankfurt, Germany. Emigrated to United States, married Therese Loeb, daughter of Solomon Loeb, founder of Kuhn, Loeb and Co. Schiff became senior partner of Kuhn, Loeb and Co., and as representative of Rothschild interests gained control of most of railway mileage in United States.

### BARON KURT VON SCHRODER (1889-    )
Adolf Hitler's personal banker; advanced funds for Hilter's accession to power in Germany in 1933; German representative of the London and New York branches of J. Henry Schroder Banking Corporation; SS Senior Group Leader; director of all German subsidiaries of I.T.T.; Himmler's Circle of Friends; advisor to board of directors, Deutsche Reichsbank (German central bank).

### ANTHONY MORTON SOLOMON (1919-    )
Educated at Harvard, economist Office of Price Administration, 1941-42; financial mission to Iran, 1942-46; Agency for International Development South America, 1965-69; president International Investment Corporation for Yugoslavia 1969-72; advisor to Chairman, Ways and Means Committee, House of Representatives, 1972-73; Undersecretary Monetary Affairs, U.S. Treasury, 1977-80; president Federal Reserve Bank of New York, 1980-

### SAMUEL UNTERMYER
A partner of the law firm of Guggenheimer and Untermyer of New York, who conducted the "Pujo Hearings" of the House Banking and Currency Committee in 1912. Counsel for Rogers and Rockefeller in many large suits against F. Augustus Heinze, Thomas W. Lawson and others. Earned a single fee of $775,000 for handling merger of Utah Copper Company. Reported in *The New York Times* May 26, 1924 as urging immediate recognition of Soviet Russia at Carnegie Hall meeting. Untermyer's prestige and power is illustrated by the fact that his front page obituary in *The New York Times* covered six columns. His listing in Who's Who was the longest for thirteen years.

### FRANK VANDERLIP
Assistant Secretary of Treasury 1897-1901; won prestige for financing

Spanish-American War by floating $200,000,000 in bonds during his incumbency for what is known as "National City Bank's War". President of National City Bank 1909-19. One of the original Jekyll Island group who wrote Federal Reserve Act in November, 1910. No mention of this important fact is made in extensive obituary in *The New York Times*, June 30, 1937.

### GEORGE SYLVESTER VIERECK (1884-1962)
Author of the definitive study *The Strangest Friendship in History, Woodrow Wilson and Col. House*, Liveright, 1932. A leading poet of the early 1900s, reviewed on the front page of *The New York Times Book Review*, and known as the leading German-American citizen of the United States.

### PAUL VOLCKER (1927-    )
Chairman of the Federal Reserve Board of Governors since 1979, appointed by President Carter, reappointed by President Reagan for another four year term beginning August 6, 1983. Educated at Princeton, Harvard and London School of Economics; employed by Federal Reserve Bank of New York, 1952-57; Chase Manhattan Bank, 1957-61; Treasury Department, 1961-74; president Federal Reserve Bank of New York, 1975-79.

### PAUL WARBURG (1868-1932)
Conceded to be the actual author of our central bank plan, the Federal Reserve System, by knowledgeable authorities. Emigrated to the United States from Germany 1904; partner, Kuhn, Loeb and Company bankers, New York; naturalized 1911. Member of the original Federal Reserve Board of Governors, 1914-1918; president Federal Advisory Council, 1918-1928. Brother of Max Warburg, who was head of German Secret Service during World War I and who represented Germany at the Peace Conference, 1918-1919, while Paul was chairman of the Federal Reserve System.

### SIR WILLIAM WISEMAN (1885-1962)
Partner of Kuhn, Loeb and Company; head of British Secret Service during World War I. Worked closely with Col. House dominating the United States and England.

# BIBLIOGRAPHY

Newspapers: *New York Times* 1858-1983
*Washington Post* 1933-1983

Periodicals: *Barron's Weekly* 1921-1983
*Business Week* 1929-1983
*Forbes Magazine* 1917-1983
*Fortune* 1930-1983
*Harper's* 1850-1983
*National Review* 1955-1983
*Newsweek* 1933-1983
*The Nation* 1865-1983
*The New Republic* 1914-1983
*Time* 1923-1983

*Federal Reserve Bulletin* 1914-1983
*The New Yorker* 1925-1983
*Saturday Evening Post* 1928-1983
*U.S. News & World Report* 1933-1983

Books:
*Current Biography* 1940-1983 H.W. Wilson Co., N.Y.
*Directionary of National Biography*, Scribners, N.Y. 1934-1965
*Directory of Directors*, London 1896-1983
*Directory of Directors In The City of New York* 1898-1918
*The Concise Dictionary of National Biography*, 1903-1979, Oxford University Press
*Congressional Record* 1910-1983
*International Index to Periodicals* 1920-1965, H.W. Wilson Co., NY
*Poole's Index to Periodical Literature* 1802-1906, Wm. T. Poole, Chicago
*Readers Guide to Periodicals* 1900-1983
*Rand McNally's Bankers Guide* 1904-1928
*Moody's Banking and Finance* 1928-1968
*Who's Who in America* 1890-1983, A.N. Marquis Co.
*Who's Who, Great Britain* 1921-1983
*Who Was Who In America* 1607-1906, A.N. Marquis Co.
*Who's Who in the World* 1972-1983, A.N. Marquis Co.
*Who's Who in Finance and Industry* 1936-1969, A.N. Marquis Co.

*Standard and Poor's Register of Directors* 1928-1983
*Senate Committee Hearings on Federal Reserve Act,* 1913
*House Committee Hearings on Federal Reserve Act,* 1913
*House Committee Hearings on the Money Trust* (Pujo Committee) 1913
*House Investigation of Federal Reserve System,* 1928
*Senate Investigation of Fitness of Eugene Meyer to be a Governor of the Federal Reserve Board,* 1930
*Senate Hearings on Office of Price Administration,* 1944
*Senate Hearings on Thomas B. McCabe to be a Governor of the Federal Reserve System,* 1948
*House Committee Hearings on Extension of Public Debt,* 1945
*Federal Reserve Directors: A Study of Corporate and Banking Influence.* Staff Report, Committee on Banking, Currency and Housing, House of Representatives, 94th Congress, 2d Session, August, 1976.
*The Federal Reserve System, Purposes and Functions,* Board of Governors, 1963
*A History of Monetary Crimes,* Alexander Del Mar, the Del Mar Society, 1899
*Fiat Money Inflation in France,* Andrew Dickson White, Foundation for Economic Education, N.Y. 1959
*The War on Gold,* Antony C. Sutton, 76 Press, California, 1977
*Wall Street and the Rise of Hitler,* Antony C. Sutton, 76 Press, California, 1976
*Collected Speeches of Louis T. McFadden,* Congressoinal Record
*The Truth About Rockefeller,* E.M. Josephson, Chedney Press, N.Y. 1964
*The Strange Death of Franklin D. Roosevelt,* E.M. Josephson, Chedney Press, N.Y. 1948
*Behind the Throne,* Paul Emden, Hoddard Stoughton, London, 1934
*The Money Power of Europe,* Paul Emden, Hoddard Stoughton, London
*The Robber Barons,* Mathew Josephson, Harcourt Brace, N.Y. 1934
*The Rothschilds,* Frederic Morton, Curtis Publishing Co., 1961
*The Magnificent Rothschilds,* Cecil Roth, Robert Hale Co., 1939
*Pawns In The Game,* William Guy Carr, (privately printed), 1956
*Tearing Away the Veils,* Francois Coty, Paris, 1940
*Writers on English Monetary History, 1626-1730,* London, 1896
*The Federal Reserve System After Fifty Years,* Committee on Banking and Currency, Jan., Feb. 1964
*The Bankers' Conspiracy,* Arthur Kitson, 1933
*Laws Of The United States Relating to Currency, Finance and Banking From 1789 to 1891,* Charles F. Dunbar, Ginn & Co., Boston, 1893
*Monetary Policy of Plenty Instead of Scarcity,* Committee on Banking and Currency, 1937-1938
*The Strangest Friendship In History, Woodrow Wilson and Col. House,* George Sylvester Viereck, Liveright, N.Y. 1932

*Federal Reserve Policy Making*, G.L. Bach, Knapf, N.Y. 1950
*Rulers of America, A Study of Finance Capital*, Anna Rockester, International Publishers, N.Y. 1936
*Banking in the United States Before the Civil War*, National Monetary Commission, 1911
*National Banking System*, National Monetary Commission, 1911
*The Federal Reserve System*, Paul Warburg, Macmillan, N.Y. 1930
*Roosevelt, Wilson and the Federal Reserve Law*, Col. Elisha Garrison, Christopher Publishing House, Boston, 1931
*Men Who Run America*, Arthur D. Howden Smith, Bobbs Merrill, N.Y. 1935
*Financial Giants of America*, George F. Redmond, Stratford, Boston, 1922
*The Great Soviet Encyclopaedia*, Macmillan, London, 1973
*Encyclopaedia Brittanica*, 1979
*Encyclopaedia Americana*, 1982
*Dope, Inc.*, Goldman, Steinberg et al, New Benjamin Franklin House Publishing Company, N.Y. 1978
*Banking and Currency and the Money Trust*, Charles A. Lindbergh, Sr. 1913
*The Strange Career of Mr. Hoover Under Two Flags*, John Hamill, William Faro, N.Y. 1931
*The Federal Reserve System*, H. Parker Willis, Ronald Co., 1923
*A.B.C. of the Federal Reserve System*, E.W. Kemmerer, Princeton Univ., 1919
*Adventures in Constructive Finance*, Carter Glass, Doubleday, N.Y. 1927
*Banking Reform in the United States*, Paul Warburg, Columbia Univ., 1914
*U.S. Money vs. Corporation Currency*, Alfred Crozier, Cleveland, 1912
*Philip Dru, Administrator*, E.M. House, B.W. Huebsch, N.Y. 1912
*The Intimate Papers of Col. House*, edited by Charles Seymour, 4 v. 1926-1928, Houghton Mifflin Co.
*The Great Conspiracy of the House of Morgan*, H.W. Loucks, 1916
*Capital City*, McRae and Cairncross, Eyre Methuen, London, 1963
*Aggression*, Otto Lehmann-Russbeldt, Hutchinson, London, 1934
*The Empire of High Finance*, Victor Perlo, International Pub., 1957
*Memoirs of Max Warburg*, Berlin, 1936
*Letters and Friendships of Sir Cecil Spring-Rice*
*Tragedy and Hope*, Carroll Quigley, Macmillan, N.Y.
*The Politics of Money*, Brian Johnson, McGraw Hill, N.Y. 1970
*A Primer on Money*, House Banking and Currency Committee, 1964
*Pierpont Morgan and Friends, The Anatomy of A Myth*, George Wheeler, Prentice Hall, N.J., 1973
*J. Pierpont Morgan*, Herbert Satterlee, Macmillan, N.Y. 1940
*Morgan the Magnificent*, John K. Winkler, Vanguard, N.Y., 1930
*Wilson*, Arthur Link (5 vol.) Princeton University Press, Princeton, N.J.
*Historical Beginning...The Federal Reserve*, Roger T. Johnson, Federal

Reserve Bank of Boston, 1977 (7 printings, 1977-1982, totaling 92,000 copies.) [It is noteworthy that this 64 page booklet makes no mention of Jekyll Island, Paul Warburg's authorship, or source of promotion funds which resulted in enactment of the Federal Reserve Act on December 23, 1913.]

*The Federal Reserve and Our Manipulated Dollar*, Martin A. Larson, Devin Adair Co., Old Greenwich, Conn., 1975

*Chain Banking*, Stockholder and Loan Links of 200 Largest Member Banks, House Banking and Currency Committee, Jan. 3, 1963

*International Banking*, Staff Report, Committee on Banking Currency and Housing, May 1976

*Audit of the Federal Reserve System*, Hearings Before the House Banking and Currency Committee, 1975.

# INDEX

## A

Abbot, Lawrence—22
Adams, John Quincy—48
Aldrich, Nelson—1, 2, 3, 6, 7, 8, 9, 10, 11, 19, 21, 22, 30, 33, 36
Aldrich-Vreeland Emergency Currency Bill—12, 19, 20, 22
American Acceptance Council—128
Allen, W.H.—33
American Bankers Association—13, 127
American Relief Administration—74, 78
Andrew, A. Piatt—1
Astor, John Jacob—64, 65
Auchincloss, Gordon—107

## B

Bagdikian, Ben H.—61
Baker, George F.—16, 42, 43, 47, 66, 67
Baker, George F., Jr.—66
Bank of England—32, 42, 51, 52, 58, 59, 68, 69, 80, 123, 129, 131, 133, 142, 146, 180
Bank of France—32, 135
Banking Act of 1935—29, 159
Barnes, Julius—73, 74
Baruch, Bernard—17, 26, 28, 74, 86, 89, 90, 94, 99, 109, 111, 112, 139, 147, 151
Barron, Clarence W.—30
Bechtel Corporation—77, 79
Belgian Relief Commission—69, 70, 72, 73, 74, 78, 83
Belmont, August—53
Biddle, Nicholas—6, 50
Bilderbergers—54, 172
Bleichroder, Samuel—59
Blumenthal, George—14

Brandeis, Justice Louis—87, 109
Bristow, Senator—38
Brookhart, Senator—117
Brown, Alexander—49
Alex Brown & Son—49
Brown Brothers Bankers—22, 49, 131
Brown Brothers Harriman—22, 48, 49, 61, 68, 79, 131, 171, 172, 175
Brown Shipley & Company—49, 68
Bryan, William Jennings—26, 29, 82, 83, 118
Bull Moose Party—18
Bush, George—49
Bush, Prescott—49
Byrnes, James—17

## C

Canaris, Admiral—62
Carr, William Guy—53, 55
Carter, Jimmy—171, 172, 173
Cassel, Ernest—59
Cavell, Edith—72, 73
Central Bank—5
Chamberlain, Neville—78
Churchill, Winston—78, 123
Clark, Champ—29
Clay, John—182
Clews, Henry—50
Cooper, Kent—60
Council on Foreign Relations—35, 54, 81, 172
Crissinger, D.R.—141
Cromwell, Oliver—58
Crozier, Alfred—20

## D

Dabney, Charles H.—50, 51
Davison, Daniel—63

Davison, Henry P.—1, 2, 4, 33, 43, 44, 66, 103
Debs, Eugene—105
Delano, F.A.—36, 114
Delano, Warren—36
Drexel, Anthony—53
Drexel & Company—48, 54
Dodge, Cleveland H.—103, 105,
Dulles, Allen—62, 75, 76
Dulles, John Foster—75, 81
Duncan Sherman Company—50

### E
Eccles, Marriner—122, 126, 159, 162, 163, 164, 167, 168, 169
Eisenhower, Dwight D.—75, 81
Ellery, William—48
Emden, Paul—36, 60

### F
Federal Advisory Council—6, 19, 40, 41, 42, 43, 44, 45, 113, 116, 117, 119, 128, 129, 144
Federal Reserve Act—7, 9, 15, 16, 18, 19, 21, 23, 26, 27, 28, 29, 30, 31, 33, 34, 35, 40, 45, 64, 82, 125, 126, 139, 162, 168, 171
Federal Reserve Banks—6, 8, 34, 35, 40, 41, 44, 83
Federal Reserve Board of Governors—6, 14, 19, 23, 29, 31, 32, 34, 35, 36, 37, 38, 39, 41, 42, 44, 45, 64, 68, 74, 86, 87, 95, 112, 119, 124, 125, 126, 128, 129, 133, 139, 140, 143, 144, 145, 146, 149, 154, 157, 159, 162, 163, 165, 169, 171, 172, 180
Federal Reserve System—5, 6, 7, 8, 19, 21, 29, 30, 32, 33, 35, 40, 41, 42, 42, 63, 67, 82, 84, 113, 114, 115, 118, 119, 120, 121, 122, 127, 128, 132, 134, 139, 140, 141, 143, 146, 158, 162, 163, 164, 165, 166, 168, 169, 170, 176, 180

Ferdinand, Archduke—69
First Name Club—3, 8, 33
First National Bank of N.Y.—1, 34, 41, 42, 44, 47, 64, 66, 67
Forbes, B.C.—2, 7
Forbes, Malcolm—2
Forgan, James B.—41, 42
Frame, Andrew—13, 14
Francqui, Emile—69, 70, 71, 72

### G
Garfield, James A.—20
Garrison, Col. Ely—22, 23, 120
Gates, Thomas S.—48
Glass, Carter—13, 14, 19, 21, 22, 29, 30, 34, 40, 45, 114, 116, 117, 138, 160
Glass-Steagall Banking Act—159
Goldenweiser, Emanuel—118, 136, 146, 148
Graham, Katherine—97
Gray, Prentiss—73, 78
Guggenheim—90

### H
Hamill, John—69, 70
Hamlin, Charles S.—36, 129, 138, 147
Hamilton, Alexander—5
Hanauer, Jerome J.—87, 95, 99
Harding, W.P.G.—36, 103, 121, 157
Harriman, E.H.—67, 90
Harriman, Mary—67
Harrison, George L.—132
Herrick, Myron T.—117
Hess, Rudolf—78
Hill, James J.—47
Hiss, Alger—24, 83
Hiss, Donald—24
Hitler, Adolf—75, 76, 77, 78, 79, 81
Hoover, Herbert H.—69, 70, 71, 72, 73, 74, 78, 139, 149, 150, 151, 158
House, Col. Edward Mandel—21, 23, 24, 25, 26, 27, 29, 30, 31, 36, 79, 88, 107, 109, 111
Hull, Cordell—84

195

## I

International Acceptance Bank—128, 144
Insull, Samuel—148

## J

Jackson, Andrew—5, 50
Jaffray, C.T.—43
James, F. Cyril—42
Jefferson, Thomas—5, 7, 35
Jekyll Island—2, 3, 4, 5, 8, 9, 10, 11, 12, 20, 29, 33, 41, 44, 171
Jekyl Island Club—3
Jones, Thomas D.—36, 38, 39
Josephson, Matthew—60, 67
Juillard, A.D.—67

## K

Kahn, Otto—19, 38, 66, 107
Kains, Archibald—43
Kaiping Coal Mines—70
Kemmerer, E.W.—85, 124
Kreuger, Ivar—71, 148, 149
Kuhn-Loeb Company—1, 17, 18, 21, 33, 35, 36, 37, 38, 39, 41, 44, 47, 48, 61, 66, 67, 71, 72, 74, 81, 83, 85, 86, 87, 88, 89, 99, 101, 103, 119, 127, 128, 146, 174, 175

## L

LaFollette, Senator Robert M.—16, 17, 18
Lamont, T.W.—2, 109, 111, 128
Laughlin, J. Lawrence—10, 11, 33
Lazard Freres—14, 34, 53, 61, 68, 74, 76, 94, 99, 152
League of Nations—136, 143, 170
Leguia, Juan—155
Lehman, Herbert—101
Lehman Brothers—35, 66, 101, 175
Lincoln, Abraham—20, 65
Lindbergh, Charles A., Sr.—11, 16, 17, 18, 28, 112
Loeb, Solomon—33
Lovett, Robert—48
Lundberg, Ferdinand—32

## M

Manati Sugar Corporation—73, 80, 81
Marbury, Bessie—155
Markoe, James—131
Marshall, Louis—29
Martin, William McChesney—163
McAdoo, William—19, 21, 26, 29, 32, 39, 99, 101, 114
McFadden, Louis—71, 72, 74, 75, 95, 127, 128, 133, 134, 135, 136, 137, 150, 151, 152, 153, 154
McIntosh, J.W.—103
Mellon, Andrew—142, 147, 150
Meyer, Eugene—14, 17, 34, 61, 72, 74, 75, 94, 95, 99, 118, 122, 150, 151, 152, 153, 159, 171
Miller, Adolph C.—36, 129, 133, 134, 135, 136, 157, 166
Minsky—67
Moody, John—47, 52
Money Trust—11, 12, 16
Montague, Samuel & Co.—38, 68
Morgan Grenfell Company—63, 68
Morgan, Joseph—51
Morgan Harjes Company—54
Morgan, J.P.—1, 2, 3, 10, 16, 17, 18, 26, 32, 35, 41, 42, 43, 44, 47, 48, 49, 50, 51, 52, 53, 54, 66, 67, 75, 83, 101, 129, 146, 150, 160, 174, 176
Morgan, J.P. Company—1, 33, 35, 41, 47, 48, 53, 66, 123, 148, 174
Morgan, Junius S.—50, 51, 53, 65, 66
Morton, Frederic—56
Morton, Levi P.—67
Mountbatten, Philip—60

## N

Nation, The—12, 16, 19, 30, 37
National Bank Act of 1864—125
National Citizen's League—10, 11
National City Bank—21, 33, 34, 41, 64, 65, 66, 112, 126, 127
National Monetary Commission—1,

4, 5, 10, 11, 12, 13, 14, 15, 33, 124, 125
National Recovery Act—159, 168
National Reserve Plan—7
Napoleon de Bonaparte—57
New York Times—27, 28, 29, 33, 35, 37, 40, 44, 61, 71, 74, 75, 80, 112, 119, 126, 144, 166, 171
Norman, Lord Montagu—49, 76, 77, 123, 129, 131, 132, 133, 142, 150
Norten, Charles D.—1, 33

## O

O'Gorman, Senator—14, 38
Owen, Robert L.—17, 19, 29, 38, 39, 40, 41, 116, 119, 138, 157, 161
Owen-Glass Bill—21

## P

Panic of 1837—5, 50, 51, 65
Panic of 1857—51, 52, 65
Panic of 1907—1, 2, 5, 10, 12, 21
Paterson, William—58, 59
Patman, Wright—34, 164, 165, 167
Page, Walter Hines—83
Peabody, George—49, 50, 51, 52, 54, 65, 171
Peabody, Riggs & Co.—49
Pegler, Westbrook—23
Pemberton, Robert Leigh—80
Pound, Ezra—58
Pressman, Lee—24
Princeps, Gavrel—69
Pujo, Arsene—16
Pujo Committee—16, 17, 18, 149
Pyne, Moses Taylor—66
Pyne, Percy—65, 66

## Q

Quigley, Dr. Carrol—53, 131

## R

Reagan, Ronald—77, 79, 80, 173, 175
Reichsbank—12, 132
Rhodes, Cecil—53

Rickard, Edgar—74
Richardson, Sir Gordon—80
Rionda, M.E.—73
Rockefeller, David—171, 172, 176
Rockefeller, John D.—47, 65
Rockefeller, William—47, 65
Rockefeller, William Jr.—65
Roosa, Robert—54, 171, 172
Roosevelt, Franklin Delano—23, 24, 30, 31, 84, 129, 137, 139, 145, 151, 155, 156, 158, 159, 162, 169, 170
Roosevelt, Theodore—1, 18, 19, 22, 38, 82
Rosebury, Lord—53
Rothschild, Baron Alfred—23, 60
Rothschild, James—5, 50, 57, 59, 61, 66, 109
Rothschild, House of—17, 47, 48, 50, 52, 53, 54, 60
Rothschild, Leopold—60
Rothschild, Mayer Amschel—55, 56
Rothschild, N.M.—48, 49, 51, 53, 57, 58, 59, 68, 171
Round Table—53, 54, 62
Rowe, W.S.—43, 70
Rue, Levi L.—42
Ryan, John Barry—66
Ryan, Thomas Fortune—66, 89
Ryan, Virginia Fortune—66

## S

Schiff, Jacob—17, 19, 26, 29, 42, 47, 66, 67, 86, 87, 90, 149
Schiff, John—66
Schiff, Ludwig—87
Schiff, Philip—87
Schoellkopf Family—34
Scholey, David—182
Schroder, Baron Bruno Von—69, 76
Schroder, Baron Rudolph Von—76
Schroder, J. Henry Co.—48, 67, 68, 69, 71, 73, 74, 75, 76, 77, 78, 79, 80, 81, 175, 176, 179, 180
Schultz, George—79
Seligman, E.R.A.—9
Seligman, J. & W.—9, 17, 71, 109, 114, 155

Seymour, Charles—31
Shaw, Leslie—14
Shelton—1, 2
Sieff, Israel—34
Simpson, John Lowery—78
Smith, Rixey—29, 112
Sontag, Susan—61
Sprague, O.M.W.—11, 114, 161
Spring-Rice, Sir Cecil—89
St. George, George F.—66
St. George, Katherine—66
Sterling, John W.—66
Stillman, Don Carlos—65
Stillman, James—8, 47, 65, 66
Stimson, Henry L.—161
Strauss, Albert—112, 114, 122, 140, 141, 157
Stone, Senator—21
Strong, Benjamin—1, 3, 32, 33, 44, 118, 123, 129, 131, 132, 133, 137, 138
Sugar Equalization Board—74
Swinney, E.F.—43

## T

Taft, William Howard—18, 19, 38, 82
Taylor, Congressman—14
Taylor, H.A.C.—66
Taylor, Moses—64, 65, 66
Tavistock Institute—80, 184, 185
Thalmann, Ladenburg—17
Tobacco Trust—89
Tiarks, Frank Cyril—69, 73, 76, 77
Tientsin Railroad—72
Trilateral Commission—35, 54, 172
Tugwell, Rexford Guy—162

## U

Untermeyer, Samuel—17, 18
U.S. Food Administration—73, 74, 78, 87

## V

Vanderlip, Frank—1, 2, 3, 8, 9, 19, 33, 44, 161

Vickers Sons & Maxim—60
Viereck, George—23, 25, 27
Volcker, Paul—34, 171, 172, 173, 183
Vreeland, Edward—12

## W

War Finance Corporation—24, 86, 94, 95, 97, 99, 151, 153
War Industries Board—74, 86, 90, 151
Warburg, Felix—38, 86, 87, 128, 129
Warburg, James Paul—128, 129, 156, 161
Warburg, Max—84, 86, 87, 88, 111
Warburg, M.M. Company—12, 17, 34, 54
Warburg, Paul Moritz—1, 2, 3, 4, 5, 6, 7, 8, 9, 12, 14, 19, 21, 22, 23, 24, 26, 28, 29, 30, 33, 34, 36, 37, 38, 40, 41, 42, 43, 44, 48, 66, 71, 74, 84, 86, 87, 88, 89, 99, 111, 112, 115, 117, 119, 120, 122, 126, 127, 128, 138, 144, 148, 156, 157, 164
Weinberger, Caspar—79
Wetmore, Frank O.—42
White, Harry Dexter—24
Williams, John Skelton—21, 32, 39, 101, 103, 140
Willis, H. Parker—132, 140, 142
Wilson, Woodrow—10, 17, 18, 19, 22, 23, 24, 25, 26, 28, 29, 30, 32, 36, 38, 39, 41, 82, 83, 84, 85, 86, 87, 88, 89, 90, 99, 101, 103, 105, 107, 109, 111, 112, 117, 137, 139, 140, 141, 156
Wing, Daniel S.—43
Wiseman, Sir William—73, 88, 105, 107, 111

## Z

Zabriskie, G.A.—73, 74